THE U.S. ARMY COMBAT HISTORIAN AND COMBAT HISTORY OPERATIONS

THE U.S. ARMY COMBAT HISTORIAN AND COMBAT HISTORY OPERATIONS

World War I to the Vietnam War

KATHRYN ROE COKER
& JASON WETZEL

CASEMATE

Philadelphia & Oxford

Published in Great Britain and the United States of America in 2023 by
CASEMATE PUBLISHERS
1950 Lawrence Road, Havertown, PA 19083, USA
and
The Old Music Hall, 106–108 Cowley Road, Oxford OX4 1JE, UK

Hardcover Edition: ISBN 978-1-63624-329-0
Digital Edition: ISBN 978-1-63624-330-6

A CIP record for this book is available from the British Library

Printed and bound in the United Kingdom by CPI Group (UK) Ltd, Croydon, CR0 4YY

Typeset in India by Lapiz Digital Services, Chennai.

For a complete list of Casemate titles, please contact:

CASEMATE PUBLISHERS (US)
Telephone (610) 853-9131
Fax (610) 853-9146
Email: casemate@casematepublishers.com
www.casematepublishers.com

CASEMATE PUBLISHERS (UK)
Telephone (0)1226 734350
Email: casemate-uk@casematepublishers.co.uk
www.casematepublishers.co.uk

Contents

Preface

> If you know your enemy and know yourself, you need not fear the result of a hundred battles. If you know yourself but not the enemy, for every victory gained you will also suffer a defeat.
>
> SUN TZU, 6TH CENTURY BCE

Sun Tzu was a Chinese general, strategist and philosopher who lived from 771 to 256 BCE. He wrote *The Art of War* on military strategy. In his book he lists nine lessons of war. Lesson three is "Know yourself, Know your enemy."[1] "If you know your enemy and know yourself, you need not fear the result of a hundred battles. If you know yourself but not the enemy, for every victory gained you will also suffer a defeat."[2] Combat historians provide after action reports, other narratives, and analyzes that give intelligence for the modern warrior. Knowing the enemy gives one the upper hand.

This book is a history of the evolution of American combat historians from World War I to the Vietnam War. Combat historians are the unsung heroes of modern warfare. Their timely record of combat helps to reduce casualties in future wars. Brigadier General S. L. A. Marshall said in 1968, "The lessons learned are not being recorded and passed on, and we are taking unnecessary casualties as a result of it."[3]

Today's combat historians are on the battlefield interviewing soldiers and writing about events, usually within days of the action. They study the action and record lessons learned. Timely analysis of lessons learned is a combat success multiplier. Without up-to-date knowledge of an enemy, a warrior is in a reaction mode. The enemy gains the initiative. Knowing the enemy gives warriors the advantage.

Notable examples of the dangers of intelligence failures—not knowing your enemy—include the World War II British surrender of Singapore (February 15, 1942) to Imperial Japan. This was the largest and most humiliating defeat in British history. Singapore was the leading British military base and seaport in Asia. Military intelligence was divided into navy, army, and air force headquarter units.

> These headquarters were served by an intelligence service which hardly lived up to its name. Just before the Japanese attack (December 1941), George Hammonds [responsible for air raid civil defense (termed Air Raid Precautions, ARP, by the British)] had gone with several spare-time ARP wardens to a lecture, where an RAF [Royal Air Force] officer had insisted that there

was no need to man ARP stations at night as the Japanese pilots could not fly in the dark. On another occasion a Colonel Ward had given a lecture stressing the magnificent fighting qualities and intensive training of Japanese troops. He was not invited back to air "defeatist" views.

Another instance of the intelligence service's abysmal talent for misinformation came six months before the war broke out [December 1941] in Malaya, when the navy had asked the Chiefs-of-Staff for some Hurricane fighters, [excellent British single-seat fighter planes]. The Vice-Chief of the Air Staff on their advice had retorted that British Buffalo fighters [outdated single-seat fighter planes] "would be more than a match for the Japanese aircraft which were not of the latest type."

This unfortunate appraisal was made only a month before a Japanese Zero [one of the best single-seat fighter planes in the world at that time] had made a forced landing in China and details of its armaments, tankage, [and] performance were passed to Whitehall [the Cabinet War Rooms, the command center of Britain's war effort]. But "this valuable report remained unshifted" with the consequence that when the first Buffalo planes found themselves facing Zeros in combat, the British pilots were still under the delusion they were flying the better machine.[4]

The Buffaloes were destroyed. This example shows the disasters that can occur without dedicated combat historians providing timely and accurate "lessons learned" to war fighters.

Another example of not knowing one's enemy is the United States' defeat in the Battle of Tassafaronga (November 30, 1942). In this night battle the United States Navy had 4 heavy cruisers; 1 light cruiser; and 6 destroyers. The Japanese Navy had 8 destroyers. Japanese night fighting excellence and torpedo superiority devasted the American ships. The Japanese lost 1 destroyer sunk, and 211 men killed. The Americans lost 1 heavy cruiser sunk and 3 heavy cruisers severely damaged, with 395 men killed.[5] The Japanese "Long Lance" torpedo was far superior to the American Mark IV torpedo. Its warhead was double that of the Mark IV. Plus, it had a range of 22,000 yards compared to the Mark IV's 9,000 yards.[6] James D. Hornfischer wrote in *Neptune's Inferno—The U.S. Navy at Guadalcanal*:

[Rear Admiral Carleton H.] Wright understood little of the combat capability of his enemy. In his December 9 after-action report, he concluded that torpedoing of the *Pensacola* and *Northampton* had been lucky shots from submarines. "The observed positions of the enemy surface vessels before and during the gun action makes it seem improbable that torpedoes with speed-distance characteristics similar to our own could have reached the cruisers." Of course, Wright's torpedoes were nothing like those of the Japanese.

Nearly a year into the war, and four months into a bitter campaign against Japanese surface forces, it seems incomprehensible that an American cruiser commander could be unaware of the enemy advantage in torpedo warfare. [Rear Admiral] Norman Scott had called it specifically to Admiral Halsey's attention in October. The reports were there to be read. Before he rode to his death in the naval campaign for Java, the captain of the heavy cruiser *[USS] Houston,* Captain Albert H. Rooks, turned over to a colleague in Darwin [Australia] an analysis he had written three weeks before the Pearl Harbor attack [December 7, 1941]. It discussed at length Japan's prowess in torpedo combat and described their aggressively realistic night battle training. Their mastery of this specialty had been recommended to them by their experience in the Russo–Japanese War [1904–1905]. Rook's prewar report, which was based substantially on existing work of the Office of Naval Intelligence, never found its way into the battle plans. Not even

Halsey grasped the superiority of Japanese surface-ship torpedoes. After [Battle of] Tassafaronga he endorsed Wright's view that the outcome to have been the result of submarines. Norman Scott's October [1942] victory over a surprised Japanese force that failed to get its torpedoes in the water might have led the Americans to underestimate the weapon [torpedo] and placed undue importance on [naval] gunnery.

The reward for this ignorance was to see four proud ships, two of them fitted with the new radar that had proven decisive in more capable hands, "picked off like mechanical ducks in a carnival shooting Gallery," as [Admiral] Samuel Eliot Morrison would put it.[7]

If combat historians had been in place, at that time, knowledge of the enemy's superior tactics and weapons would have been available. History unrecorded is history lost and forgotten. By providing lessons learned, combat historians have a direct impact on the success of future combat. The combat historian's work is dynamic history in action—it is applied history.

In the years before World War I, combat histories came from soldiers' letters and diaries, and books written sometimes years after the conflict. An example are the official records of the American Civil War, entitled *The Official Records of the Union and Confederate Armies in the War of the Rebellion*. This was 128 volumes of 138,579 pages, written between 1881 to 1901. A complete history was finished 36 years after the civil war ended in 1865. This is not timely reporting of combat actions and lessons learned. Modern combat historians provide reporting within days, or at least months, of the action.

In the early and mid-20th century a combat historian may have been recruited from the halls of academia, such as Korean War historian Bevin Alexander; from a newspaper office, as in the case of Marshall; a novelist, or a good storyteller. Many had no training as soldiers. They were civilians with research and writing skills who joined up or who were drafted by the War Department to fulfill a need for documenting combat operations. Most never had training to prepare them for combat history. Many became combat historians due to "other duty as assigned."

With the formation of Military History Detachments came more thorough training. More comprehensive combat historian training began in the 1980s. Active-duty and reserve soldiers were recruited. The contemporary combat historian is first and foremost a soldier. He is also a combination of a storyteller, journalist, novelist, and scholar for 10 percent of the time, but for 90 percent, the combat historian is like a detective. Colonel David Hackworth had a four-month Vietnam assignment training combat historians in 1968. It led him to later write in *About Face*: "General Marshall and I went to work immediately, setting up the first of four 'schools' to teach his postcombat interviewing technique. Essentially a copy of the system police uses for reconstructing a crime, Marshall's method entailed bringing together the participants of whatever action was to be reviewed, and, with a trained interviewer guiding the discussion, reconstructing that action as a group."[8]

A journalist can write about what happened, novelist or storyteller can be entertaining, a scholar can be informative—the soldier/detective/combat historian records facts and observations that will help determine what went right and wrong, what can be changed to improve combat efficiency and ultimately save lives. It is this analysis of the action that will determine the lessons learned.

As a soldier, the combat historian can relate to other warriors by understanding their language, technology, mindset, culture, and traditions. In past wars, a combat historian's ammunition were words and his weapon a typewriter … (jokingly, the only thing missing was the bayonet lug). Modern combat historians walk in the footsteps of Clio, the muse of memory. Legendary Greek and Roman historians Herodotus and Tacitus covered the blood-red iron battlefields of yore; without those ancient combat historians, there would be no record of Achilles or Helen of Troy. Their legacy lives on in today's combat historians.

Acknowledgements

This book would have been impossible without the substantial Historical Research Collection and Historical Manuscripts Collection at the U.S. Army Center of Military History (CMH). Frank Shirer willingly shared his extensive knowledge of the records. He worked tirelessly to locate invaluable resources and "nuggets" in these two vast collections. The entire CMH staff was cooperative and supportive. The National Archives and Records Administration (NARA) has numerous federal records essential to telling this story. We appreciate the dedication of NARA's archivists. NARA's online catalog, much improved during the Pandemic shutdown, was easier to navigate, rendering relevant documents and photographs.

Claudia Rivers, Head Special Collections Department at The University of Texas at El Paso Library and Archivist Anne Allis were exceptionally accommodating. They located records within the Eva Spencer Osterberg Papers, and the SLA Marshal Papers used in the manuscript. Anne had several students scan numerous records and photographs. Without their assistance we could not tell the story of T/5 (Technician fifth grade) Eva Spencer. Melissa Davis at The George C. Marshall Foundation, Lexington, Virginia, located and scanned the photograph of Forrest Pogue entering Paris. Katie Carey, Hodson Curator of the Johns Hopkin University Archives graciously provided a photograph of Kent Roberts Greenfield.

And a special thank you to Pamela Ottesen for her excellent proofreading and her ongoing encouragement.

CHAPTER I

World War I and the Beginnings of Army Combat Historians

Collecting historical combat records predates the Civil War (April 12, 1861–April 9, 1865). American military historian and author Dr. Robert K. Wright, Jr. traces it back to April 1775. The Massachusetts Provincial Congress collected oral interviews, conducted in the field, to write about the Battles of Lexington and Concord.[1] They were the first military skirmishes of the American Revolutionary War (1775–1783).

Major General John J. Pershing immediately after he landed at Boulogne, France. Major James G. Harbord is behind the French civilian at General Pershing's left. (Courtesy National Archives and Records Administration)

During the American Civil War, General in Chief Henry W. Halleck encouraged collecting and publishing military records. From 1860 to 1901, the War Department published 128 volumes of *The War of the Rebellion: The Official Records of the Union and Confederate Armies*.[2]

A dedicated in-theater Army historical office dates from World War I. In September 1917, Major General John J. Pershing wanted a historical office within the headquarters of the American Expeditionary Forces (AEF). He discussed his idea with his chief of staff, Major General James G. Harbord. Harbord suggested the function would be writing a war diary—an officer experienced in historical research methods would write the diary. He recommended West Point professor Colonel Cornelis Willcox to head the office.

Willcox traveled to France. After two weeks of observations, he agreed with Harbord. A war diary should be prepared together with a "refined narrative" to be completed later. The office should collect records, maps, photographs, and related material. He recommended the staff consist of one qualified "military author" to write the war diary and maybe a "civilian assistant."[3]

On February 9, 1918, the War Department reorganized the General Staff to include a Historical Branch in the War Plans Division. The branch was organized into military history and archives, and placed under the leadership of Lieutenant Colonel Charles W. Weeks. It was located with the rest of the division in the Army War College building in Washington, D.C. Initially the branch was authorized 7 officers, 15 enlisted soldiers, and 5 civilians. Among the first to arrive was Harvard University Assistant Professor Robert Matteson Johnston, a proponent and long-time "vigorous crusader" of military history.[4] Among his pre-World War I publications were *American Soldiers; The French Revolution;* and *Bull Run*.[5]

A week later the AEF issued its own general order. It formed a historical subsection reporting to the Secretary of the General Staff to "collect data for an official history of the war and to keep a war diary."[6] The War Department notified Pershing of its plans to create a historical branch "after which the necessary personnel will be detailed for service at your headquarters."[7] The department asked him for advice on the branch's organization and whether or not he had "initiated any similar activity."[8] Pershing recommended the Washington office be staffed with 5 officers and 2 civilians along with a number of enlisted soldiers and that the office be sent to his headquarters in France "where the work [on a history of the war] should be conducted."[9] Actually, three months before the Historical Branch was organized Pershing had recommended the establishment of a historical section in his headquarters.[10]

On March 19, 1918, Captain Joseph Hanson arrived at Headquarters AEF to establish the historical office. It was responsible for recording "the nature and repositories of all important documents and communications, not secret, originating in or coming to the staff sections and the administrative and technical branches of General Headquarters."[11] Before Hanson's arrival, Major Frederick L. Palmer, a news correspondent and writer and Pershing's friend, had written a censorship plan and was given the job of preparing the headquarters' war diary. In April, Hanson's office was moved to the Intelligence Section. Meanwhile, work on the war diary remained under the Secretary of the General Staff.[12]

Enroute to Chaumont, France, Johnston, now a major, and his team were torpedoed while aboard the SS *Leviathan*.[13] The formidable SS *Vaterland*, pride of Germany's merchant marine, had been seized while in American waters when the U.S. declared war on Germany; it was renamed *Leviathan*, "huge and formidable," and converted into a U.S. Army transport ship.[14] Fortunately, it did not sink. This incident illustrates that combat "service support personnel" (those usually in the rear of a battlefield) were not immune from enemy attacks.

Upon Johnston's arrival on June 8, Hanson became his assistant. Johnston became what is now called the theater historian.[15] His chief was his friend and colleague, Harvard University graduate Colonel Arthur L. Conger, who was a veteran of the Spanish–American War, Philippine–American War, Boxer Rebellion, and the Pancho Villa Expedition. While on the AEF staff, Conger was the principal planner for a summer 1918 deception known as the Belfort Ruse. This attempt was to mislead German commanders into assigning forces away from Saint-Mihiel, thereby, enhancing Allied forces.

At the succeeding Battle of Saint-Mihiel, the Allied numerical dominance created by Conger's plan stunned the Germans, triggering a quick Allied victory. According

USS *Allen* convoying USS *Leviathan*. (Courtesy NARA)

to Johnston, Conger "spent most of his time in the field."[16] Was Conger then the first World War I combat historian? Johnston thought Conger's battlefield activities hampered his own plans. Johnston was not allowed access to confidential documents, which undoubtedly frustrated him.[17] His only recourse was to "arrange with The Adjutant General to have tabs placed on those of historical significance so that they could be found and used later."[18]

Pershing ordered the Historical Section to "prepare short statements on military operations."[19] Two of these were nearly completed when, on July 12th, Conger returned to headquarters and informally approved Johnston's proposed program. Johnston wanted a general order to support his plan calling for:

Colonel Arthur L. Conger. From 1920's *Soldiers All: portraits and sketches of the men of the AEF.* (Courtesy Wikipedia)

1. the creation of a war diary system at the headquarters and "its several staff and technical sections, with all of the work to be assigned to officers detailed from the Historical Subsection but with Palmer left in charge of the public relations type of war diary that he was then superintending";

2. establishment of "similar journals at the headquarters of the Service of Supply and of major field units";

3. prepar[ation] [of] monographs on operations for the general reader based on unclassified material only, similar to a German General Staff series then being produced, and with the first one to be on Origins of the AEF (June 1917–1918);

4. investigat[ion of] the archival and historical systems of the British and French armies.[20]

Headquarters approved preparing the monographs and the archival search but not the war diaries. According to Stetson Conn, former chief historian at the U.S. Army Center of Military History and general editor of the *United States Army in World War II,* "More and more it seemed to Johnston that history was an unwanted stepchild at General Headquarters, and one kept under close check by a complete lack of transportation facilities."[21]

Another problem was the alignment of the AEF Historical Section. Washington said it fell under the Historical Branch's Operations Section, War Plans Division. Headquarters AEF said it was the command's "historical Subsection of G-2 [Plans]."

In October 1918, Johnston went to the chief of staff who directed the Historical Section. A general order placed the office under the Secretary of the General Staff. Johnston "defined [the office's] mission as collecting data for an official history of the war and keeping a war diary." Johnston would have to wait until after the armistice for the completing of the "reassignment of the history office and realignment of its functions…." At that time, the office had 9 officers, 12 field clerks, and several enlisted soldiers. "Perhaps," wrote Conn, "the most important result was the establishment within what was now termed the Historical Section of orderly archives to which all AEF offices and units were directed to turn in documents of historical value."[22] That was a huge step forward in the combat operations history program.

Meanwhile, Johnston's monograph program ran into roadblocks. Headquarters had approved their writing, but not yet their publication. One monograph, *A Survey of German Tactics, 1918* was completed. On October 22, Johnston sought official support of his monograph program. Pershing responded: "Am doubtful, Very, of the wisdom of this at this time. Think this should be very carefully considered. I want to know more about it." A key problem was not allowing authors to go to the front. [23]

Johnston was told Pershing required "brief articles on subjects, not too lengthy, and suitable for reproduction not only as monographs but also as newspaper articles." Johnston also was told plainly that the "G-3 [Operations], G-5 [Plans], and G-2 [Intelligence] will all assist in outlining the frame for these studies, G-3 being primarily responsible for the tactical correctness. The C-in-C [Commander in Chief] desires to see each one of these studies in the rough draft before any work

Tanks on the move. American tanks moving forward to the battle line in the Argonne Forest in 1918. (Courtesy Army Art Collection, U.S. Army Center of Military History)

on any of them is put into print." Pershing wanted them completed as soon as possible. What Pershing required were "short statements on the Argonne operations that could be used to brief negotiators of a now prospective armistice."[24] So, World War I combat historians contributed to the armistice negotiations. But the authors of the brief studies were not allowed to visit the front lines.

"Mopping up Cierges, 1918," by Wallace Morgan. (Courtesy Army Art Collection, CMH)

One of the guns of Battery D, 105th Field Artillery, showing the American flag hoisted after the last shot had been fired when the armistice took effect. Etraye, France. (Courtesy NARA)

CHAPTER 2

Post-World War I
Army Military History Operations

Pershing defined the Post-World War I Historical Section's duties in a cablegram dated November 20, 1918. He said the section had archival and historical responsibilities. Archival duties included:

> the collection and preservation of all historical documents of General Staff after their period of actual use. To classify and organize these documents in such a way as to make them immediately available when the General Staff requires to refer to them. To make them the nucleus of the historical records of the Army, adding to them related documents and publications, such as war diaries, etc.[1]

Johnston knew the monographs were subject to review. But he could make changes. Pershing said nothing was to be published without his "full review and approval...."[2] Perhaps unaware of Pershing's directive, Johnston vented his frustration in a letter dated December 1918 to Weeks:

> It is difficult to convey the deadweight that the Section is always up against. This deadweight is the complete absence of understanding on the part of almost everybody that the work we are trying to do has a scientific basis. We are always viewed, automatically, as a sort of halting adjunct of propaganda. When, at infrequent intervals, it occurs to someone that we may be useful for something, that usefulness is inevitably for propaganda purposes.[3]

In utter irritation, Johnston pulled one monograph because he considered the feedback unacceptable. Weeks said monographs were over; the focus was on preparing the planned five volumes of operational history. Doubting that the volumes could be written in Europe as Johnston planned, Weeks wrote, "History must tell the truth ... and it is obvious that the officers with whom you are dealing at GHQ consider history as a report of their conduct of the campaign.... A report is a piece of special pleading."[4]

On February 4, 1919, Brigadier General Oliver Lyman Spaulding, Jr. succeeded Johnston, but Johnston remained with the office; he was hospitalized in April and on extended convalescent leave. Spalding thought the historical office's primary duty was to collect "historical documents" and conduct "field surveys to improve the documentation of operations."[5] Although historical documents were to be sent to the Historical Section, that was not happening all the time. Instead, documents were flowing through The Adjutant General to the Washington Historical Branch. In March, the War Department ordered that all documents were to be sent to the AEF headquarters' Historical Section "for immediate use...." Ultimately, the Washington Historical Branch would get them "for use in completing the projected Army history of the war."[6]

Spaulding wanted to conduct "a survey of the ground [battlefield]...."[7] Each officer chosen for the mission initially studied the records of his area of operation, and then visited the area. "The evidence gathered was put into the form of maps, sketches, photographs and written field notes" and eventually sent to the Washington Historical Branch for reference. Unfortunately, by 1930 most of the field notes were missing.[8] This shows that officers acting as historians went "down range," albeit not into combat. They worked at or near the front lines, but not in harm's way.

On May 20, 1919, the Historical Section was closed. Spaulding, Johnston and eight other officers were ordered to the Washington Historical Branch. They took with them the "field data" that they had collected. Four junior officers were to stay in Chaumont "to handle the flow of AEF historical documents." The Washington Historical Branch assumed control of "all historical work on AEF operations...."[9]

What was to become of that work? On July 29, the war plans chief appointed Spaulding, Johnston, Conger, and Fred M. Fling to a committee. They were to determine the future of the army's historical work. The committee made several recommendations:

1. Make the Historical Branch a "permanent institution responsible for dealing with all the wars of the United States";
2. Keep a plan for a World War I history "subject to modification";
3. Use the World War I history plan "as a guide for collecting data and ... writing ... monographs ... from which ... complete volumes would be constructed" [similar to Pershing's objectives];
4. Reorganize the branch according to Spaulding's plan, "except ... some civilian experts might be added to the staff";
5. Ensure the branch chief "maintain[s] close relations with the American Historical Association."[10]

The report was sent to Secretary of War Newton D. Baker, Jr.[11] On August 4, 1919, Baker wrote to Army Chief of Staff General Peyton C. March:

> The work of the Historical Branch should in my judgment be limited to the collection, indexing, and preservation of records and the preparation of such monographs as are purely military in character and are designed to be of use to the War Department. The War Department ought not to undertake the preparation, either by way of monograph or connected discourse, of a narrative history of the war. Such a history would be incomplete unless it undertook to discuss

economic, political, and diplomatic questions, and the discussion of such questions by military men would necessarily be controversial, and many of the questions appropriate to be discussed in a narrative history would be impolitic and indiscreet for treatment by the War Department.[12]

In short, for now there would be no official interpretative narrative history of World War I.

Spaulding became the chief of the Historical Branch. He said the branch's functions were to "preserve historical documents relating to the wars of the United States; make these documents and the information … accessible to agencies of the War Department, and to students and investigators when properly accredited; and to prepare monographs on matters of military history of interest to agencies of the War Department."[13]

Meanwhile, Major Henry duR Phelan was appointed as theater historian in November 1919. He was the Washington Historical Branch's "liaison between the American and the French armies' historical offices; he also copied material from the French archives relating to American operations in France."[14] This office continued until 1940. Presumably, Phelan sent the records to the Historical Branch. The branch had relocated to what is now Fort McNair. That "provid[ed] enough space for the anticipated flow of records from France and the existing collection."[15] In 1922 historical offices began operating in London and Berlin. The London effort lasted until 1924 while the Berlin operation continued to 1938.[16]

By 1920 the "flow of historical documents into the Washington Historical Branch almost stopped. Even so, the branch continued anticipating that eventually it would acquire custody of all AEF records, including the large collection of historical documents amassed in France by the Historical Section…."[17]

The Washington Historical Branch received documents from the Berlin operation, led by Colonel Walter Krueger, who worked in concert "with the military attaches."[18] "In a typical year (1935–1936), Krueger sent 200 documents totaling 2,632 pages and 156 map tracings."[19] The Berlin office collected most of the historically significant documents relating to German combat units.[20] Krueger and the military attaches were serving as combat historians.

Over the next few years, the Washington office faced several challenges. Among them were:

1. physical separation from the rest of the War Plans Division;
2. relationship with other War Department historical offices while functioning as the War Department's central historical office;
3. oversight of the publications of other offices;
4. internal reorganization and re-designation in 1921 as the Historical Section and transfer to the Army War College;
5. criticism from others for using "officers who were not trained historians" to write monographs;

6. changing manpower;
7. attempts by The Adjutant General to take over its control;
8. struggle with The Adjutant General over control of the records.

The War Department's decision in 1922 to make The Adjutant General the "custodian of all historical records," including those held by the section further complicated matters between the Historical Branch and The Adjutant General.[21]

On July 16, 1929, the Army War College and the Historical Section accepted the end of the monograph program. The focus was on compiling and publishing documents. "Any 'synoptical studies' (the word 'monographs' would be eschewed) undertaken from this time forward would be for internal reference use."[22]

In August 1929, Army Chief of Staff General Charles P. Summerall weighed in on the section's primary mission to collect the army's World War I records for publication as was done with Civil War records. In fact, Summerall directed the "suppression of monographs already prepared, forbade any printing until all of the documentary work was completed." He authorized the preparation of "synopses of facts" by officers in charge of combat units.[23] "The synopses were censored by a General Staff Advisory Committee…." They were not published until all synopses and documentary collections were finalized. This became an official directive on August 14, 1929. The section, which remained with the Army War College, examined over 12,000,000 records and selected about 100,000 AEF records for indexing. This work took more than four years.[24]

The second stage of compiling the documents began in December 1933. The section selected documents from the 100,000 items acquired during the initial screening. These were the AEF documents the historical organization in France had collected in 1918 and 1919. Also included were foreign documents gathered for the Historical Section since 1920.[25] In 1947 the U.S. Army Center of Military History published 16 volumes of World War I documents and one volume of the order of battle.[26]

The stateside document collection and cataloging was the major focus of the Army War College's Historical Section during the interwar years.[27] No official World War I narrative history remained the policy.

In 1928, the army issued Army Regulation (AR) 345-105, *Military Records: Historical Records and Histories of Organizations*. It was a major new doctrinal initiative with numerous directives.

> Units ranging from a regiment and battalion to a battery must keep a detailed organizational history. The commanding officer managed the history's preparation. The history included information on the unit's formation, recruitment, organizational changes, strength, station arrivals and departures, marches, campaigns, battles, and related data.
>
> The unit history contained the names of commanders in significant engagements, the names of men killed and wounded in action and the names of those who had distinguished themselves along with their rewards and decorations.

Efforts were made to obtain photographs.

Written after action reports were forwarded to The Adjutant General.

General staff officers kept journals of operations used to create operational reports.

All journals and other original papers of historical interest dealing with operations (e.g. war diaries, maps, intelligence summaries) were forwarded to the Army War College's Historical Branch.

Copies of journals of marches were sent to The Adjutant General.

In campaigns, war diaries replaced the journals.

The regulation also governed the destruction of old books and papers, disposition of data used in preparing organizational histories, commanding officers' talks to troops to promote esprit de corps and the organizational history of regimental days.[28]

In 1930, Army War College student Major Julian F. Barnes designed a historical program plan for future wars. He suggested mobilization plans including forming a War Department historical agency (called the Historical Branch) upon mobilization as part of the General Staff.[29] The branch would have several divisions including an Operations Section. The section would "make and preserve field notes on each battle or campaign by actual field study of the ground over which the operation takes place and by personal interview with the key participants in the operation as soon after the operation as practicable."[30] This was a harbinger of what combat historians would do in World War II.

Unfortunately, his plan was not well received. Major General W. D. Connor, commandant of the Army War College, wrote:

> When I recall the mud-and-rain and darkness and guttering candles of dugouts … the dirt and difficulties in which we had to do all that we did accomplish, this plan to write up "historical data" in the heat of military operations makes me feel more than ever that officers at GHQ did not know how the war was being fought. All the important data is somewhere—and there is more time to look it up after the war than there is to make a beautiful record of events in the difficult situation of active operations. I lack sympathy with this whole idea.[31]

In 1935, Army Chief of Staff Major General Malin Craig seconded Connor's assessment quipping, "Me too."[32] This was the general opinion on the eve of World War II. The U.S. Army's historical function was limited to the collection, collation, and publication of documents. There was no place for narrative, interpretive writing.

CHAPTER 3

Developing the World War II Army Historical Program

The December 7, 1941, Japanese attack on Pearl Harbor and President Franklin D. Roosevelt's declaration of war on Japan the next day transformed America and its people forever. That change altered military history too. In the fall of 1941, Director of the Bureau of the Budget Harold Smith instructed Dr. E. P. Pendleton Herring, secretary of the Graduate School at Harvard University, to write the history of the war's administrative events. This was a lesson learned from the poor administrative recordkeeping in World War I.

Prominent scholars and organizations, such as the National Archives and the American Historical Association, responded favorably.[1] Then came support from none other than President Roosevelt. On March 4, 1942, Roosevelt wrote to the Bureau of the Budget's director, "I am very much interested in the steps that you have been taking to keep a current record of the war administration. I suggest that you carry this program further by covering the field more intensively, drawing on whatever scholarly talent may be necessary."[2] He wanted the program to be broadened so Roosevelt proposed a committee "on records of war administration, to be composed of representatives of appropriate learned societies and perhaps two or three agencies of the Government which might be interested in such a program."[3] Roosevelt believed:

> The present program strengthened in this manner might be helpful to the work of the Bureau of the Budget in planning current improvements in administration in addition to its main objective of preserving for those who come after us an accurate and objective account of our present experience. I hope that officials in war agencies will bear in mind the importance of systematic records, and to the extent commensurate with their heavy duties, cooperate in this undertaking.[4]

Roosevelt learned in January 1944 from the Bureau of the Budget that significant progress was not being made. He reiterated his concern for "a full and objective account … of the way the Federal Government is carrying out its wartime duties."[5] More was needed than the collection of documents; a candid, straightforward narrative of administrative events was unmistakably the central objective.

On June 11, 1942, Herring was the advisory committee's acting executive secretary. He asked Assistant Secretary of War John J. McCloy how best to gather information about the War Department's role in the war. McCloy told Herring he would see what he could do. Spaulding took the lead. He appointed historical officers in the War Department. They would "prepare an outline for an administrative history." The Army War College's Historical Section would direct all historical activities. Historical officers would submit their outlines to the section for approval. Each bureau's history would be a narrative, backed by summaries of official documents.[6] This was a notable change from the no-narrative approach of World War I.

The Adjutant General established historical offices in the Army Ground Forces, the Army Air Forces, and the Services of Supply.[7] They focused on administrative history. On August 4, 1942, Spaulding explained why a history of military operations was excluded. He told the historical officers: "Military operations will be covered when the documents become available. Systematic plans have already been made for handling these documents in accordance with the same methods now being employed for the records of World War I."[8]

On November 16, 1942, Historical Officer for the Army Ground Forces Major Kent Roberts Greenfield made a case for an operational as well as an administrative history:

> [I]t is evident that the history of a war is impossible without first assembling a record of operations. The armed forces of the nation have been engaged for more than a year, but no provision has been made for creating an organized record of their operations on which a history of the present war can be based. The fate that has overtaken efforts to write a history or compile a record of the part taken by American forces in World War I is a warning that such provisions should be made without delay.[9]

Greenfield argued that historical reporting of the war must include combat operations. "The military historian needs a record covering decisions, organization and administration, and training and combat operations." He said there was no "provision ... for preparing a historical record of [vital] decisions or actions in ... the high command.... It would seem then," he added, "that the purpose and scope of historical activity in the military agencies needs to be extended in two directions: outwards, to cover operations and upwards, to embrace the high command."[10] Greenfield said the record "should be designed for current reference; to meet the historical requirements of the service schools after the war; and to meet the eventual requirements of historians. There is agreement," he believed, "among the present historical officers that they should create two kinds of records: select file of primary documents and first narratives."[11]

Greenfield continued:

> *The preparation of the record must begin while action is going on.* [Italics added] That the documents must not be too few requires no argument. The serious problem is to keep them from becoming

A young Kent Roberts Greenfield seated at the head of a classroom table. (Special Collections, Sheridan Libraries, Johns Hopkins)

too many…. The mechanical problem of handling records and the intellectual problem of digesting and interpreting them in their present volume threatens history with suffocation under mountains of the material on which it feeds.[12]

Greenfield warned that verbal and fragmentary orders were replacing written orders. "Nowadays … important decisions are recorded and the motives for them stated in vibrations of air [telephone] instead of words on paper." He said written reports would not be "adequate [and dependable] … [given] the stress of critical action, and the memory of men, recorded in memoirs written long after the event…." Greenfield urged "immediate action to get" those records. He said:

> [T]he Historical Sections regard it as part of their duty to devise means of obtaining a record of decisions and events as quickly as possible … *In the sphere of operations, it is highly desirable to have historical officers on the ground at the time of action. Only if they are on the scene can they recognize the form in which the evidence of action emerges in modern warfare or take measures to see that it gets into the record* [Italics added].[13]

Greenfield cited the example of Admiral William Snowden Sims. During World War I, Sims recognized that "oral expressions" could help prevent the loss of important material not in "official documents." He noted the Navy "has decided to send historical officers to key points on sea-fronts and battle units and is equipping them with sound-recording machines to take the statements of officers and seamen who have been in action. It is recording in the same way statements of officers returning to Washington from scenes of actions." Testimony should not be restricted to officers but extended to all ranks. "Otherwise," Sims said, "history is written solely or largely from the Staff point of view. It is all the more important to get such testimony because of the limitations put on personal letters and diaries in this war."[14]

Historical officers of the three commands saw the need to write narratives soon after a battle. Greenfield wrote his 1942 memorandum specifically for the Army Ground Forces' historical program. In time, his ideas resonated throughout the U.S. Army. His ideas were incorporated into the August 2, 1943, War Department memorandum establishing the history program.[15]

Coincidentally two days after Greenfield's memorandum, Assistant Chief of staff, G-2, European Theater of Operations (ETO) Brigadier General Robert A. McClure wrote to the War Department's G-2 about capturing the ETO's history. He pointed out that the records of World War I remained unpublished; McClure was convinced "the preparation of documents for eventual publication was started too late and somewhat as an afterthought." He noted the British and the Canadians had historians working on operational histories.[16] McClure said the Canadians had "a splendid cataloging system...." He proposed the adoption of straightforward measures, beginning with the indexing and cataloging of the war's records. "It would seem desirable," he opined, "to have someone start that work here, insofar as it pertains to troops in this area. The buildup of Headquarters, ETO and AFHQ [Allied Forces Headquarters] was so recent that records are now neither too voluminous nor scattered and are readily accessible."[17]

On December 11, 1942, Spaulding sent a Memorandum on Historical Records in Theaters of Operations Overseas to the War Department's G-2. He "suggested that machinery be set up at Headquarters European Theater (and inferentially in other theaters) for classifying documents relating to activities in each theater, as a first step toward eventual publication." This should be done "before the records become too voluminous as to be cumbersome, and before they are subjected to further risk of loss or damage."[18] In addition, he recommended: "the commanding general of each theater should appoint a historical officer, with necessary assistants," to "compile synopsis of documents, and send them to the Historical Section."[19] He ordered:

> No attempt should be made to write narrative historical studies at this time; the experience of the Historical Section indicates that it would be premature. The collection of American documents will be incomplete; military secrecy will prevent the free use of even those on hand; and documents presenting the enemy's point of view will be unavailable. Until some of these handicaps are removed, it will be best to postpone writing.[20]

Clearly, Spaulding saw no change in the document collection function, reminiscent of the World War I approach.[21]

Then on January 2, 1943, Spaulding presented his plan to Colonel Thomas North of the Operations Division (OPD), General Staff. He offered to write a procedure for its execution. After some discussion, North agreed with Spaulding, with one exception. Historical officers would be appointed within theater, and they would execute the historical work as an additional duty.

Fourteen days later Assistant Chief of Staff, OPD, Major General Thomas T. Handy contacted the deputy chief of staff recommending Spaulding's plan. Handy included a proposed directive for the deputy's signature committing the army's historical program to the *status quo*. *There still would be no narrative operational history—only an index to the records*.[22] Handy believed "that sending historical officers to the Theaters is not justifiable; the proposed tasks can be performed in addition to their other duties by officers already overseas."[23]

Assistant Deputy Chief of Staff Colonel Otto L. Nelson, Jr. objected. A graduate of the U.S. Military Academy, a former instructor at West Point, with a doctorate from Harvard University, Nelson had experience in the army's organization and administration. He had his own progressive idea about recording the war. Based on his foresight, Nelson recommended the War Department establish an "organization ... to serve the needs of the war, by writing the history of both operations and administration."[24] He pointed to the British and the U.S. Navy's programs.[25]

On February 20, 1943, Nelson sent his recommendation and plan to Deputy Chief of Staff Lieutenant General Joseph T. McNarney. Nelson thought he needed McNarney's support "because the tendency was for everyone to feel that they were too busy fighting the war that they could not take the time to preserve historical records and compile a history."[26]

McNarney recommended to Army Chief of Staff George C. Marshall that some prominent men of academic, journalistic, and military backgrounds be recruited. They would "organize a system of writing a history of our military operations that will provide a first narrative and a proper documentation of source material, and that an appropriate organization be provided in Military Intelligence, Operations Division, or the Office of the Secretary of War to direct the historical program."[27] Nelson later said "neither General Marshall nor General McNarney were very greatly interested."[28]

When no action resulted, Nelson enlisted the help of Assistant Secretary of War McCloy who admired the Navy's effort. Dr. Samuel Eliot Morison directed that program. McCloy was interested.[29] On April 23, McCloy called an informal meeting in his office to "discuss the formation of a historical office for the current war."[30] It was agreed that the Historical Section's system for collecting key materials was sound. The meeting's attendees wanted an historian or a group to immediately begin the preliminary effort towards "a large-scale history [to be] written later. They also wanted work to begin on 'produc[ing]' the smaller studies on particular operations or aspects while the war was still in progress."[31]

McCloy told the five officers attending the conference to submit their ideas. The ideas of Major Charles H. Taylor of the Military Intelligence Service had the most influence in designing the organization. Taylor's recommendation resembled the British model. The new historical activity would be under the joint directorship of an historian and a committee of civilian historians and officers. The committee would write operational monographs, and "inspirational narratives and other studies ... for current use." The historian's primary duty would "lay the basis for a definitive, large-scale history for publication after the war."[32]

Conference attendee Acting Deputy Director of the Bureau of Public Relations Colonel E. Ernest Dupuy noted on April 26, 1943, that Dr. Morison "himself is moving to theaters of operation to obtain first-hand eye-witness perspective." He suggested the army do likewise. He wrote: "It would ... seem advisable that secure research be supplemented by contemporaneous historical operations, to included screening of eye-witnesses, commissioned and enlisted." Dupuy recommended Colonel William Addleman Ganoe for "historical duty."[33] Ganoe, a West Point graduate, was a professor of military science and tactics at the University of Michigan. He wrote *The History of the United States Army,* originally published in 1924, and *Soldiers Unmasked,* first published in 1935.[34]

Spaulding told McCloy "[W]e already have, in operation, machinery which can readily be modified to give you the result you are seeking." He "understood that the General Staff was planning 'a daily summary of events....'" He thought McCloy had something like a book in mind, "not restricted in circulation, based upon documents where available, but accepting and using also secondary evidences—bearing on somewhat the same relation to a definitive history as General Pershing's preliminary report bore to his final."[35]

Spaulding recommended assigning historical officers to overseas commands. McCloy was to assist in collecting and using the material. Spaulding warned McCloy that no matter how carefully the "historical machine" was set up, "the historian will be looked upon by the fighting men as more or less a nuisance." The historian must exercise "great care and tact." He "must be selected with care, strongly backed up, and not hurried."[36] This was "not theory." Spaulding learned from his own experience in Pershing's headquarters.[37]

On April 30, 1943, Secretary of War Henry Stimson issued a directive signed by McNarney. It instructed the G-2 to: "establish in the Military Intelligence Division the necessary organization to plan and supervise the compilation of the military history of the Second World War." McNarney described the new organization's responsibilities; it would plan and supervise:

1. "preparation and publication of a first narrative of military operations":
2. handle the "dissemination of a training aid of military information concerning current operations";

3. determine the "methods to be used for…accumulat[ing] … such documentary evidence … needed in … compil[ing] … an official history of the war";

4. establish the needed personnel and organization in the theaters to "accomplish the collection and forwarding of the necessary historical data and the prescription of the methods, procedures, and levels at which compilation of historical data will take place";

5. coordinate and supervise the work of War Department agencies and commands writing administrative histories.[38]

Assistant Chief of Staff, G-2 Major General George V. Strong objected to the location of the new organization. He said it should be part of the Office of the Assistant Secretary of War. McCloy overrode his objection. Strong instructed his assistant executive officer, Lieutenant Colonel John M. Kemper, to act for him. Kemper was a West Point graduate and had a master's degree in history from Columbia University. He worked faithfully with Nelson, who communicated closely with McCloy. As a result, the Office of the Assistant Secretary of War was the leading force in designing and creating the new historical organization.[39]

McCloy, Nelson, and Kemper established a six-member planning committee: three military and three civilians. The committee was to "recommend a program of organization for the compilation of the military history of the (current) war and … act as a permanent advisory committee."[40] Spaulding was one of the members. He said the Historical Section would administer a World War II historical program. He proposed the Historical Section be transferred from the Army War College "to … an authoritative agency of the War Department, such as the Office of the Secretary or Assistant Secretary, or an appropriate section of the General Staff."[41]

In May 1943, McCloy briefed the committee on the results of the developing historical program, which included:

1. a records preservation system;
2. monographs for Army School use;
3. a popular history to be published after the war, and
4. necessary steps during the war for ultimate publication of an authoritative official history.

The committee met six times in a month. It surveyed the current historical activities of military agencies. The committee asked about the historical records of the Southwest Pacific theater. This included the Operations Division and operations of the historical section of the Army Ground, Air, and Service Forces. Committee members visited the Army War College's Historical Section and the Office of Naval Intelligence.[42]

On June 26, the committee reported to McCloy. The committee advised the prompt creation of an organization within the Military Intelligence Division, charged with planning and supervising the compilation of the war's history. The organization, known as the Historical Branch, G-2, should be led by a brigadier general. A civilian historian under the branch chief was proposed. Planned writing included operational monographs, theater and campaign histories, administrative histories, and a popular history along with the publication of documents. Spaulding filed a minority report, again disagreeing over the need for a new organization. Nevertheless, McCloy approved the committee's report. He wanted to talk to the civilian historian candidate before a final selection was made. He also wanted to be consulted on who was to be selected as the general officer.[43]

The following month Nelson approved the report. Lieutenant Colonel Kemper's appointment to head the organization came on July 16. The committee had decided that the best route was to select a colonel eligible for promotion. Four days later the Military Intelligence Divisions notified its subordinate units that the Washington, D.C., Historical Branch, G-2, had been established.[44]

The War Department's August 3, 1943, memorandum stated the Historical Branch's "functions are to plan and supervise the compilation of the military history of the Second World War...."[45] The branch was responsible for:

1. preparing operational monographs, theater and campaign histories, administrative histories, a general popular history, and an official history;
2. publishing documents;
3. developing ways to gather significant documents;
4. establishing procedures to collect and forward historical information;
5. supervising agencies involved in writing administrative histories;
6. determining the functions and responsibilities of the Army War College's Historical Section;
7. discussing with the advisory committee, editing, and approving historical manuscripts written for publication by War Department agencies.[46]

In the words of its second military chief, Colonel Allen Clark, the branch had the broad "authority to do almost anything in regard to the history of the war which it desired to do."[47]

The Historical Branch's first assignment was to write, as soon as possible, short studies on specific military operations. This answered Army Chief of Staff General George C. Marshall's April 1943 directive for easily readable accounts of combat actions to benefit training staffs, and later to inform the public. This directive eventually resulted in 14 paperback pamphlets for *The American Forces In Action* series. The first pamphlet approved for publication in 1943 was *To Bizerte with the II Corps*.[48] The branch published it in February 1944 followed in July 1944 by *Papuan Campaign*. Both reportedly did not satisfy expectations.[49] But the Historical Branch developed by Barnes and Greenfield was realized. Now was the time to implement the combat operations historical program. It began by training combat historians.

CHAPTER 4

Training the World War II Combat Historian

When Kenneth Hechler was asked whether he had any training in the duties of a combat historian, he replied, "Well, sure. I have a Ph.D. in political science and my minor was in American History at Columbia University where I got my Ph.D. in 1940 and my dissertation was on a historical subject.... So, actually I had a good deal of experience in the area of history prior to my activities as a combat historian."[1]

In 1943 the Historical Branch provided a little classroom training. By 1944 the branch tried to go beyond the sometimes-static classroom. It incorporated into the curriculum lessons learned from the practical experiences of branch members who had deployed abroad. The branch also corresponded with in theater combat historians, such as the Fifth Army's Captain Chester G. Starr, Jr. The branch learned about the difficulties of writing combat histories. Colonel Charles Taylor spent 11 months in the ETO and worked with Ganoe and his deputy Samuel Lyman Atwood Marshall (SLAM). When he returned to the Historical Branch in February 1945, Taylor gave advice on problems and solutions.[2] These became part of the evolving training guide, "Orientation Material for Theater Historians."

Hechler said he was "transferred to the [Pentagon's] history section ... which got people ready to go to Europe and our assignment there was to take some of the combat reports from the Far East and fashion ... [them] into a readable account as we would in Europe after the war. And we had some very able people there including Forrest Pogue who wrote the five-volume biography of General George C. Marshall. This was all prior to my going [in April 1944] to Europe."[3]

Forrest Pogue, a professional historian with a doctorate from Clark University, had taught history until being drafted into the army in 1942. He later referred to a three-week training course:

> When I joined the Historical Section of the War Department in March 1944 ... we heard a lot about Sam [S.L.A. Marshall] since eight or ten of us had been brought in as the first combat historians to be sent overseas.... We took a three-week course on combat interviewing with [Major Hugh] Cole as instructor. We heard a lot about Sam's work in interrogation in the Pacific. His book, based on his interviews in Kwajalein, was on the way to be printed. We heard a lot about the fact that he was in some of the island battles and afterward when men in the units had little to do [aboard ship], he interviewed large numbers of them at a time.[4]

Pogue stated that Marshall had decided to organize a unit of combat historians whose task was interviewing enlisted soldiers and officers soon after combat and collecting eyewitness stories for the narratives.[5] Pogue believed Major Cole "designed ... an extremely off-the-cuff reading program...." He thought Cole was "the only one of them that had any claim to being an experienced military historian."[6]

Samuel Lyman Atwood Marshall is perhaps the most well-known World War II combat historian. By trade a journalist, he became one of the most renowned, albeit not without some controversy, combat historians of the 20th century. Beginning in 1922 he covered sports stories for the *El Paso Herald Times* and five years later for the *Detroit News* (a post he held intermittently until 1961). The cartoonist Tad Dorgan noted that his name was perfect:

> Good God. you must be dumber than I thought. Your initials spell SLAM. and you don't realize that's money in the bank? It's perfect for a sports editor. It's perfect for anything. Nobody can forget that name.[7]

In June 1942, Marshall was summoned to Washington where he became a civilian consultant to Secretary of War Henry Stimson. In September Marshall received a commission as a major and was assigned to the army General Staff's Information Branch, Orientation Section. There he assisted in writing the *Small Guides to Foreign Countries* series. It was intended to help American soldiers stationed abroad and led to the formation of the Army News Service. Marshall was influential in creating the policy for the relocation of Japanese Americans on the West Coast. That involved recruiting the 442nd Nisei Combat Team. With help from others, Marshall wrote this unparalleled policy and, in fact, engaged in its execution.[8]

In 1939, Marshall had started a daily column analyzing and anticipating developments in the war. He gained favor as a reputable writer. His credibility increased by publishing *Blitzkrieg: Armies on Wheels,* giving his sense of German tactics.[9]

Samuel Lyman Atwood Marshall (SLAM). (Courtesy University of Texas at El Paso Library, Special Collections Department)

In 1941, at the age of 41, this high school dropout, World War I veteran, and newspaperman volunteered for active duty.[10] He joined the Special Services Division, Army Service Forces and was transferred in August 1943 to the Historical Branch. Major Marshall was involved in writing short operational narratives, eventually resulting in *The American Forces In Action* series. The first to be drafted, but not published, was Marshall's *The Tokyo Raid* of April 1942.[11]

While Marshall acknowledged the branch's training course, which he maintained was largely written by himself, he placed an emphasis on in-theater training. Three of his recently arrived combat historians in the Pacific Theater had taken the course. However, he claimed "they were as mystified as ever about how to do the work. I had them in the field with me for five days while I worked over units of the 82nd Division. Watching, they got the idea almost at once. Nothing else works half as well as on-the-job training."[12]

In the summer of 1943, an officer was assigned to start recording Ground Forces' procedures and training.[13] Lieutenant J. S. Howe deployed to V Corps' divisions. He examined training to better prepare the history teams responsible for writing combat history.[14]

On January 25, 1944, Ganoe made more than 20 training suggestions. These were included in "The Orientation Material for Theater Historians." He said, "All history personnel, whether of first line teams or having functions in the History Section, should soon be schooled" in history techniques, namely:

- Methods of maintenance and disposition or records;
- Writing … pamphlets and first narratives;
- Winnowing … records;
- Preparation of records for particular archive deposit in Washington;
- Methods of extracting information from front-line personnel;
- Navy Methods.

The skills and knowledge required to record and understand warfare were:
Near shore assembly areas and their functions;

- Methods of communication on the battlefield;
- Composition, training, and functions of assault landings;
- Influence of terrain on attack;
- Night fighting;
- Modern types of attack, especially the pinch-out;
- Composition of corps, and Army troops;
- Organization and weapons of infantry divisions, armored divisions, air support command, airborne troops, rangers, and commandos.

Ganoe thought the training course "should give only fundamentals for the history gleaners and above all be put over with life and highest type of visual aids."[15]

Marshall probably would add training on how to fire a weapon. In February 1944, Ganoe referred to a school the historical teams were attending with a "curriculum we have devised."[16]

Despite the sometimes harried training experience, "the branch's recruiting and training efforts appear to have produced results that were generally gratifying." One historian cited the example of a letter from Lieutenant Louis Morton in New Caledonia concerning a team of five historians which had arrived recently in the Pacific. "They are all good men and a catch for any historical section. They are intelligent, mature, experienced writers, adaptable, and have good backgrounds. I think the Historical Branch made a wise selection."[17]

CHAPTER 5

Organizing Historical Units and Assigning Combat Historians to Theaters

Kemper feared combat units were not maintaining sufficient records so on August 6, 1943, he left his new Washington office for the Aleutians to investigate. There he participated in the *Kiska* operation aimed at driving the Japanese from the area. His in-theater observations and the meager records in Washington convinced him that writing an adequate combat history depended on the Washington Historical Branch

Bombing damage on Kiska Island, 4 gun 120mm. G-2 report, September 13, 1943. (Courtesy NARA)

sending trained men to theaters. They needed to remedy flaws in record keeping as well as in acquiring more information through interviews. And since theaters were keeping the most significant records, it appeared that the basic research and writing would be done in theater. He thought drafts could be sent to Washington to be edited and published. "With high-level backing, Kemper obtained permission to send nine three-man teams overseas to work on combat studies, hoping at the time to keep the work of these teams under the control of his branch."[1]

In 1943, Kemper went with the first two teams to the Mediterranean. For two months he was in that theater, and in England. While there, Kemper "helped establish a separate Army historical office in what was about to become a theater under overall British command, and he drafted a directive to guide its work. The order was issued internally rather than as orders from across the Atlantic that might have been resented or ignored."[2]

Kemper wrote about his concern and the Historical Branch's infant historical program in an illuminating letter dated September 16, 1943. He sent this to Chief of the Historical Section, AFHQ, Colonel Paul Birdsall. Kemper supposed the branch's two most urgent issues were collecting combat records and operational papers.[3] Even if units complied with U.S. Army regulations and submitted records, Kemper was unsure of their use to the Historical Branch. Among his criticisms were:

1. lack of recording telephone and oral orders, the "why of decisions and plans," and the plans' execution, particularly below the battalion level;
2. not capturing the "time and place" of actions; and
3. erroneous official records.

If the criticisms were valid, then Kemper urged immediate action be taken to strengthen records and record keeping.[4] On September 18, 1943, he wrote to Ganoe about similar apprehensions. Given the magnitude of the job, Kemper believed it was "remarkable" that staff officers were able to "keep any records at all."[5]

What was Kemper's solution? He told Birdsall the "best bet" was to send historical officers to the battlefield where they could track records and note where these were inadequate, investigate rumors, conduct interviews "during lulls in the battle and when they are in reserve or rear areas and so on." They "would operate effectively without getting in the hair of the men busy fighting the war." They would serve on division or corps commanders' staffs and perhaps be responsible for preparing the commanders' final reports. Historical officers were needed on the "ground before, during, and after every operation." Only by such a system, Kemper stressed, "will we be able to get the coverage that is essential to any first narrative that will have practical value both for training and historical purposes." The Historical Branch was "concerned with the assignment of historical officers to cover specific operations rather than the assignment of permanent historical officers to lower units." Kemper asked the Historical Branch to send Major Jesse Douglas to meet with him.[6] Douglas, a military historian, had worked for the National Archives. For a year he was the chief of the Records Management Branch of The Adjutant General's Office. When he learned of the new Historical Branch Douglas quickly asked to be assigned to it. After his punctual transfer, Douglas headed the branch's records section. In that job and subsequently as a liaison and policy officer, he prepared directives and visited theaters to assist in starting historical programs overseas.

Kemper then told Birdsall about the *American Forces In Action* project. "Think that over for a minute and you realize that we've really stepped into something!" To "set up a pilot model," the branch had written a manuscript about the 2nd Corps' operations over the last three weeks of the Tunisian Campaign. The branch had used all available sources, which included records in Washington along with interviews with wounded soldiers at Walter Reed Army Medical Center and with at least one battalion commander. The result was a "decidedly sketchy" product. "Only an occasional regiment's or battalion's action … [was] … detail[ed]." The maps were bad; the photographs were dreadful. So, the branch wanted to deploy Major Douglas. Kemper told Birdsall that he certainly did not want to be "thrown out of General Marshall's office because . . . [he] couldn't produce what he asked for."[7] He was "going to try to get … [Douglas] on his way."[8] This letter, included in the "Orientation Material for Theater Historians," is an insight into the developing methodology to be used by World War II combat historians.

In October 1943, Ganoe told Kemper that in addition to his 12-member staff he needed more historians in the field. "If I can't obtain officers, I will strive to fill in with Enlisted Men, forming teams for Corps and similar units. But the Enlisted Men," he clarified, "must come up to that high standard of education, acumen, acquisitiveness, unlimited energy, and fine character which we feel we have obtained with our present personnel."[9] He had support from the G-2. Ganoe also wanted the War Department to authorize "some green bands or other insignia" for these combat historians on the front.[10]

Ganoe sent his plan to the Historical Branch for collecting information on combat operations and manpower. He proposed that a team of 2 officers and 3 enlisted men be attached to each corps headquarters. One of the officers and two enlisted men would constitute the front-line team and be responsible for pulling together the data needed for a history of combat operations. The other officer and enlisted man would be charged with preparing a pamphlet directly after each operation. That pamphlet would be part of the *American Forces In Action* series.[11]

Who did Ganoe think was "the best man [to have] down with the troops and activities"?[12] As he told British Army historian, Brigadier General Sir James E. Edmonds in September 1943, it was a man with "newspaper reportorial experience—a hustler with insatiable curiosity, merely to get facts, dates, places, hours, events, reasons, action … [who could] put them down in telegraphic style As soon as possible, he writes them down in condensed narrative form." Rewrites would be done by "historians who can write."[13]

Also in October, a month after Kemper's letter to Birdsall, the Historical Branch developed a plan to organize historical teams. The branch intended to train the teams and then assign them to the theaters. The proposal recommended "nine teams, each consisting of a major, a captain, and a sergeant—every three teams were to comprise a group, headed by a lieutenant colonel."

On December 1, 1943, the War Department approved the plan with revisions. Majors were to command the groups; team officers were to be captains and first lieutenants. That month the first group left for North Africa. The Historical Branch sent Major Douglas on his way to gather information. In January 1944, the branch deployed Major Roy Lamson to Italy.[14] Lamson, a professor in civilian life, joined the branch from the Bureau of Public Relations. He helped prepare manuscripts for publication and forged the creation of combat historical teams deployed to theaters.

Ganoe asked that he be allowed to attach historical teams to the armies. In a letter to First Army Commander Lieutenant General Omar N. Bradley, Ganoe recommended "An historian team consisting initially of a team chief, four additional

From left to right: Major General Leven C. Allen, Lieutenant General Omar Bradley, Major General John S. Wood, Lieutenant General George S. Patton and Major General Manton S. Eddy being shown a map by one of Patton's armored battalion commanders during a tour near Metz, France, November 1944. U.S. Army. (Courtesy Wikipedia)

officers and four enlisted men will be attached from the Historical Section, ETOUSA, [the European Theatre of Operations, United States Army] to each Army. The team chief will direct the historical function of his team. The Theater Historian will have technical supervision over these teams and be responsible for their efforts." Ganoe made a similar proposal to Third Army Commander Lieutenant General George S. Patton. Both commanders approved the plan.[15]

In early 1944, the Washington Historical Branch organized other teams in the Central Pacific and ETOUSA. The first teams were assigned to higher headquarters. Their main task was preparing the *Army Forces in Action* narrative pamphlets. However, a standard system still was needed to cover operations at lower levels of command.[16]

Kemper visited North Africa in January 1944. He helped the Historical Section there to prepare an order summarizing the historical program's objectives and to issue instructions detailing the unit historical reports to be submitted and information about their preparation. On March 4, 1944, Major Dwight Salmon informed the Historical Branch that four teams were in the theater; three of them were with Fifth Army headquarters. Salmon wrote to Kemper that his directive had "prove[n] of enormous help in improving the material units will be turning out in the future."[17]

On March 29, 1944, Kemper told Ganoe that the War Department was working on a Table of Organization and Equipment (T/O&E) for a publicity, information, and history detachment. One detachment was to be available for each Army, separate corps, or task force. The manpower was to include:

1. A colonel to command the headquarters and headquarters detachment;
2. 1 lieutenant colonel as the historian;
3. 1 lieutenant colonel as the executive officer;
4. 1 major as the assistant executive officer;
5. About 10 enlisted men as clerks, typists, drivers, and specialists;
6. A magazine and feature unit of 2 officers and 1 or 2 enlisted men;
7. A radio unit of 2 officers and 1 or 2 enlisted men;
8. Operating under the headquarters and headquarters detachment a group of information collecting teams: 3 historical teams of 1 captain, 1 lieutenant and 2 enlisted men acting as historians; 1 enlisted man as cartographer.

A jeep and other items like typewriters, cameras, and weapons encompassed the equipment.[18] Kemper informed Ganoe that upon approval of the T/O&E these historical detachments would "absorb the historical teams" the Washington Historical Branch had already sent to the theaters.[19]

Kemper kept struggling to find qualified historical officers. On April 13, 1944, he wrote to Salmon: "I have calls from all the theaters for officers and am breaking my neck to find them. As I find them, I will keep you advised."[20] By the summer of 1945, the Washington Historical Branch had stepped up its assignment of personnel to theaters. This is evidenced in July 26, 1945, in a letter Kemper wrote to an historian in the South Pacific:

> We have really been turning out historians at a great rate the past two months. No less than four enlisted men, some of whom spent only about four days with us, the longest 28 days, have gone through. We have had up to 22 officers at one time, none over 30 days'[sic] the quickest time was one who reported in at 9:00 A.M. and signed out at 4:00 P.M. the same day.... [I]n two cases [we] were not even able to have our enlisted men come in; the time was too short, and they reported to the ports.[21]

As the Washington Historical Branch grew its program, the War Department's Bureau of Public Relations was busy developing a system for wartime news coverage.[22] On April 18, 1944, the department published a memorandum, officially creating the wartime historical structure and its missions. The memorandum read in part:

> The War Department desires to increase the flow of certain types of information covering the frontline combat activities of ground units. This material is to be used primarily for public relations purposes ... to put greater emphasis on the combat role of ground troops, particularly infantry.
>   A secondary mission ... is ... collecti[ng] ... data to be used for historical purposes and for summaries of combat lessons learned as a result of actual operations.[23]

In April 1944, the War Department initially proposed one 42-manned headquarters detachment, known as an Information and Historical Service (I&HS). An I&HS was to be attached to each army. Its main mission was to collect, prepare and send "information of all kinds to include moving and still pictures of public or general interest" about the organization's combat activities and of individual soldiers. Selected personnel were responsible for collecting and dispatching historically interesting material to the department along with information and photographs of distinct training value.[24]

On April 23, 1944, five days after the War Department's official creation of I&HS, the ETO Historical Section attached a team to First Army's G-3 (Plans). On May 5 a team was attached to the Third Army.[25] By June 1, the Historical Section had 10 officers and 9 enlisted men staffing historical teams. The enlisted soldiers were not a "clerical force. They were, with two exceptions, combat historians whose qualifications and duties equaled those of the officers. Some of the enlisted men had two or more academic degrees, were history professors, professional writers, newspaper men, etc."[26]

Lieutenant Colonel Cleaves A. Jones commanded the First Army Historical Team. It had a 4-person headquarters detachment, and 3 historical units each with 4 people. T/5 (Technician fifth grade) Forest Pogue was in the third Historical Unit.[27] As the historical editor, Major Hugh M. Cole commanded the Third Army Team. It had a 4-person headquarters detachment with 3 historical units: one with 3 soldiers and 2 with 2 soldiers each. Captain Kenneth Hechler led the headquarters detachment.[28]

In July 1944, Taylor told Kemper that two men per corps was "ludicrously inadequate when you have continuous operations" as in the ETOUSA.[29] Then on October 3, 1944, the War Department released T/O&E 20-12S. The I&HS totaled 43 soldiers. It authorized:

1. a headquarters detachment commanded by a colonel, 5 other officers and 7 enlisted men;
2. a magazine and feature unit (2 officers/2 enlisted men);
3. a monograph unit (1 officer/3 enlisted men);
4. a radio unit (1 officer/2 enlisted men);
5. a combat information collection units (3 officers/1 enlisted man each);
6. historical units each with 2 officers and 2 enlisted men equipped with three .30 caliber carbines, one .45 caliber submachine gun, one ¼-ton trailer, and ¼- ton truck.[30]

According to a War Department memorandum dated October 18, 1944, "Historical teams will be provided on a variable basis depending upon the strength and assignment of the organization to which attached. Normally, three of these teams are required for an army." In November 1944, Ganoe referred to field teams averaging more than 2 officers and 2 men per corps. He stated, "eighty-six historical officers and men were with the armies, who receiv[ed] technical supervision and some control from the Theater Historian."[31] Manpower was fluid.[32]

CHAPTER 6

Army Combat Historians in the Pacific

Before approval of the Historical Branch's plan for historical teams, it deployed Lieutenant Colonel S. L. A. Marshall to Hawaii in October 1943. He recorded the island operations of the Seventh Infantry Division.[1] In December 1943, the Historical Branch sent a team of two officers and one enlisted man to join Marshall. Three months later the team began operating.[2]

In December 1943, Marshall informed Taylor of his misgivings about being assigned to the Pacific theater. He wrote: "[W]hereas all of my training, military knowledge and inclination are disposed toward the European Theater. Here I am a tyro. In the other field, I am about as well qualified as any man in the Army. This does not seem reasonable."[3]

On February 23, 1944, Marshall penned similar woes to Kemper: "[N]ever before have I had the experience of going into combat, and out again, then into it, and out again, with never one day of rest—not even one Sunday." The only "break in this grind" was when he made a trip to the 33rd Division to set up a "historical operation." Soldiers received five-day passes after a battle. "That I simply could not afford." He referred to "our kind of business" and the need to "show the Staffs here that we mean business. I have kept them up until midnight time after time to work with me for the completion of the record. To keep going, on other nights, I've joined them in elbow-bending. That provided an aberration and gave me a rest. There was no other way I could keep going."[4] Marshall was known for his ability to write under pressure, to write fast, to meet deadlines, to keep a demanding schedule, and to expect others to work just as hard.

Marshall explained to Kemper the relationship of the historical program to the supported units. "The men are here now. They are good men—much too good to be left in the lurch. I do not intend so to leave them." He had developed a program which could not "be passed to the Team automatically." He had established the relationships and contacts and had the "degree and support" needed. Support had been "splendid. They believe in us because they have already discovered tangible values in our work." But he added, "imponderable values enter into this working relationship—friendship, respect, the comity that comes of service together in the field, an ability to speak the same language...."[5]

Continuing, Marshall disclosed to Kemper:

> I must stay here while these men learn how to work with the friends I have made. The course must be softened up for them so that they too can get in to the commanders when necessary and enjoy the full confidence of the Staffs.... Too, it is necessary to take them by the hand and train them, demonstrating the working method rather than telling about it.... At my request ... [they were] transferred ... to the 7th Division. They are now housed and officed there and ... will be working there. I will school them a while, then turn them loose. The Kwajalein job will be completed in this manner. The worst 60 percent is already done. Before I give over, I will see to it that they know all ... the commanders and their Staffs in person.[6]

Marshall had "crews of draftsmen" from the 7th and 27th Infantry Divisions working "to make complete sets of operations maps in the field."[7]

He used his journalistic skills to perfect a new way to write a military "story"/operation. The captivating development of this technique and the historical program in the Pacific is found in correspondence between Marshall and the Washington Historical Branch. It was included in "Orientation Material for Theater Historians." He wrote to Kemper on December 7, 1943, about the Makin Island operation,

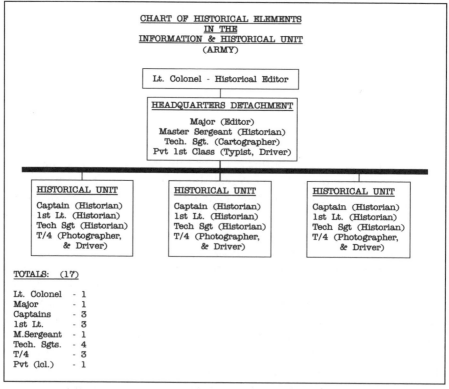

Historical Elements in the Information & Historical Unit, February 2–March 27, 1944.

Marshall informing Kemper how he analyzed the assignment. It was a "chance to cover an action from first to last." In doing so, "we might have something … unique in the [army's] records…." He "laid the groundwork" by doing complete background studies of the G2 [Intelligence], G3 [Operations and Plans] and G4 [Logistics]. He asked for details and knew "the operation in its entirety from each GI's viewpoint." Marshall told Kemper he "worked out for [himself] a tentative plan" that included "study[ing] preliminary bombardment, witnessing … landings," visiting the front lines, examining "enemy works," "retur[ning] to the front lines … mak[ing a] further check with Division [if feasible], talk[ing] with natives." He "spent about half of [his] time at the front and the other half elsewhere." Marshall saw "no other way to make a fair test of the records and journals." From them, he wrote, "we will never get more than 40 percent of what we need…. Where [was] the rest to be had"? "Well," he informed Kemper, "from a multifarious variety of people," ranging from the tankers and artillery to the beachmasters. It would come from interviews.

Marshall made several points about his interview technique.

> First … It is an error to believe that soldiers and commanders do not wish to talk right after an action. That is when they want to talk most. They are ready to tell what happened to them and they don't hold anything back.
>
> Second: They will talk readily to a non-commissioned officer under these circumstances, provided he has credentials.
>
> Third: Details begin to slip away from them within a day or two. It is surprising how I found everyone from the General to the greenest private forgetting the Day on which something took place even though remembering the HOUR.
>
> Fourth: The journals not only are scant from 60 to 80 percent of what is needed to interpret [an] operation but in many cases the entries are misleading because they bear on a fancied situation which is never corrected by an entry further along.
>
> Fifth: There are categories of vital information which are not touched by the records and which are lost to history unless gathered by the historians.[8]

Those categories included information on landings at Makin, enemy works and plans, battle tactics, and the effect of terrain on those tactics. All this Marshall "check[ed] in detail," to include studying the ground and the vegetation. Consequently, the operation he claimed was "more fully and accurately" covered "than any action fought elsewhere by our arms….." Marshall argued that was "because the historian was given full liberty of action and permitted to employ all of his time to utmost advantage."[9]

"As for coverage from other sources," Marshall wrote, "to wit, press correspondents. I have checked their stories and about 80 percent of what they have written is journalistic flapdoodle."[10] This was coming from a former newspaper man. The letter became part of the "Orientation Material for Theater Historians."[11]

On December 28, 1943, Marshall wrote to Taylor, making his case for group interviews. Marshall believed "higher headquarters can give them [combat historians] only the sketchiest ideas of what has gone on…." Regiments had a better idea than divisions. "But the battalion commander's accounting of the situation becomes almost a 'fixing bath' for our process. He can detail the major points and the reasons for decisions affecting the smaller units." From that dates and hours could be determined. Then he recommended going down to the company level "to get the expanded stories of local happenings...." Then the combat historian would know "where to begin the questioning."

Continuing, he wrote: "Group discussion is a good thing. I found it fruitful to get company officers together with some of their non-coms and privates who had been at a good point of observation and get them all talking about a given situation. What the men have to say is usually quite as pertinent as anything the officers have to say." He stressed the need for the combat historian to "look for direct quotes. What a commander or man actually says in a battle situation should be put down in his own words as nearly as possible."[12]

Marshall elaborated on January 9, 1944. "In the battalions concerned, I got the battalion commander, executive, S2 and the officers immediately concerned together with each group of enlisted men who had participated in each incident. Then, thread by thread, all of the parts were woven together. Being in the group, each man spoke

Anti-aircraft crew man a 37mm gun on Makin Island, Gilbert Islands, 1943. (Courtesy NARA)

fairly." The story then could be pulled together. Marshall cited his own experience in World War I as evidence of not knowing more than the "one-man" story. He reasoned these interviews could be used to supplement and correct written reports. Marshall said he "sat down and interviewed" soldiers who had completed reports and "found that the best part of what they knew had not been included in the report." He read "scores of reports which were completely sterile and have briefed the writers and elicited from them the most vital kind of information." The interviews were lessons learned. And they supplied "a sound basis for the writing of tactical history."[13]

Marshall explained his interview technique in *Island Victory: The Battle of Kwajalein*. He wrote about the "tactical confusions" over the Makin night operation in November 1943. That operation involved the 3rd Battalion, 165th Infantry and its advance to Butaritari Island. He compared it to a puzzle. Nobody seemed to know how the different combat actions related to each other. Facts were succumbing to "fable." The only way he saw to uncover the "truth of battle" was to interview those soldiers involved. This would determine "for once whether the small tactical fogs of war were as impenetrable as we had always imagined they were."

Over four days he talked individually to each member of the gun crews while the company officers and battalion staff were there. The fogs of war were penetrated. "[E]very fact of the fight was procurable—the facts lay dormant in the minds of men and officers, waiting to be developed." He compared it to "like fitting together a jigsaw puzzle, a puzzle with no missing pieces but with so many curious and difficult twists and turns that only with care and patience could we make it into a single picture of combat."

Continuing in *Victory Island* Marshall wrote:

> We discovered other things as we went along—important things. We found that the memory of the average soldier is unusually vivid as to what he has personally heard, seen, felt and done in the battle. We found that he recognizes the dignity of an official inquiry where the one purpose is to find the truth of battle, and that he is not likely to exaggerate or to be unduly modest. We discovered also that he will respond best when his fellows are present, that the greater the number of witnesses present at the inquiry the more complete and accurate becomes the record, since the recollection of all present is a check on the memory of any one witness.[14]

Marshall wrote to Kemper again on March 9, 1944. He referred to his interview technique as a "critique." Marshall thought anyone considering it in the "abstract" in the War Department might contend it led to "confusion." Using capitalization evidently to underscore his argument, Marshall stated it was the "ONLY WAY TO GET ORDER OUT OF CONFUSION." A man thinking "on his feet" could get soldiers to "let their hair down." Those thinking they knew soldiers had not "given thought to the meaning of the word." His "former associates talk[ed] that way." He said they "reminded … [him] of some of … [his] favorite characters in Alice in Wonderland."[15] This letter also was included in "Orientation Material for Theater Historians."

S. L. A. Marshall interviews two soldiers in the Pacific, no date. (Courtesy University of Texas at El Paso Library, Special Collections Department)

The result was the group interview after combat technique. Marshall thought it was "the most important discovery of all—the immediate *tactical* value gained by seeking the full detailed history of an action. The companies themselves were direct and immediate beneficiaries of all that was learned." Each man knew what "personal role" he played in the larger scheme of the battle. "Direct tactical and moral dividends … came out of every company interview held."[16] This was contemporary on-the-battleground use of the combat historian's work.

Marshall included in *Island Victory* a "how to do it" manual for historical officers, giving more details about his methodology and interviewing techniques. Firstly, the historian must determine if an interview was warranted. If a company's action in a battle was "confused" or when its participation was of particular significance "deserving of the most minute searching so that the battle history may be organized with balance and perspective" an interview was needed. Next, the historical officer must do the research "by examining the regimental and battalion journals" and listening to what was being said about the action. He could then determine which companies to interview. The interviewer must know the details and view of the battle from the company to the battalion level, and their interactions; know the terrain by going there or by examining maps. He then could "relate all that he hears to the context of the battle, without having to be led by the hand by the company itself."

When should the interviews begin? Marshall wrote: "Companies have been interviewed … beginning within thirty minutes after leaving the front and their battalion officers have participated willingly." The interview should follow the natural course of the battle from "the starting point—the point where some individual soldier (or squad) of the company first fires upon the enemy or is fired upon by the enemy" and then continue in chronological order. That would dictate the order in which soldiers were called. That order "depend[ed] upon the time sequence of the combat story and never upon the rank of those who are telling it. All soldiers including officers," Marshall adjudged, "are equal in the informal court. Relative rank does not bear on the weight of the evidence as to what happened during the fight."

Once the company was assembled, with all the officers present and preferably with the commander or his executive, the interviewer explained his objective. He made it clear that "we are here today to determine the facts." Each interviewee was equal. If something, in the view of an interviewee, was stated erroneously regardless of the rank that man held, it was his "duty to stand up and speak … [his] piece."

The interviewing officer then called his first witness. As each man mentioned the names of others, they should be called upon. The interviewing officer would "guide" the interview along. The historical officer need not ask all the questions. The company commander might take the lead, while the historical officer saw that what he determined necessary was being covered.

What about the questions? "The interviewing officer must look constantly for cause and effect." He must seek to know the how, what, and why of an action. For instance, "It is not enough to know that men fell back; there must be reasons brought out why they did fall." A blackboard or wall with chalk in hand or a "pot of sand or clear sand" should be available so that interviewees could plot their positions. A sketch should be developed. Marshall imagined combat historians "should be able to sketch in their situation maps—even in rough form—as they set down their facts. Unless they are prepared to do this, their accounts will not be clear and … they themselves will become confused about what they have written. It is the only way," he emphasized, "to preserve the story and they cannot depend upon others in the field to do this work for them. Maps done some time after are as inaccurate as narratives written some time after. And on that point," he added, "I want to make it even more definite that what is said, thought or remembered 3 or 4 weeks later has less [than] half the value of what is said and thought AT THE TIME. Men forget, and likewise, they want to change their stories."[17]

How long did the interview process take? "To reconstruct one day of vigorous battle," Marshall wrote, "will usually take about two days of briefing [interviews] (five to six hours each day), provided the men are given the opportunity to do most of the talking. They will always be keener and will participate more freely on the second day, and, if a third day is needed the response will again rise."

How much training should the historical officer have in interviewing? "None of this," opined Marshall, "calls for an expert trained in such briefing, or for special training in conducting such interviews. Any company officer who has the respect of his men and a reasonable amount of horse sense can do it. If he is fitted to lead them into battle, he is fitted to lead them in re-living the battle experience." In many cases "less than ten minutes of coaching" would do it.

"Above all," Marshall wrote, "the interviewer must remember he is there to get the facts. He is not conducting a critique, takes no part in tactical debate, and does not become personal or emotional. He avoids any reflection on individuals as he would the plague."[18] Yet, Marshall did take part in tactical debate. Marshall told Taylor in December 1943, "I do not feel that I can undertake that [writing narratives] here. First, because I have no help of any kind, and second, because the work of getting the basic stuff together simply grinds one's brains to powder." He said he had written some "40,00 [sic] words and made notes to an additional 20,000. Any writing hack could take my basic and turn out a book from it." Marshall explained that he "could do such a book in 10 days. But here, I don't have the days…. It is not possible to do finished work in the field under these present circumstances." He maintained: "That is far beyond the compass of one man." The three-man historical team sent from the Washington Historical Branch, which he retrained, was not operational until March 1944.[19]

Major General Ralph C. Smith, commander of the 27th Infantry Division, valued Marshall's work. On December 12, 1943, he wrote to Assistant Chief of Staff, G-2, Major General George V. Strong, who supervised the Historical Section. As a "commander of a task force in active operation," he had received "material assistance" from Marshall. During the Makin Operation, Marshall had "spent some time with the 27th Division during the preparation phase; then he accompanied the landing force, was present throughout the brief operation, then retired with the landing force to the base in Hawaii. He [Marshall] gathered what appears to me to be highly important data. His tact and keenness as an observer made him a most valuable member of the expedition." Smith considered "that the pattern he has set for collecting historical data on the spot should prove of greatest value, both to the Army in its present training problems and to the future for basic historical data. If the Historical Section can send officers on such missions who are the equivalent of Colonel Marshall in judgment and tact, I think they will always be welcomed by commanders."[20]

Smith realized that Marshall's data could be used at once. As an illustration, Marshall had discovered that failing to place a tank platoon under the infantry unit to which it was attached often resulted in the tank platoon's exit from the operation before the enemy's defeat; the infantry unit was left without heavy weapons. In one case Marshall concluded that the tank platoon leader had not checked the ammunition supply. When he realized the need to resupply, he just removed the whole platoon from the action without warning the infantry. As a result of Marshall's work, tank platoons were placed under the infantry commander to conserve ammunition and to restock by section rather than by the entire platoon.[21] That was a valuable lesson learned from Marshall's work.

What type of "historical material" was Marshall gathering? He listed several types when he wrote to Kemper in February 1944. Among them were:

Signal Corps maps;
Air Photo Interpretation maps and charts made before an operation;
other tactical maps;
captured enemy maps;
special maps created by the headquarters for his team;
G-2 estimates of enemy strength;
G-2 recapitulations of enemy situation following operation, relating to armament, positions, conduction of troops, etc.,
Special training orders in anticipation of operation.

He said the list "could go on almost endlessly." These were the most significant. Two central sources were: "(1) The official records [and] (2) Our narrative records…. [T]he teams should understand there … is no limit to the search."[22]

On June 27, 1944, Taylor wrote to Kemper that he had studied Marshall's Kwajalein and Makin works and believed "nobody but Sam could have done it" because of his "battle experience, knowledge of what to look for, aggressiveness, and reportorial skill … Sam is really doing, in a remarkable way, what all the elements in the Information and Historical units are supposed to do." Marshall produced history, battle stories and "direct analysis for tactical lessons and statement of the same." While others could follow Marshall's lead with the first two, Taylor supposed it was the "third feature … that it will be hard for anyone to follow in Sam's footsteps." He thought that was just a bridge too far for most of the men.[23]

In July 1944, Kemper responded to Taylor. War Department policy required "factual narratives, without criticism or statement of lessons, conclusions, or opinions by the writer … case history material."[24] Kemper agreed that Marshall had "accomplished all the objectives set up for the Information and Historical Services and he acknowledged 'that our boys should not attempt to emulate Sam's efforts to draw conclusions and develop lessons. We are in business first and last, to establish the facts. That done, there are plenty of people to analyze those facts.'"[25]

Marshall thought the battlefield uncovered more advantages of the historian's work. Among them were:

1. sharing information between organizations,
2. providing "tactical research" with him as an advisor, and
3. "spreading new methods."

Marshall believed "a man coming out here has to work at first like an aluminum pan salesman."[26] He realized the added importance of the records he amassed. They were of immediate use in determining awards and decorations "so that men heretofore unrecognized will get their just due."[27]

Added to that list was easing friction between organizations when one blamed the other for an action. "[F]act-finding stops recrimination and restores mutual confidence." Through "redressing of the records" the historian could advise those keeping poor records like journals. "When I see one doing a faulty job and the next regiment doing a proper job, I sometimes call that to the official attention so that the Division will become interested in establishing a general level of reports. We are interested in the records and we <u>can</u> tactfully work toward bringing the level up."[28]

On July 13, 1944, the War Department notified the Central Pacific Area commander, General Robert Charlwood Richardson Jr., about the organization of the 1st Information and Historical Service (I&HS). The unit was activated on August 5, 1944, at Fort Shafter, Oahu, for the Central Pacific Area. On September 17, 1944, the unit moved to Fort Ruger, Oahu. It was aligned under the G-2. The unit had: 3 news teams, 3 historical teams, a headquarters, and a headquarters detachment. That should have totaled 49 personnel—but the 1st I&HS never reached its full authorized strength.

Some of the initial historians and news reporters of the 1st I&HS were experienced, having served in the Gilbert and Marianna Islands. One of the first two historians was assigned to the 81st Infantry Division for the Mariana and Palau Islands campaign (June–November 1944); the other historian continued work on a monograph about the Battle of Saipan (June 15–July 9, 1944). In September 1944, Major Hugh Lytle, a public relations officer and former Associated Press bureau chief, assumed command of the 1st I&HS. A mechanic temporarily filled the clerk typist position.[29]

On October 3, 1944, the officer strength was reduced by three. A clerk typist replaced a radio technician in the headquarters detachment. In each historical team,

American personnel inspecting a destroyed Japanese pillbox on Ebeye Island, Kwajalein Atoll, painted by Coast Guard Combat Artist Ken Riley, April 4, 1944. (Courtesy NARA)

Army reinforcements disembarking from LSTs form a graceful curve as they proceed across coral reef towards the beach. Saipan. *ca.* 6/1944–*ca.* 7 /1944. (Courtesy NARA)

a technician who had been carried as a photographer was designated the historian. The news teams were reorganized into five teams. A historical pool was formed with assignment of individuals to various headquarters. In November 1944, the Historical Branch assigned three historians to the 1st I&HS. The unit remained with the Tenth Army until August 30, 1945. It was assigned to XXIV Corps for the occupation of Korea.[30]

Historians were deployed to the Philippines to prepare histories for the Leyte Operation (October 17, 1944–July 1, 1945). Their principal mission was collecting, preparing, and forwarding material about combat operations to the War Department.[31] Their expanded assignment developed a rough framework for the theater history.[32]

In December 1944, a group of historians was attached to armored-unit-participants in the battle of Saipan. Their job was to write the units' history. Second Lieutenant Russell Gugeler was among them. Before soldiers left for Okinawa, most Tenth Army combat historians were assigned to units for the coming battle.

Marine historians were already attached to III Amphibious Corps headquarters and to the Marine divisions assigned for the battle. Lieutenant Colonel John Stevens commanded the Army historians. Master Sergeant James M. Burns, author of *Guam* in the *American Forces In Action* series, was his chief assistant. They accompanied Tenth Army Headquarters. Captain Donald L. Mulford arrived from Leyte with

On the beach of Leyte Island, Philippines, members of the 21st Infantry Regiment, 24th Infantry Division, unload supplies from small craft. (Courtesy NARA)

XXIV Corps and stayed with the corps until late May. Then he was assigned to the 96th Division, replacing its historian, Sergeant Bert Balmer, who had been wounded in action.[33]

To synchronize their work, Army historians held regular conferences throughout and following the campaign. They quickly formed a liaison with the Marine historians, continuing it during the operation. The Army historians acquired additional details and perspectives from U.S. Navy personnel. Following the campaign, the historians chronicled the operations of the four U.S. Army divisions and of the 6th Marine Division. Major Roy E. Appleman, XXIX Corps headquarters, wrote a history of the XXIV Corps on Okinawa; U.S. Marine Corps Reserve Captain James R. Stockman recorded a history of the 1st Marine Division on Okinawa.

A group of Army historians was with the 1st I&HS. By January 1945, the unit was attached to the Tenth Army to cover the Battle of Okinawa (March 26–July 2, 1945). By March 1946, Appleman completed the narrative of XXIV Corps' operations on Okinawa. Gugeler finished the 7th Division's participation in the campaign. Stevens, Appleman, and Gugeler were qualified for separation—but they decided to return to Washington with the Okinawa records. They continued their work in the War Department Special Staff's Historical Division. With Sergeant Burns, a civilian by then, they finished the Okinawa history by the end of June 1946. The men

Army amphibian tractor and tank battalions in the Battle of Saipan, June15–July 9, 1944, 1st Lieutenant Russell A. Gugeler, 1st I&HS, January 20, 1945. (Courtesy CMH)

handed the manuscript over to the Pacific Section of the Historical Division, War Department Special Staff, for finalization. The final product, published in 1948, was *Okinawa: The Last Battle*.[34]

On February 14, 1945, in the wake of the Ryukyus operations, two more news teams were authorized.[35] Their mission was providing a "flexible unit which could be attached to an army or task force for a specific operation to handle public relations, news gathering and the preparation of the official War Department history."[36]

In July 1945, following the Battle of Okinawa, Colonel Stevens and Sergeant Burns were separated from the 1st I&HS. They returned to Oahu to write about all army units in the battle. Captain Edmund G. Love, 27th Division, an experienced historian of operations in the Central Pacific wrote the division's history by July 1945. He returned to Washington. The other army combat historians remained with their units, interviewing soldiers, writing division and corps histories, and awaiting new assignments.[37] The 60th Historical Team, I&HS, also served in the Pacific theater. The unit was constituted on July 21, 1945, and activated in the Philippines on August 9, 1945, just before the end of World II. The 60th served with the occupation forces before it was inactivated on May 31, 1946. On November 1, 1948, the unit was redesignated as the 305th History Team and allocated to the Organized Reserve Corps.[38]

After the war the work continued. Captain Paul R. Leach who had served with the 77th Division on Leyte, finished the operational history of the 77th Division. Captains Mulford and Jesse L. Rogers wrote the 96th Division's operational history. Major Appleman and Captain Russell Gugeler were deployed to Oahu in late 1945. There they completed their respective corps and division histories. Later they traveled with the XXIV Corps and the 7th Division to Korea.[39]

Details on I&HS are scant. The 4th and 5th I&HS were organized in the Pacific on July 13, 1944. They had the same structure as the 1st I&HS. However, 3 officers and 1 enlisted man were added to the news teams. That totaled 28 officers, plus 1 warrant officer and 24 enlisted men.[40] In time, the 4th, 5th, and 6th I&HS were activated in the Ninth, Seventh, and Fifteenth Armies, respectively.[41]

According to the after action report dated August 1, 1945, in the Ryukyus campaign, the organization with personnel vacancies had the mission of preparing the theater history of U.S. Army Forces, Pacific Ocean Areas along with the operational narratives for the Central Pacific campaigns. Seven officers and two enlisted men were available for combat historical coverage of the Ryukyus campaign. Combat historians were attached to Headquarters Tenth Army, 7th Division, 27th Division, 77th Division, 96th Division, and to XXIV Corps. The combat historians held regular meetings at Tenth Army Headquarters. They coordinated their work, discussing problems, arranging for photographic and cartographic coverage, gathered enemy material and developed an outline of the history to be written. Tenth Army told the division historians before they began their interviews which phases of the operation should be covered from squad and company level and which phases should be recorded from the battalion and regimental level.[42]

Tenth Army Historian John Stevens' work was hampered by not being included in the passenger list of the Tenth Army command ship. Consequently, he did not have contact with the Army command on the voyage to the area of operation, nor in the operation's initial stages. He stayed at XXIV Corps Headquarters, visiting the Tenth Army command ship as often as practical until headquarters moved ashore. Then he attended the daily general staff meetings. With another combat historian, he interviewed various staff members. He studied copious reports and documents and toured the front lines with the division historians.

The division and corps historians kept daily journals of their activities and interviews. They sent copies to the Tenth Army historian. The division historians were at the front lines almost daily. They observed the action and kept close contact with the battalion in line. The operation's history was written at the battalion level. The historians kept in touch with their G-2 and G-3, other staff sections and attached units, and the commanding general. They emphasized the need to get the command point of view, decision making, and on using intelligence about enemy plans and tactics. The Tenth Army historian contacted the Marine divisions' historians to review their submitted reports. The 1st I&HS officers revised and enlarged a manual written before the operation by another historian. It was issued as "A Guide for Historical Officers in the Field."[43]

The after action report included a section on lessons learned. This streamlined the work of future combat historians. Another section included recommendations on assigning historians at different command levels. The report suggested wider distribution of "preliminary, unofficial drafts" among an action's participants. That would elicit "more comment, criticism, and additional information." This would give lessons learned to soldiers engaged in future actions. It would also promote the Pacific's historical program and further its acceptance "by demonstrating its accomplishments." The report recommended the appointment of a major as the senior historian. That rank was because of the "importance of the position and high qualifications demanded." Plus, "much of the historian's work is done with very high ranking officers."[44]

The 10th I&HS, attached to Headquarters, Eighth Army, also served in the Pacific.[45] The unit's monthly reports made in 1943 and 1944 were detailed operational narratives, along with a section called "comments."

The 10th I&HS prepared a 14-page action report of the operation on Panay Island, with maps and charts. The report outlined the situation before the American landing, defense preparations, the operation's progress after the landing, activities following the Japanese surrender, observations, and a tactical critique. A supplement included an interrogation of a Japanese officer, along with his biography. The 10th I&HS also produced a staff study of the operation.[46]

Roy E. Appleman, James M. Burns, Russell A. Gugeler, and John Stevens, *Okinawa: The Last Battle* (*United States Army in World War II: The War in the Pacific*). (Courtesy CMH)

The 10th I&HS did a staff study of Japanese operations on Mindanao Island. The narratives were based on accounts prepared by Japanese officers, including interrogations of the officers at Eighth Army headquarters in Yokohama. Wiring diagrams and maps were part of the study.[47] This well-organized study shows the historians' breadth of research and knowledge of the operation.

U.S. LCM carries troops of Company I, 34th Infantry Regiment, 24th Infantry Division up the Mindanao River for the assault on Fort Pikit. (Courtesy CMH)

CHAPTER 7

Army Combat Historians in Europe

A historical section existed in the European theater of operations, U.S. Army (ETOUSA) *before* creation of the Washington Historical Branch. As mentioned in Chapter 3, Developing The World War II Army Historical Program, the idea for a historical program had existed in the ETOUSA at least since April 5, 1943. On that day, ETOUSA Commander Lieutenant General Frank M. Andrews asked the War Department to assign Colonel William A. Ganoe to his command. Andrews wanted Ganoe "to start an historical record of ETO."[1]

Ganoe arrived in London on May 8, 1943. He was assigned to the Censorship and Information Section, however, nobody knew what he was supposed to do because

U.S. Army personnel remove bodies from the wreckage of Lieutenant General Frank M. Andrews' B-24 after it struck a mountain side in Iceland, May 3, 1943. (Air Force Historical Research Agency, Wikipedia)

Andrews and Colonel Morrow Krum from the Public Relations Office, who had been involved in formulating the historical program concept, had been killed in an airplane crash.[2] According to the Washington Historical Branch, the primary mission was collecting data to supplement unit and staff records. A secondary mission was writing brief operational narratives (e.g., pamphlets) for immediate War Department publication.[3] This sounds like the WWI historical program.

Ganoe, essentially the theater historian, did not hesitate. On May 20, 1943, he presented his "Proposed Initial Plan for Producing the History of the ETO." It was the Historical Section's objective, he wrote, "… to produce a history of the ETO which is at once accurate, balanced, and readable."[4] Ganoe added the Historical Section would need access to confidential and secret information.[5]

The section was be divided into four subsections with the following personnel:

1. Past Affairs; (2 officers);
2. Current Affairs (4 officers);
3. Compilation (1 officer);
4. Illustration (1 officer).

The Compilation Subsection would "write drafts of the narrative and seek in every way to have the truth control the balance and perspective."[6] Continuing, Ganoe stated:

> It shall be the constant effort of the History Section to obtain constructive criticism from the principal participants in the ETO by personal interviews and correspondence….The … plan, if followed should produce the first contemporary history accomplished during any of our wars—*history on the spot and at the time* [Italics added].[7]

He believed the section's primary mission was obtaining—on the ground and at the time—those happenings and statements which had a chance of being lost or distorted later.[8] On May 27, 1943, Ganoe related in his "Notes on Importance and Possible Extension of this Section" that he did not want to "over-emphasize the importance of the Section charged with recording that history [of the ETO]…." Nonetheless, "it is … clear that the conception of researching and drafting the story of the ETO contemporaneously with passing events is probably one of the most signal advances in the writing of American history."[9] He said, "It is probable that representatives of this Section should accompany at least rear echelons of any task force or forces to be used against the common enemy in the near future."[10] The section might even have to send soldiers to North Africa.[11]

On June 7, 1943, the chief of staff approved his plan. By that time Ganoe was appointed to the Office of the Assistant Chief of Staff, G-3.[12] Ganoe added more recommendations:

1. [S]eek … interpretations, explanations, elaborations and firsthand knowledge of happenings … as may be needed for a full understanding of them;

2. [S]ubmit narrative drafts of major occurrences for criticism to the main characters in the story of the ETOUSA as soon after the particular occurrence as possible;

3. Give at least one officer in the History Section … access to … secret and confidential information … allow[ing] him to obtain the proper balance and perspective for the … narrative drafts;

4. Select every member of the History Section … carefully … [ensuring] he is so thoroughly impressed with the solemn obligation of secrecy that he will not be tempted to discuss any of the material outside of the official research and preparation.[13]

ETOUSA Commanding General Lieutenant General Jacob L. Devers, approved the recommendations on June 9, 1943.[14] On October 4, V Corps issued a directive stating the History Section was "directly responsible for the history of V Corps and … its representatives were to have access to commanders for questioning."[15] Historical officers were to be appointed. In addition to their other assignments, their historical duties were "mainly … cooperating with the ETOUSA history representative in seeing that oral and written matters of historical interest were not lost."[16]

The History Section was responsible for compiling the theater's history. The staff was to have "access to records and opportunities to question" personnel. In another directive, general officers were asked to keep a concise account of significant events, conferences and explanations for their key decision making. These two directives were the first to field forces on historical matters.[17] Ganoe had Devers' support, which attested to Devers' historical-mindedness and to Ganoe's resilience. At one point, Ganoe released this statement: "Under War Department directives and the Sixth Army Group Commander's specific instructions the Theater Historian is given supervision over all Information and Historical Units in the Theater."[18]

Ganoe and his historical officers coupled the directives with personal appeals. On August 18, 1943, Ganoe gave a 10-minute talk to commanders. He stated that the War Department and the ETO had historical officers to gather records and to write history. He said a current history would be more accurate and just to commanders "than termite stuff years afterward."[19]

When the ETO Historical Section was created, Kemper contacted Ganoe.[20] In August 1943, Assistant Deputy Chief of Staff Colonel Nelson was in the ETO. He had carried a letter from Major Taylor, acting chief of the Historical Branch. Nelson and Ganoe met that month whereupon Ganoe learned of Taylor's letter. Taylor made it clear that he wanted transparency between Ganoe and the Historical Branch. Taylor wrote that due to the Historical Branch's responsibility "and in order to devise an immediate working program, (the Branch was) vitally interested in the setup, for historical purposes, at present existing or in process of organization in all theaters." Taylor also wanted information on each theater's writing program.

He explained the information was essential to efficient program planning "from the standpoint both of records and of production, and one which will make of greatest service to the country the work of the theater organizations."[21] Taylor then asked for specific material.

Three days later Ganoe replied to Taylor telling him of the program's progress, status and answering Taylor's questions. Taylor wanted to know if there were directives defining the program and directives executing the program concerning records and writing. He inquired about the types of proposed historical studies (e.g., battle studies, campaign studies, theater history, unit histories, and administrative history). And he wanted to learn about the writing in progress or planned. Ganoe replied that he had not issued formal directives. Instead, he relied on "verbal orders and informal memoranda...." He explained the casual and successful cooperation between the component commanders made official directives unnecessary. But there were directives relative to writing and collecting war diaries, journals, and the order of battle.[22]

Ganoe planned combat studies; an operational current history of the ETO; monographs of organization and methods of current theater and general headquarters history and collecting and indexing material for unit histories. He was primarily interested in writing a monograph. The section was inventorying repositories; collecting war diaries and journals; obtaining leads; locating records and diaries; and creating a broad clipping service of all British news releases, the *Stars and Stripes* and *Yank* magazines, and clippings sent from the homeland.[23] Undoubtedly, the emphasis was on historians writing in theater, locating and collecting source material. The historians advised staff sections and units on the creation, maintenance, and preservation of records.

Taylor also inquired about manpower. Ganoe reported there were 6 officers; all except one had a graduate degree. There was also 1 warrant officer, 1 civilian secretary, and 3 enlisted artists. The artists provided "historical photographs, paintings executed in the field, photostats, etc." There were no personnel to establish the Past Affairs subsection.[24]

Taylor asked if units were methodically keeping operation reports, journals, and other records. Ganoe told Taylor that instructions addressed noncompliance with regulatory requirements. Records were not centralized at the theater headquarters, but the section was trying to correct that. Although there were no directions about the disposition of The Adjutant General files, theater historical officers had access to them. Copies of war diaries, journals and operational reports were forwarded to Washington. Units maintained administrative records until the War Department authorized their disposition.[25]

On September 18, 1943, Ganoe again wrote to Taylor. He explained the ETO program in more detail. "Our representative sells to the commanders in the field the idea of recording and preservation by appeal to their desires for the future veneration of the Unit." He was "slowly convincing the generals to preserve their remarks, reactions and discussions with others not to be found in documents [and] … ask[ing] them to dictate for not over ten minutes first thing in the morning these oral matters which will be lost or tragically mutilated later."

Four generals were doing just that, including General Devers. Ganoe was promoting the idea "that such dictation will help them to coordinate and crystallize scattered happenings for the benefit of their own decisions." The generals believed it aided them. "One of them," he wrote, "is highly enthusiastic."[26] And, Ganoe informed Taylor, his three artists assisted not only by taking photographs, but also by scouting out "critical happenings." These "happenings" were not recorded elsewhere.[27] Earlier Ganoe stated the need for the section to work closely with the Pictorial Service.[28]

On that same day, and included in "Orientation Material for Theater Historians," Ganoe issued "Notes on Our Present Objective and Plans" intended for his staff. He also sent the notes to Taylor. The notes on procedures to follow in writing monographs, and beneficial ideas and suggestions were:

1. Amply illustrate manuscripts;
2. Seek documented and substantiated facts;
3. Limit notes and observations while gathering information;
4. Write a short and abbreviated "first narrative" when visual, oral and written research was adequate to have any part ready for a well-connected account;
5. Critique the "first narrative" and then revise it until all inaccuracies are eliminated and gaps filled;
6. Start work on the final monograph once all narratives are completed;
7. Submit the final monograph to the high command for criticism and final approval.[29]

Ganoe wrote that these were grounded on the actual experiences of historians, "the outstanding historian of the British Army, Brigadier General Sir James E. Edmonds, and [on] German publication and production of [post World War I history]…." Declaring oral testimony critical, he wrote:

> Contemporary or current history cannot be written from documents alone. Those concerned must be consulted at the time and if possible, the historical representative should be on the scene for main occurrences to obtain general atmosphere, conditions, and temper of the military men as well as specific facts. Every effort must be given by the representative to obtain those statements, reasons or estimates which will never appear in writing and which would otherwise be lost.[30]

They were writing "first narratives … the work of faithful reporters. The finished history will probably be an assembly of these monographs elaborated and pieced together by historians who are also writers." One must be "able to rustle and hustle prodigiously, drudging often until late hours;" avoid being "'writey' or verbose." "Remember," Ganoe cautioned, "not to get lost in the trees. Let your criterion be 'Does it affect the ETO as a whole?' Work closely with unit historians. Pertinent Allied and enemy material will be set down in notebooks wherever found." Finally, Ganoe instructed, "We must not have correspondence with commentators on our narratives. Personal contact must prevail. Have interviews over disagreements."[31]

"Notes on the Methods of Production of the History of the ETO" was also part of the "Orientation Material for Theater Historians." It was a guide for Ganoe's staff. The historians were to be mindful in their research and writing that the intent of the ETO's history was "not a recital of the intimate details of any particular unit...."[32] Instead, the focus was on the actions coming from the headquarters. While the narrative was to be unified, there was no problem in "introducing human interest and contemporary features...." Finding ways to fill in gaps might be problematic. Initially, it may be "puzzling" to know where to close the account of the "ETO's share in the North African campaign." The "order of procedure" was:

1. Interview people familiar with records and happenings;
2. Obtain leads to repositories and people;
3. Locate repositories and pictures;
4. Make a general inventory of repositories;
5. Research interview and correspondence;
6. Write a draft;
7. Obtain criticism of drafts from authorities;
8. Write the final copy.

Forget rank and position. Each job was significant and their success in accomplishing them would affect those in the future. Be open-minded. Include facts rather than predetermined impressions or views. Ganoe told his staff, "We will oftentimes be like prospectors digging through sand and silt. But when we unearth a nugget, we will be repaid for all our back-breaking, and not without a romantic thrill." They were "writing interpretive] history—not annuals or chronicles [and not] ... a mere succession of facts and happenings." Identify conjectures or assumptions. Annotate the writing. Document the logistical aspects of the war. Document the war's logistical operations." In another set of instructions on research procedures and filing, he told each researcher to keep a notebook and detailed how to use it.[33]

In the fall of 1943, the Historical Section established an Oral History Subsection. Major Cleaves A. Jones (mentioned in Chapter 5 when he had been promoted to Lieutenant Colonel) was the responsible officer.[34] Ganoe thought oral history was the "real mortar," the "whys and hows." Unless it was captured, it was "allowed to wash away almost as fast as it was spoken."[35] This was a lesson learned from World War I. "Generals [Tasker Howard] Bliss and Pershing felt that much of their talk had a smack of importance; and brigadiers felt generally that theirs was drivel."[36]

Ganoe supposed, "The mortar was often more important than the brick ['decisions and effects.']."[37] Ganoe and Jones visited general officers such as Lieutenant General Omar N. Bradley, Brigadier General Norman D. Cota, Brigadier General Leonard T. Gerow, and Brigadier General Edwin L. Sibert, to whom they explained the history program and enlisted their support.[38] Ganoe had permission "to attend and record the high-level discussions and decision briefings at Headquarters, Supreme Allied Command."[39]

By October 1943, Ganoe sent a memorandum to 80 general officers. He explained the Historical Section's mission in gathering oral interviews. It resembled a pre-briefing statement used by some 21st-century military history detachments.[40] Ganoe asked the generals to dictate daily their "telephone and other conversations with important persons on subjects pertaining to ETO." He told them this information had been "largely lost in previous wars." Ganoe stated the information would be [useful] in the service schools and of "personal benefit" to them by:

1. Helping verify statements later;
2. Fixing and crystallizing past conversations;
3. Refreshing the memory later;
4. Aiding in rendering reports;
5. Yielding proof against imputations or accusations.[41]

In a similar letter to other general officers, Ganoe described the Historical Section's objectives in "obtaining on the ground and at the time those happenings and statements that may be lost or distorted later." The section would not be "underfoot...." Ganoe explained the Historical Section found it was possible to get "the essence of otherwise vanished car or phone conversations" through the assistance of secretaries, aids, and executives. "All we ask," he wrote, "is that, when your aide nudges you in a recess moment, you do not refuse a few crystallizing sentences." Narrative drafts would be submitted soon after combat.[42]

Ganoe boldly and straightforwardly told the officers how his work could benefit them in the short and long term. By May 22, 1944, Ganoe had persuaded 128 general officers and colonels to use his plan. And he developed a system to check the note-taking practice.[43] This was part of his objective: to preserve records of conferences, conversations and oral orders made by key officers.[44]

Ganoe's October 1943 guidance applied to units down to battalion level. They were to keep "war diaries and journals and to designate an officer 'to oversee the keeping of historical data.'"[45] That officer was a liaison to his staff. A staff member was to be assigned to Eighth Air Force; Services of Supply; Ground Forces; and Chief of Staff, Supreme Allied Commander (COSSAC) to assist historical officers, secure "data which will otherwise not be recorded," and report on the status of record keeping.[46]

Ganoe tried to get trained historical officers suited to the work. "The addition of a dud causes the morale and enthusiasm to lag."[47] So, he was establishing contacts between his London office and field unit historians down to the battalion. They were forming a network of combat historical operations and a coordinated historical program. The Army Air Force had a comparable program.[48]

What about covering small unit actions in the ETO? Although Taylor at one time "blew the bugle for small unit action," by late June 1944, he questioned that approach. Small unit actions below the battalion level were the hardest to obtain, so it was important to get the most significant points. He told Kemper combat historians could not "specialize on small unit stuff—they have also the problem of filling the gaps out at higher echelons."[49] Kemper concurred with Taylor (and Ganoe) "that the boys have too big a job to get very many small unit stories." However, he wanted as many of those accounts "as we can get, either by our combat historians when they have the opportunity, or from the units themselves whenever and wherever they can be persuaded to prepare them, without jeopardizing other necessary historical work."[50]

In November 1944, Ganoe submitted to the G-1 a "Study and Plan for Future Army Coverage." He summarized the background of the ETO historical program. He said, "Theater was the first organization ever to approve and implement the gathering of facts … on the spot and at the time, material which had been lost in previous wars and was being lost in other theaters." The Historical Section had 51 officers and men. There were 86 field historical officers and men assigned to the armies.

Ganoe reported on the program's status. Field teams averaged more than 2 officers and 2 men per Army Corps. Their "stamina … not necessarily [being] an editor, writer or researcher" was crucial. Because of the history program's late start, not all history personnel had the proper credentials. Overall, they had "worked out extraordinarily well … even though each Army Corps has had its own peculiar equation." He explained that the teams and the History Section's sub-sections had worked "in their separate niches with little need for collaboration."[51]

Ganoe offered his ideas about the future situation.

1. All the "scattered gleanings and gleaners" must be pulled together into "a single storehouse" so that material could be inventoried, assessed for gaps, organized, filed and used to write "at least the first draft of a definitive integrated and exhaustive history of the Theater;"
2. Field research must continue;
3. "Reports, pamphlets, short histories, monographs, and combat narratives" must be "coordinated, checked and completed but often compiled into a more general exposition;"
4. Existing personnel were inadequate;

5. "Team members as we have seen are diggers and not necessarily builders." Many of the most qualified would "disappear" due to "private and official causes;"

6. While army and corps headquarters would be dissolved, the History Section's work would increase as it tried to retrieve the historical record, thereby increasing the need for qualified personnel;

7. At the end of the war, corps teams should "revert" to the theater historian's control. He would "cull" the unqualified and replace them with competent personnel;

8. Instead of attaching historical teams, personnel should be centralized and controlled so that the official records and combat narratives were under historical scrutiny.[52]

Next Ganoe detailed a personnel plan. The Historical Section's functions in postwar hostilities would drive personnel needs. An Occupation Subsection would be needed. Additional historical information would have to be collected. Campaign and logistical narratives would conform with theater programs. All historical materials would be catalogued and indexed. The Historical Section would assist small units to prepare their histories.

An executive should study and review all writing and collected materials and make field personnel assignments to include:

1. 1 historical editor;
2. 1 art editor;
3. 40 officer field historians;
4. 40 enlisted assistants;
5. 12 research assistants;
6. 4 librarians;
7. 2 officers and 2 enlisted men to assist units with their histories;
8. 12 officer or enlisted historian-writers;
9. 1 officer in charge;
10. 8 artists;
11. 4 cartographers in the art section;
12. a pool of 5 stenographers and typists;
13. 2 enlisted messengers and runners;
14. 2 officers and 2 enlisted men to cover heretofore neglected areas.

In addition to these 138, among the personnel to remain were the 5 officers, 4 enlisted men and 1 enlisted woman in the Communications Zone Subsection; 2 officers and 8 enlisted men in the Past Affairs Subsection; and the team of 3 officers, 3 enlisted men and 3 civilian stenographers used in interviewing the wounded in the hospitals and prisoners of war (POWs) for combat data. That totaled 167 needed for "post-bellum" history, whereas the current total in November 1944 was 137.

Ganoe called for a post-war education program. He also recommended the formation of The Army of Occupation Subsection mirroring a field army history team.[53] The fact that Marshall later reported in *Bringing Up the Rear* that he had a staff of 152 may indicate the G-1 was sympathetic to Ganoe's proposal. Or was it due to a similar plan Marshall submitted on December 13, 1944, to the G-1 calling for a staff of 167?[54]

As for deployment, corps teams would remain at or near the corps headquarters before an action. They would become acquainted with the makeup, potential and uses of all corps troops and learn about the plans, decisions, and orders of corps commanders. They would arrange for the preservation of vital documents, secure significant oral information and establish relationships with key personnel. "After the jump-off or landings, corps teams would spread out among divisional headquarters in strength proportional to the critical nature of the task." For instance, 1 officer and 2 enlisted men would go to the division involved in the main effort; 1 officer and 1 enlisted man to the supporting division; and none to the division in reserve. As the action continued, combat historians would be "switched to divisions which develop engagements of unforeseen importance" as in the case when the reserve division was sent in on a flank. At least 1 officer and 1 enlisted man then should try to reach that division's headquarters.

Normally combat historians would remain at divisional headquarters until lower echelons were reorganizing; consolidating its position; preparing a defensive position; withdrawing to a "protected area; holding a quiet sector; extend[ing] halt in a zone of action." During these situations, team members should conduct their interviews, remembering that "the best moments to approach a man who has been in the fight are after a meal, while smoking, during rest and recreation, while he is in good humor...." From then until "active operations teams should be visiting their front-line units for the double purpose of becoming friends with small unit leaders and in schooling them in profitable and economical methods of keeping and rendering diaries, journals and overlays for their future benefit." These general guidelines "illustrated the principles of approach and requirements of facts. Battle is a mixed-up affair at best. Teams must use initiative, resourcefulness, and adaptability to circumstances in order to get the facts without undue risks. It will be hard for them to realize they are not out there to fight."[55]

In October 1943 the Past Affairs Subsection was under the supervision of Women's Army Corps (WAC) Lieutenant Susie J. Thurman. She and her staff of three enlisted WACs, began "extracting material from documents in The Adjutant General Records Section ... maintain[ing] 'a chronology and index of available material....'" The WACs performed other jobs such as surveying diverse theater document depositories.[56] And comparable to other ETO Historical Section soldiers they went into the field, serving as combat historians.

Eva Carol Spencer was one of those WACs. On September 30, 1943, she enlisted as a private at Rapid City, South Dakota.[57] After basic training, Spencer deployed to England. She was one of 50 WACs from the London WAC headquarters selected to:

> accompany the first of the ComZ [Communications Zone] troops into Normandy. We were the FE/ComZ group [Forward Element/Communications Zone] … to go into Normandy after D-Day and set up housekeeping for the rest of the CZ troops. Our training started before D-Day…. The WACs were slated to go to the Continent/Far Shore with the first group of ComZ troops to set up the service of supply for the troops to follow.[58]

Spencer was a stenographer to Ganoe and to Marshall. One of her jobs was to assist the Historical Section in producing unit history pamphlets. Ganoe described Spencer's work as "extraordinary" and of "immense help" to him. He thought her efforts were "indefatigable."[59] On August 31, 1946, Ganoe wrote to Spencer from Sarasota, Florida. He praised Spencer for her "loyalty and attitude in those trying times." He had been living in Florida for almost a year.[60] That means by 1945 Ganoe had redeployed from the ETO.

William A. Ganoe, *U.S. Military Academy Yearbook, The Howitzer*, 1907. (https://www.findagrave.com/memorial/88517692/william-addleman-ganoe/photo)

Eva Carol Spencer, Basic Training, September 1943. (Courtesy University of Texas at El Paso Library, Special Collections Department)

Marshall spoke to Spencer about returning to the War Department once her enlistment ended. He later wrote in *Bringing Up the Rear* that Spencer was the "most diligent and cheerful woman ... [he] ever knew in service."[61] He and Ganoe knew stenographers were in high demand during the war. Spencer also knew this. She wrote to her parents from Frankfurt, Germany, on December 16, 1945: "I think I have it cinched. Could go back right now, but don't think I shall desert this sinking ship for a while. Good typists (and good telephone operators) are almost out-of-this-world. I have a job, perhaps with a raise, awaiting me when I return to the Stateside part of the world."

The first group of U.S. Army WACs to be assigned to duty in France unload from a troop transport onto an LCM off the French coast, at Normandy. (Courtesy NARA)

Spencer also wrote that the "History Branch of G-2 (Intelligence) in D.C. recently got a break. We're now History Division, a special staff section and not a sub-section of G-2. We should get it organized on an operational status in time for the next war."[62]

Spencer told her parents that she had been in Germany for "almost a week. Am beginning to like our HQ [headquarters] here very much but am afraid I shall have to leave by Tuesday morning. The office crowd is wonderful ... and the whole place is guarded by 82nd Airborne Division paratroopers, and I got a date with one of them for tomorrow night."[63] She described a London office:

> We live in an old mansion—marble floors in the halls and bath—lots of marble fireplaces, but I live so close to the attic I could jump out with a parachute—and there's no elevator. The craziest plumbing I've ever seen—we don't know if we should expect hot or cold water out of either pipe, and we just don't seem to mind much. The only thing I get hungry for and can't get is strawberry ice cream. We have the custom of serving tea in the office late in the afternoon. It really peps us up, too, and saves dashing out for coffee.[64]

Spencer described her idea for the ETO historian patch.

The open book represents history in-the-making—the present. The pen and the gun are of equal size—of equal importance in this war. The emblem in the left side of the book, in this case the Service of Supply (ASF) Star, is for the history of the SOS. The emblem may be that of SHAEF [Supreme Headquarters Allied Expeditionary Force] or HQ ETO—that is the star with the chain, etc., depending upon the particular branch the historian is associated with.[65]

On September 1, 1945, T/3 Spencer was awarded the Bronze Star; the next month she was separated from the WACs. Spencer became a published writer and historian. She wrote about her experiences in Great Britain, France (Normandy), Switzerland, and Germany. A copious writer, Spencer's work was published in several magazines.[66]

In 1944, Master Sergeant Forrest Pogue (*see also* Chapter 4) was deployed to England and then to Normandy "as one of the most highly educated active-duty Soldiers. He was the first historian of D-Day." Pogue began interviewing wounded soldiers on June 7, while aboard a Landing Ship for Tanks (LST) that had been converted into a hospital ship. The next day Pogue went ashore at Omaha Beach.[67] Pogue and fellow combat historian Lieutenant William J. Fox were attached to V Corps. Franklin D. Anderson, wrote in the Preface to *Pogue's War: Diaries of a WWII Combat Historian*:

> He lived in the field at or near the front from D-Day until after the breakout at Saint-Lô and entered Paris very soon after the Allies recaptured that famous city. He returned to the field in September in time to record the Hürtgen Forest battle and then experienced the famous Battle of the Bulge. He was present at Torgau, Germany, when the U.S. Army met the Russian Army. He was one of the first witnesses to the holocaust that had taken place at Buchenwald. After the Germans surrendered in May 1945, he was ordered back to Paris to start the history that had been collected by the combat historians.[68]

First Army's combat history team also accompanied the troops on the Normandy invasion. The Third Army combat history team followed them on June 26.[69]

As previously noted, the 4th I&HS was organized in the Pacific on July 13, 1944. The unit was activated on August 19, 1944, at Bristol in England and became operational on September 4, 1944, in Périers, France. Lieutenant Colonel Cleaves A. Jones was the commander. The unit was attached to the Ninth Army's Headquarters Special Troops for rations, quarters, and administrative needs. By December 1944, the unit totaled 23 officers and 24 enlisted men, more resembling the TO&E authorization.[70]

At the time the 4th I&HS was formed, the recently activated Ninth Army was engaged in the final reduction of the German forces at Brest in France; 2 officers from the 4th I&HS were assigned to the 29th Division; 2 to the 2nd Division; and 1 officer each to the 8th Division, VIII Corps, and Task Force A. These officers remained with their respective commands until completion of the Brest and Crozon operations.[71] The 4th I&HS, 9th Army, wrote "Operations IV, Offensive in November."[72]

"Messing in the Open on Okinawa," by John A. Ruge. (Courtesy Army Art Collection, CMH)

With the fall of Brest and Crozon, the teams returned to headquarters to begin recording combat actions. A three-man team was detailed to the 8th Infantry Division when it moved on the line in Luxembourg. By mid-October 1944, the 4th I&HS had given 35 assignments to historical teams. Normally these teams used the division command post "as a base of operations, going down to regiment and battalion to gain interviews, observe battle sites of recent operations, and talk to officers and [the] men involved." The teams wrote and reproduced "three volumes, totaling over 650 pages." The 4th I&HS sent copies to the commanding general, each unit, the ETO Historical Section, and to the War Department.[73]

When organized on July 13, 1944, the 2nd I&HS was activated in the First Army.[74] The 3rd I&HS also was activated in the Third Army. As noted previously, they "absorbed" the combat history teams already there.[75]

In June 1944, the Washington Historical Branch sent Marshall to the ETO against his will. He later wrote:

> The word had already come that I would be hauled out and sent to ETO in time for Normandy. I didn't like it; we had a going concern in the Pacific and I wanted no more *troubleshooting* [Italics added]....We had a system that was repairing mistakes in operations as we moved along.... I had become reconciled to my fate and was ready enough in time to turn to a new horizon, but I was still griping. The Pacific had proved to be my dish. We were doing well there.[76]

Marshall's task was to teach his interview method to historical teams in France. He was also to tour Europe and the Mediterranean. Then he would return to Washington to

Saint Lô Patrol, 35th Infantry Division, Normandy 1944, by Olin Dows. (Courtesy Army Art Collection, CMH.)

Members of the WACs at operations center, 1943. (Courtesy NARA)

write a brief, popular history of the war. Marshall arrived in England two weeks after the Normandy invasion. He immediately began to use his interview technique.[77]

Captain John Westover, who served with Marshall, later wrote: "I watched Marshall at work and then I used it [the technique] in three wars and a variety of non-military uses. It simply cannot be beaten as a method of collecting accurate information." After the Normandy invasion, Marshall showed the technique to some battalion commanders. One who used it after the Arnhem Operation "claimed it worked as well for him as for Marshall."[78]

However, Marshall had critics. Commanding General of the 82nd Airborne Division

Master Sergeant Forrest Pogue on his entrance to Paris, August 28, 1944. (Courtesy of the George C. Marshall Foundation, Lexington, Virginia)

Lieutenant General James M. Gavin wrote that at least on one occasion the troops resented Marshall's prying. Some thought Marshall was not always accurate in his details when his work was based on interviews.[79] The methodology Marshall used to collect facts and statistics for *Men Against Fire* came under scrutiny. One critic wrote "While Marshall's books make excellent reading regarding battle on a soldier's level ... [his] work seems to have lacked even rudimentary attention to accepted standards of scientific inquiry. In essence, there seems to be no evidence of ANY definitive research into individual soldier firing rates in SLA Marshall's wartime efforts."[80]

Certainly, Marshall was not the first to use eyewitnesses. Dr. Joseph Dawson III wrote in his 2001 introduction to Marshall's *Victory Island: The Battle of Kwajalein*, "but his approach to analyzing battles was more focused and systematic than ... any authors had used before. His design ... to interview groups of soldiers soon after combat … contrast[ed] to standard methods of asking questions months or years after the event."[81]

Ganoe endorsed Marshall's interview technique. Historians in the Army Historical Section and British military historian, John Keegan, thought Marshall's technique was one of his "genuine contributions to the U.S. war effort in World War II and to the study of military history thereafter."[82] In the 1970s, Keegan described Marshall as "an author, not a scientist." In his opinion, Marshall was a first-rate writer, "but not as someone who carefully mustered facts, percentages, charts, and graphs." Keegan emphasized "that as a writer, Marshall used 'elaborate detail' to paint his impressions of soldiers."

Pogue agreed. He believed Marshall "was splendid on small level details." In pulsating accounts, Marshall told the soldier's story as he saw it and made it more personal.[83] Pogue wrote:

> None of us had his success. He had been a young lieutenant in the first war, was called back as a lieutenant colonel, had extensive experience as a newspaperman, [and] had written a lot about the war…. He could get battalion and regimental officers to bring together dozens and even hundreds of men…. None of us had his rank, we lacked his skill and reputation…. However, so far as we could, we tried to practice some of the lessons he had to teach.[84]

Major Kenneth W. Hechler (*see* Chapter 4) was born in Roslyn, New York, on September 20, 1914, and was of German descent. He earned a BA from Swarthmore College, and an MA and PhD from Columbia University in history and government.

While hundreds of others move towards the beach in landing craft, American assault troops, with full equipment, move onto Omaha Beach, in Northern France. (Courtesy NARA)

Before World War II, Hechler was on the faculty of Columbia University, Princeton University, and Barnard College. He also held some federal civil service positions.

In July 1942, Hechler was drafted into the U.S. Army. After graduating from Armored Force Officer Candidate School, he was assigned as a combat historian in the ETO. Hechler assisted in documenting the Normandy invasion, liberation of France, the Battle of the Bulge, and the U.S. Army's entrance into Nazi Germany. He was attached to the 9th Armored Division.

Major Kenneth W. Hechler

Unexpectedly, the 9th captured the Ludendorff Bridge, over the Rhine River, during the Battle of Remagen. Hechler interviewed American and German soldiers involved. When he was a captain, Hechler later remembered getting "a tongue-lashing from Gen. George Patton for smearing the shiny officer's insignia on his uniform with grease to deter snipers." He was awarded a Bronze Star and five battle stars.[85]

Hechler said combat historians "who were sent to the field were urged to follow G-2 reports, check frequently with G-2 officers, analyze intelligence reports and summaries, and assemble the most educated guesses on the enemy." There would be time after the war to use "captured enemy documents for a more comprehensive fill-in on German intentions and operations."[86] Some of those enemy documents made their way to higher headquarters "when German command posts were overrun. Occasionally—usually by accident—the historians would fall heir to more important nuggets." Hechler gave an example. In the summer of 1944, Taylor was working at the First Army headquarters. He "overheard news that the German Seventh Army Telephone Diary had been captured. Col. Taylor latched on to a copy of this important document, and had it translated for use of the historical section of ETO."[87]

In early November 1944, Hechler took command of the VIII Corps Historical Team attached to the First Army. Captain Richard Shappell was the team's chief. The two of them attended a briefing with Deputy Chief of Staff Colonel Walter Stanton. There was a short discussion of the VIII Corps historical team's plans. Stanton asked them "what measures the historians were taking and might take in order to fill in the enemy picture."[88] Hechler said their reply did not satisfy Stanton or himself.

Afterwards Hechler suggested to Shappell that "several German-speaking officers and enlisted men be attached to each corps historical team to conduct interrogations which might secure tactical information of historical value from German prisoners of war."[89] Shappell believed G-2 interrogations of these POWs were problematic in that they focused on "getting intelligence which might be useful in future operations. Most G-2s did not care what had happened in detail unless it had a possible bearing on the future." Hechler thought, "that these historical interrogators could get German prisoners to tell us something more of the tactical picture on their side, as soon as we could convince them that we were not after information which would prove injurious to the Fatherland during operations."[90]

Hechler "hammered and hammered" his proposal to others and evidently to Kemper who was visiting the corps. It was rejected for several reasons including "our own historians were so busy with American operations that they could not adequately cover their own operations, let alone enemy operations."[91] Hechler's idea became a reality after V-E Day when he was involved in interviewing German POWs. For more information *see* Appendix B.

There were other obstacles facing combat historians. One was the historian's desire for classified information and the backlash they got.[92] Hechler recounted his own experience:

> When I got to the 15th Corps I asked to be assigned to the G-3 section because I knew that was where … most of the history was being made, but instead of that they assigned me to the G-2, which was headed by a real sourpuss…. He was so security conscious that he would always be hanging around to watch what I was doing. I started out there by simply going through all of the incoming messages and this disturbed him a great deal and he said, "I don't like the way you're wandering around in our secret documents." He said, "From now on you will write me a memorandum on which document you want to see and why." And I said, "Colonel, I don't know what documents I want to see in advance." And he said, "Those are my orders." It made me infuriated because I couldn't perform my mission.[93]

In April 1945, the ETO Adjutant General echoed Hechler's position. He thought the Information and Historical Services should have access to classified material in writing the official history between tactical operations and command actions and responsibilities.[94]

Hechler and his counterparts faced the problem of being aligned most effectively within a command's organization. Alignment under the commander or chief of staff usually meant more support than alignment under the G-2. When Hechler interviewed German POWs after the war, Hechler wrote that he occasionally had to follow the "same 'hat-in-hand policy' which the combat historians had sometimes been forced to use during operations…" to get what they needed. He said Marshall "favor[ed] a more direct approach to the top commander … Col. Marshall in fact resented the implication that any historian had to apologize for doing his duty, and took the position that the 'hat-in-hand' approach enabled other officers to walk over the historians."[95]

Hechler returned after the war twice to interview German participants in the Battle of Remagen. He discovered Captain Willi Bratge, one of two captured officers who had not been killed on Hitler's orders. Hechler spent a week with him in the Remagen area, gathering details about the battle.[96] Hechler was assigned to interview several key German Third Reich leaders before they were charged and tried for war crimes in Nuremberg. Among them were Field Marshals Albert Kesselring and Wilhelm Keitel; General Alfred Jodl; Foreign Minister Joachim von Ribbentrop; and Supreme Marshal Hermann Goering. Hechler recorded Goering making a deranged suggestion to join the American side and "knock hell out of the Russians."[97]

In 1949, he wrote for the U.S. Army *The Enemy Side of the Hill: The 1945 Background on the Interrogation of German Commanders as Seen Subjectively by Major Kenneth W. Hechler*. In 1957 he published *The Bridge at Remagen: The Amazing Story of March 7, 1945*. In was adapted into a film in 1969. He also wrote a biography of the Remagen commander, *Hero of the Rhine: The Karl Timmermann Story*; an account of

First U.S. Army men and equipment pour across the Remagen Bridge; two knocked-out jeeps in foreground. Germany. March 11, 1945. (Courtesy NARA)

one battalion's role during the *Battle of the Bulge—Holding the Line: The 51st Engineer Combat Battalion*, and the *Battle of the Bulge, December 1944–January 1945*.[98]

As Hechler noted in *The Enemy Side of the Hill*, alignment of the Historical Section was problematic. On June 13, 1944, a Standard Operations and Procedures (SOP) placed the public relations officer in command of the I&HS. Public Relations Officer Colonel J. B. L. Lawrence and Colonel Ganoe had approved. The historical units were allowed to "function strictly for their particular mission, insofar as practicable." They were under the immediate supervision of the ranking historical editor and under the technical supervision of the theater historian.[99]

Some combat historians were troubled about having a public relations officer in charge. On May 11, 1944, Major Dwight Salmon wrote to Kemper, "The new T/O is dismaying to behold. I don't like the looks of it for I fear what the PRO [Public Relations Office] boys will do with it and I have visions of a PRO colonel running the show with scant regards for our needs."[100]

Ganoe expressed his own concerns to Kemper. In June 1944, Kemper wrote to Ganoe that he "appreciate[ed]" his viewpoint. As Kemper put it, the "historian may have his wings clipped if he is too close to the Public Relations people." The deputy chief of staff had advised Kemper of the decision to "set up combat correspondents" who "would operate as teams." Kemper had been asked if these teams could also "collect historical data." Kemper "reacted violently" to no avail. He had to "combine the historical teams with the combat correspondent teams under one administrative head." He had argued to include "a lieutenant colonel and a major historian" to "protect the historical teams." Together they "could operate almost independent [sic]" within the Information and Historical Service.

Kemper further told Ganoe, "There was no other choice but to make the most of it and take advantage for all we were worth of the opportunity for increased vacancies and organic equipment for combat historians." He did not know how this arrangement would work but was determined to "convert the whole thing somehow to our advantage." He thought if the officer chosen to lead each I&HS was a "good feller" they "still ought to go places." Anyway "by the time all this is an established fact, these boys with the Armies will be so well dug in that they ought to be hard to shake." At the time, the Washington Historical Branch was trying to deploy 11 historians. Three had left just two days earlier.[101]

Another hindrance to the combat historian occurred when others mistook him for a public information officer, tour guide, lecturer, statistician, or expert on local history or mores.[102] Ganoe was asked "to address officer candidates, to lecture at senior officers' and liaison schools, and to sit on a board considering designs for a new theater shoulder patch," all of which detracted from the core mission.[103] Sometimes there was no cooperation and support from the higher echelons. Several thought their S-3s or G-3s could do the job. Combat historians had to ensure their functions were separated from those of "unofficial" historians.

Transportation was tricky. Many times, the TO&E allocated no jeep. Injuries and transfers were setbacks.[104] And there were those who obstructed the historian's work. They were just too busy to be bothered by historians.[105] To them Ganoe wrote his now famous reply: "History is the last thing we care about during operations and the first thing we want afterward. Then it is too little, too late and too untrue."[106]

Then there was the problem of qualified personnel. Hechler wrote about his view of Ganoe in *The Enemy Side of the Hill:*

> At the start, the Historical Section in the European Theater lacked leadership. Its objectives were never stated with clarity and precision. Neither the War Department, nor the Theater Historian, nor the teams in the field could agree on a simple and direct set of objectives.… By the end of the war, when the Historical Section had aggressive leadership and had formulated clear objectives, redeployment siphoned off the trained personnel, a series of moves of the office and records lost precious time, and the Section fought a losing battle to meet an impossible deadline.[107]

Hechler believed Ganoe had what he considered to be:

> a less than competent staff that clearly didn't have a very clear idea about what they were doing. And so I went to Colonel Ganoe one morning and I said, "Look, I don't have anything to do. I don't have any assignment; I don't have any mission." And so he said to me, "Well, just make a list of all the units in the European theater and the names of their commanders," which I thought was kind of a make work policy but then Ganoe was eased out. Apparently, somebody got the idea that he was incompetent and he was eased out and replaced by a real ball of fire … a colonel later promoted to brigadier general, S. L. A. Marshall.[108]

Hechler described Marshall as "a very dynamic leader…. And he assembled a much more competent staff and our mission then became very clear." Perhaps defending his opinion of Ganoe, Hechler recalled, "I was in a position to be very critical of Colonel Ganoe because I wanted to get started, because I was full of adrenaline and I didn't think he knew what he was—why he was there or what he was doing."[109]

Apparently Ganoe's plans for the ETO historical program had either deteriorated or were never fully realized. Why is not clear. At one time, the Washington Historical Branch must have thought Ganoe's program was a model. It included examples of the ETO's program in "Orientation Material for Theater Historians." In notes made on August 18, 1943, Ganoe stated that although the War Department was "suddenly becoming history conscious" and other theaters were scrambling, the ETO did not have "much to make up because it was among the first." He said Professor Commager, a member of the War Department's Advisory Committee, set up to monitor the Washington Historical Branch, had visited his section and "approved what we are doing. Couldn't get from him any adverse criticism."[110] An early news release from the Headquarters, ETO, lauded Ganoe's ability and that of his staff, calling him a "pioneer." "In Colonel Ganoe," the release stated, "the United States Army has one of its most constructive military historians."[111] In June 1944, Kemper wrote to Ganoe that under his "leadership we can expect great things."[112] The next month Kemper wrote to Taylor, "Thanks to Colonel

Ganoe's vision and understanding, fine men are on the ground, established and at work."[113]

Four months later Kemper traveled to Europe to "correct deficiencies" in the program. Apparently in December 1944, Kemper wrote: "The lack of supervision is appalling. Coupled with a lack of any plan, it is a wonder anything has been done. Fortunately, here and there good men have done good work." More investigation supported Kemper's viewpoint. Consequently, Kemper made plans to have Marshall chosen as deputy theater historian. The theater G-1 assured Kemper that Marshall, "would be given a free hand in bringing the theater's historical program up to desirable standards." Kemper left the theater on December 29, 1944, but not before he and Marshall had designed a "general plan for corrective action."[114]

Perhaps Ganoe's reliance on verbal, rather than on written directives, was a factor. Ganoe saw himself as an advisor to the First Army historical team's commander.[115] "No one gives orders," he wrote, "but yourself. Nor are you to be interfered with. If I come down, I expect only to suggest and advise. You are answerable administratively only to G-3 and technically to me." The First Army historical team commander told Ganoe in June 1944, there was some dissention in the historical team.[116] But was that enough to cripple Ganoe's program?

Further clouding the situation was a letter dated January 1, 1945, from Ganoe to all history teams entitled "clarification of objectives." He stated that the section's and teams' mission was to "bring forward a comprehensive and well-proportioned history of military operations by our forces. The final objective is the writing and publication of such history."[117] His idea about what comprehensive history was to be written differed from the Historical Branch's expectations.

By March 1945, it was obvious to the Historical Section that after action reports, needed in writing for an official history of the ETO, were not being submitted. Ganoe was getting questions and cries for help from those charged with writing the reports. He sent to all historical officers a memorandum detailing some of the problems with the reports and how to correct them.[118] Marshall enlisted the support of The Adjutant General to correct this "particular delinquency."[119] He also received messages from some of the historians about the reports.

In April 1945, The Adjutant General unmistakably stated the theater historian was responsible for the "technical supervision of all historical work...." But, regulatory after action reports were the responsibility of the given commander, not the mission of what became the I&HS.[120] Combat historians still prepared after action reports. On September 19, 1945, Marshall officially became the ETO theater historian.[121]

A clue as to the possible cause of the problem is a statement dated March 10, 1945, from the ETO to The Adjutant General. It claimed the I&HS was following the Washington Historical Branch's instructions. An August 3, 1943, War Department memorandum outlined the basic functions of the branch. It was to prepare and publish operational memoranda, a popular history, and an official history.

The I&HS argued that the 1943 memorandum did not "delegate" to the ETO "headquarters responsibility for … complet[ing] … the program with which" the Historical Branch was charged. The I&HS had not received any "instructions to that affect, either written or oral…." Until the ETO headquarters received the "basic communication … [it] was not aware of its responsibility [to] … prepare … as a comprehensive summary … all aspects of the history of the Theater." Instead, the I&HS was focusing on the theater's administrative history and on collecting and supplementing "vital historical materials concerning combat operations … for subsequent general use by the Historical Branch…." Accordingly, the I&HS was working on operational studies. The I&HS maintained that an administrative history was not possible until the war ended.[122]

On January 19, 1945, The Adjutant General wrote a letter entitled "Historical Program in European Theater of Operations." It cited a progress report submitted on October 14, 1944, by the theater historian. The letter read: "[I]t is noted that the historical program of your theater does not conform in several particulars to the standards for historical work" set forth in the August 3, 1943, War Department memorandum. The Historical Branch was to "exercise technical supervision" over projects and was "prepared to assist in the reorganization of the theater historical program." The letter explained the requirement for a "*single narrative account of United States Forces in the European Theater of Operations … as a comprehensive summary of all aspects of the history of the theater* [Italics added]."[123] The concentration was to be on:

> administrative organization, major policies, problems, accomplishments, and lessons learned, and combat operations should be treated only as necessary to present a balanced study of the theater as a whole. This history may be supported by a series of more detailed monographic studies of topics (other than combat operations, which should be covered in accordance with paragraph 3 below) or organizations of particular interest or significance.[124] Nothing was to be published without the Historical Branch's approval. The branch required regular progress reports.[125]

Paragraph 3 was about operational histories for inclusion in *American Forces In Action*. They were to be descriptive accounts. Since relevant records were both in theater and at the War Department, cooperation between the two offices was essential. The historical units in the I&HS were to assist. The Historical Section was to prepare the basic studies. The Historical Branch was to add more information and prepare the final study for publication. By March 1, 1945, the Historical Section was to submit to the Historical Branch a list of studies for inclusion in *American Forces In Action*.[126]

On February 26, 1945, a report submitted, evidently by Marshall, defended the Historical Section's program. The section argued it was complying with the August 3, 1943, War Department memorandum. It had received a charge from the Historical Branch to write operational monographs.[127]

The Historical Section considered The Adjutant General's January 1945 memorandum to be an expansion of its mission. The section was working to comply but due to its personnel shortfall, with assistance from higher commands, and coping with security issues "which hamper all efforts to obtain accurate and complete military history during a period of active operations." Personnel from the Historical Section and from the I&HS were not "procured" to support such a requested mission. Mission accomplishment could not be assured unless the theater historical organization was maintained "for a prolonged period after the cessation of combat and unless a re-organization of all personnel … [was] permitted by higher authority." The section had given priority to finishing operational studies, "suitable for monographs."[128] So, the Historical Branch wanted a comprehensive narrative; the Historical Section focused on operational studies.

In March 1945, Marshall asked for assistance with "editorial problems." The Historical Branch sent Major Roy Lamson (*see also* Chapter 5). During his four-month visit, Lamson told Marshall the branch's "objectives and policies, helped edit operational monographs, and drew up plans for an editorial organization in the Historical Division, Headquarters, ETO." Before he left, he wrote to Taylor: "I fell [*sic*] that our critical outposts in this theater have now been established, even though on a small scale."[129]

Hechler's *The Enemy Side of the Hill* monograph provided more evidence that things in the ETO Historical Section were amiss. When trying to answer his own question as to why the section had not been thinking about interviewing German POWs, he stated there was a "crisis spirit" gripping the section in 1945.[130] Yet, he believed the section "produced remarkable results in the face of a series of obstacles and recurring crises." He had only "admiration and amazement" for the section.[131]

The "crisis spirit" probably began on February 1, 1945, when Marshall gave the First, Third, and Ninth Army I&HS commanders seven days to dispatch to the Historical Section all interview material obtained covering the December 16, 1944, to January 13, 1945, Ardennes Operation (Battle of the Bulge). He suggested the same procedure for other operations.[132] On May 1, 1945, Marshall sent a memorandum to all detachment commanders about documenting the occupation as completely as the tactical phase.[133]

Then there was Major Lamson's idea for the section to produce a 500-page volume of selected interviews. Included would be a chapter on the method of getting the interviews, the operations of the historical teams and a descriptive catalog-index of all interviews. This volume "should not," Lamson wrote to Marshall, "preclude publication of interviews as appendixes to historical monographs or as articles in service journals or other periodicals of high quality."[134]

Another cause for the "crisis spirit" may have been Marshall's memorandum of May 29, 1945, to I&HS commanders. He issued seven directives.

1. Submit to the Historical Section all interviews and supporting documents collected since activation of the I&HSs;
2. Prepare a list of all interview materials;

3. Catalog interviews to standard;
4. Search and deliver to the section top secret control files;
5. Publish a recommended directive advising the need to screen and preserve significant historical documents;
6. Submit a report to the section estimating the time needed to complete "historical coverage of tactical units" along with a "statement as to when" the I&HS would be ready to "devote its entire attention to the writing of the history of the Occupation;"
7. Obtain complete files of troop movement orders and forward them to the section.[135]

Wow! What a task list.

Added to that was Third Army Team Commander Major Hugh Cole's plans announced in his July 1, 1945, letter. He wanted to produce a tactical history of the ETO down to the division level using after action reports, interviews, maps and supporting documents. Because most of the writers were not professional historians, Cole realized the writing must be closely supervised.[136] The "crisis spirit" must have skyrocketed. Colonel Allen Clark (Kemper's successor) read a July 1945 report about the section. He exclaimed it "made my hair stand on end."[137]

CHAPTER 8

The Enemy Side of the Hill

In July 1949, while on temporary duty at the Washington Historical Branch, Ken Hechler wrote *The Enemy Side of the Hill: The 1945 Background on Interrogation of German Commanders: As seen subjectively by Major Kenneth W. Hechler.*[1] In the Foreword, he stated: "So much has been accomplished by the Foreign Studies Section of the Army Historical Division, and by the Operational History Section of EUCOM in the collection and analysis of interrogations and reports by German commanders that it was felt useful to recapture some of the details of how this project started in 1945."[2]

As in the years following World War I there were efforts by combat historians to collect foreign documents, in this case German documents as detailed in Hechler's monograph. In late April 1945, as the Germans were in "wild retreat," the War Department and the ETO Historical Section began to focus on the "possible accession and exploitation of German documents." In a letter dated April 27, 1945, Cole "noted in his diary of activities, 'Had Ex. O. request information on present location of Historical Section, German General Staff, and plans for its seizure and use.'" Then on May 9, 1945, one day after V-E Day, "the War Department asked the ETO Historical Section to keep a finger on what was being done with German documents." Colonel Clark (*see* Chapter 3) wrote to Marshall, "I don't care how the records are obtained as long as we end up with sufficient documentary evidence to fill in the German side of the operational picture. Anything you can do to assist in this will be of great value to the future historical program."

According to Hechler, before V-E Day the Historical Section was too involved in other work to pay much attention to preserving enemy documents. By the time Clark expressed interest, Marshall was already in London lobbying to do just that. "But, the collection of documents for use in war crimes investigations was seen as more important…. [P]roposals of giving the historians prior claim on documents were exceedingly dim." The focus had been on their intelligence value. Marshall wrote, "The question is whether we can now make them realize that they must change their focus and recognize that the historical interest in documents and archives has become paramount." To do so, he believed, would take a directive from the War Department. Clark, for his part, was making little progress, noting the lack of manpower and organization to pursue document collection.[3]

Meanwhile Marshall had problems of his own, including the redeployment of combat historians "with the intention, which never materialized, of sending them on to the Pacific," and proposed plans to move the Historical Section, which by that time was in Paris. If that happened, Marshall threatened to leave.[4] The Historical Section did move on July 28, 1945, to Saint-Germain-en-Laye.[5] "During such a crisis, the problem of securing German materials seemed peculiarly out of season."[6]

According to Hechler, "none of the initial thinking" either in the Washington Historical Branch or the ETO Historical Section called for a plan to interview German commanders or to have them write reports. The emphasis at that point was on collecting documents. "It does not seem surprising that individuals well-grounded in historical tradition should be thinking primarily along documentary lines." He believed Cole was "the only qualified professional military historian" in the section; he knew what documents meant in "the writing of adequate history." But the people in the Historical Section "had been trained and had recognized the value of the interview technique as applied to American operations." "Why," Hechler questioned in *The Enemy Side of the Hill*, "was not the technique that was so successfully employed to 'fill in the gaps' and get a clearer perspective on American operations also used for the same purpose in respect to enemy operations?"

By V-E Day, the Theater Historian and his Deputy were buckling down to the single task of turning out a narrative of European operations. They did not want to be distracted by any frills which might interfere with the main job at hand. They had too much experience with those who would ride off in many directions in pursuit of interesting but unproductive schemes. "'First things first' was the determined policy of the Historical Section."[7] Hechler said if Marshall and Cole doubted they could complete the narrative in time, they did not tell the rest of the staff.[8]

But there were those in the Historical Branch who saw after V-E Day the value of interviewing German commanders and leaders. One, Dr. Troyer Anderson, was attached to the Office of the Undersecretary of War Robert Patterson. Patterson, too, became convinced of the value of such interviews. He raised the concern that given the nature of the Nazi government and its decline, much historical information "can never be reconstructed from paper records…." He thought there was an urgency to interviewing German commanders as they would become "widely dispersed" and that with time they would "probably develop a sort of party line explanation of events."[9] These concerns led to the creation of the Shuster Commission, composed of four subject matter experts. When conducting interviews, they were to focus on economics, politics, and diplomacy; the commission initially lacked an expert on military operations.[10]

It left on July 1, 1945, for Paris and visited Marshall at his headquarters. "With nonpareil salesmanship … Marshall convinced Shuster that an officer from the ETO Historical Section would also be of assistance to the Commission." Marshall wrote to Clark that "It is our intention to attach an officer to this party to carry out interrogations on our own behalf."[11]

After some deliberation, Marshall tapped Hechler to serve on the commission as the military operations subject matter expert. Hechler had rejoined the Paris headquarters after 10 months in Czechoslovakia. Cole voiced his objections to depleting the staff when the main job was to finish the "first narrative history of tactical and administrative operations in the [ETO]...." All else in his mind was a "side issue." Nevertheless, Hechler remained on the commission even though Cole wanted to recall him to write.[12]

Hechler later wrote "the fact that the War Department objected to my inclusion on the Commission probably strengthened Col. Marshall's determination to keep me there, because Col. Marshall was the kind of commanding officer who always went to bat for his subordinates—particularly when they were criticized at headquarters with which he had engaged in some tiffs."[13]

In July 1945, the commission began to interview prominent German officers in Mondorf-les-Bains, Luxembourg. Hechler asserted that "the War Department had decided they wanted to send this commission over to Europe to interview these Nazi leaders before they developed a party line of their own and to try to get things very, very fresh and quickly before they even knew they were going to be sent to Nuremberg."[14]

Hechler armed himself with his questions. Usually, an enlisted man who took notes accompanied him along with an interpreter. As previously noted, Hechler interviewed influential German military commanders such as Hermann Goering, a leading member of the Nazi Party who had supervised the creation of the Gestapo. Another interviewee was Alfred Jodl (*see* Chapter 7), chief of the Operations Staff of the German Armed Forces High Command. And Hechler interviewed General Wilhelm Keitel, chief of the German Armed Forces High Command. No wonder sometimes the day began at 07:00 and ended past midnight.[15]

What was his methodology? First Hechler discussed the questions with the two enlisted men. The men were:

> thoroughly briefed on the ... operations.... Most of the questions came from ... the Historical Section in Paris developed out of their research into field operations, which Marshall said "pertain[ed] to enemy action ... [and] pertinent to our own success or failure....The state of the enemy archives being what it is and with the chance that these fellows will clam up the moment they face trial as war criminals that is about the one main chance of relating cause to effect in field operations."[16]

Later the section had more questions. Marshall made sure Hechler was "supplied with questions on tactical and non-tactical operations."[17]

The Third Army's historical team also provided questions. They were "regrouped and rephrased to meet the particular level of knowledge and interest of the PW we were to interrogate. All of the questions were gone over in German (orally), and ...

[he] pointed out some of the follow-up questions which would be likely to arise depending on the initial responses of the PW."[18] He did apparently, at least sometimes, talk to an interviewee before the actual interview, decided what to concentrate on, and then drafted his questions.[19]

General Walter Warlimont was his first interviewee. He was former deputy chief of the Operations Staff, Armed Forces High Command. Hechler gave him a short "explanation of the aims and activities of the Historical Section…" which became part of the SOP. "We then plunged into the interview, and my eyes widened as I saw for the first time what had taken place 'on the other side of the hill.'"[20]

"Each response," wrote Hechler, "opened a new vista. Hitler alone had felt we would land in Normandy…. The other Germans thought it would be closer to Pas de Calais…. Some direct quotes from Hitler about the decisiveness of the invasion of France…. Rommel wasn't on hand on June 6, 1944, because it was his wife's birthday and he went home to Stuttgart…."[21] Hechler learned to "be careful in pitching … [his] questions to the level of knowledge of the person … [he] was interviewing."[22]

What was one of Hechler's lessons learned? The interviewer must not "give the PW the impression he is to 'tell everything he knows about everything,' or else the interview will get completely out of hand. It is comparable to reeling in a large fish, and the PW has to be given the proper amount of play with the line, but never too much, or else he either will wander or get started on his personal difficulties as a PW."[23] This is similar to today's training to maintain control of the interview and avoid getting off on tangents.

Not only did Hechler and his team conduct interviews and prepare interview reports they also "prepared and translated … manuscripts" written by the Germans. That is, he left questions with a prisoner and "let him alone to prepare his answers with the assistance of maps." He had "grabbed a single set of maps to cover most of the operations in which the Historical Section was interested." Some manuscripts seemed to have been made by more than one prisoner, as in the case of Jodl's and Keitel's account of the Ardennes offensive. "In some respects [these] … took less time…." Hechler considered the time well spent in translating the manuscripts thereby making them more useful for the Historical Section. "[T]he time element loomed large." But valuable time was not wasted on "extensive checking of unit designations, the spelling of the names of towns and items of this character" because such details "could be checked [by the Historical Section] without too much trouble."

Time seems to have "dictated the policy on manuscripts and oral interrogations," that is, on which method to use. Consider the time it must have taken to conduct the interview; take notes, sometimes "word-for-word;" translate them, and then put that into a report. Hechler believed the oral interviews did have some advantages in that he could explain the historical program's goals to the prisoners, get to know them, tell them he was searching for historical information and not "collecting data to support war crimes trials," and could better share the "burden of translation...." Insufficient maps were a factor in the number of manuscripts "which we could have prepared at the same time."[24]

Hechler did not know for sure how long he was to stay at Mondorf, nor how long the prisoners were to be there before the war crimes trials. Time was spent on creating a final product, as that was crucial to getting support for the program. The decision had to be made whether to prepare "a series of short reports on various subjects, or a very few long reports on a limited number of topics."[25] Hechler chose the former "to try and cover the entire sphere of operations in the European Theater...." Marshall liked the idea; Cole did not. Apparently, Cole supported the program after reading SS Commander General Fritz Kraemer's October 1945 manuscript, Sixth Panzer Army in the Ardennes Offensive.[26] Obviously, the ETO Historical Section's needs in writing about European operations at the tactical level influenced which manuscripts to prepare.[27]

Nine days after beginning the project at Mondorf, Hechler had completed eight manuscripts and eight oral interviews.[28] The enlisted men had typed indices to the interviews, arranged, labeled, and catalogued them.[29]

The Historical Section's reaction to these reports was "somewhat mixed." The "entire Historical Section was gripped in a vise—they had a deadline to meet and an objective to accomplish." One member of the section told him: "The days of the combat interview are now over. Any further collection of material will be governed by the law of diminishing returns. We now must write with the documents we have in our possession, and forget about outside materials, which will be available in the War Department later."[30] On the contrary, Hechler stated, when the interviews were "forwarded to General Eisenhower's headquarters, they went wild over them...."[31]

In mid-August 1945 Hechler began to search for German documents. He saw this as an opportunity to support "the use of German materials," possibly with reference to his interview and manuscript reports. He wondered how the Historical Section could even produce "a preliminary draft without certain key documents." And he was unaware of the agreement between Great Britain and the United States in late May "for the exploitation and shipment of most of the documents to the United States." Other than Cole's advice to find out what he could through the interviews about the disposition of the military archives, he pursued this search on his own. He found a goldmine of boxed records, especially maps, operational orders, and intelligence reports at the document center in Fechenheim. He believed the Historical Section could use them so he managed to borrow a duplicate set of maps for the Normandy, northern France, and Ardennes campaigns; "... they were put to good use by the Historical Section at St. Germain."

"At that time—both during and immediately after the war—the Historical Section was in the humble position of having to beg for its information when it should have been able to command support." Through "'hammer-and-crowbar work,'" ...

[he with help] unearthed" more treasures there and in other places, such as the Seventh Army Documents Center at Heidelberg and G-2 offices. At one point, he wrote: "I opened the box and leafed through the documents with scarcely concealed pleasure. In those days, the documents collection agencies were so swamped with truckloads of material that it was difficult to keep track of everything."[32]

From mid-August to mid-December 1945, Hechler interviewed German POWs at the Seventh and Third Army Interrogation Centers using the same methodology as at Mordorf.[33] His formal work with the Shuster Commission ended in late August.[34] He had tried to promote the program and thought at first the idea would sell itself, "but this did not prove to be true because some of the members of the Historical Section felt they already had <u>too many</u> raw materials if they were going to finish their first narratives on time."[35]

Nonetheless, Hechler's next move to sell the Historical Section on the German program was to have German POWs actually visit the Historical Section. Talk about going to the source! This, of course, was before Nuremberg. When he arrived at the section with Major Herbert Buechs, Jodl's air aide, the reactions were: "(1) amused tolerance; (2) deep skepticism; (3) bitter hatred." However, sub-sections did make use of him through interviews, for example, the Ardennes Section interviewed him "on the planning of the Ardennes Offensive and the use of the Luftwaffe...." The results were "'passable' as far as the information we derived from him was concerned." Others followed. Generally, the historians interviewed them; the Germans wrote briefs. By "November, the writers all faced early deadlines, and they were not interested in well-rounded and lengthily oral interviews; they were searching for specific information which they needed in a hurry." Hechler thought the reports the Germans wrote were "superior in character," leading to "the emphasis which was later placed on the written reports, and the lack of emphasis on oral interrogations as a source." The latter "at St. Germain were generally an unfortunate phase of the program."[36]

Following this Hechler returned to the Historical Section to write about the VII Corps in Operation COBRA. Although that was his main mission, he tried to locate German POWs for the Historical Section's desire of having a pool of German officers write a history of the war. Marshall and Cole went to Nuremberg and met with Colonel Robert Gill, the executive officer of the U.S. Chief of Counsel for Prosecution of Axis Criminality in an effort to postpone the indictment of the German officers identified as needed by the Historical Section. Marshall wrote to Hechler; "I was afraid that we might suddenly lose most of our key men.... You can say that we got 100 percent intelligent understanding from the Nuremberg people." Hechler then drafted a plan for Marshall. Gill later told Marshall that he could not count on releasing any of the German officers "until conclusion of the first trials...." As late as January 1946, Hechler was interviewing German officers.

The program continued with more participation by Marshall, Cole and other officers in the section; the objective was a German history of operations. Hechler's role was trying to locate German officers.[37] Hechler wrote:

> Col. Marshall was the type of officer who seized readily on new ideas. He had done a pioneering job in the Pacific in showing the practicability of combat interviews to reconstruct the battle details. The pure-bred historians never received him wholeheartedly into their clique because he was basically a journalist in his approach. To the historian, a journalist sometimes sacrifices completeness for human interest. Col. Marshall shared the strong feeling which Theodore Roosevelt expresses in his *Autobiography* that history does not necessarily have to be dry to retain its name. It was very fortunate that a man of Col. Marshall's nature was in a position where he could give the needed support to the German project. He had the foresight to see its potentialities and refused to abandon the idea despite the fact that the Historical Section was to complete a history of European operations as quickly as possible.[38]

As noted, Cole's support of the program was latent. In 1948, he commended it:

> Every effort is being made to distill the collective memory of the German officer corps into useable historical material. Here we are running what is often a losing race with the hangman's noose, senility, alcohol, and the "star-craziness" of the PW cages. But something has been accomplished. The files of the Historical Division now contain five hundred narratives prepared for us by German officers, from Field Marshal to Major, and more are on the way. Preliminary examination, made with German and American documents at hand, indicates that in this collection we have one of the most important contributions to the history of World War II.[39]

Greenfield, as it may be recalled, was instrumental in proposing the need for an operational history of the war. In 1946 he became the chief historian. Greenfield seconded Cole's opinion of the program in determining what had happened "on the other side of the hill." Referring to skepticism over the interviews and using them to write history, Greenfield wrote:

> The testimony of ex-officers of German and Japanese forces was, of course, subject to suspicion as historical evidence. But it could be controlled. So many officers, of all ranks, were at our disposal that when they wrote, it was possible to confront them with inconsistencies in narratives of the same event by different officers. Erroneous statements and misrepresentations were thus brought to light for further investigation. Later we were permitted to confront them with their own records, a check on their accuracy and candor. The narratives we have obtained from German and Japanese generals are memoirs. But they are controlled memoirs and … are far more valuable than those published independently by enemy individuals…. [H]istorians normally had to depend for their knowledge of the other side.[40]

That was quite an endorsement!

CHAPTER 9

Army Combat History Operations in the Mediterranean Theater

A December 13, 1943, letter from Captain Chester Gibbs Starr, Jr., Historical Section, Headquarters Fifth Army, sent to Lieutenant Colonel Kemper (previously mentioned in Chapter 3) told what combat historians were doing in the Mediterranean Theater of Operations. Starr was a professional historian and authority on ancient studies. He had earned a Ph.D. in 1938 from Cornell University. Starr interrupted a teaching career at the University of Illinois at Urbana to serve as a combat historian.[1] At the time, Kemper was with the Allied Forces Headquarters Historical Section.[2]

Starr told Kemper that the team had "been busy as beavers...." They were working on the Salerno Operation and had run "into the drop by the 509th Parachute Battalion on the vicinity of Avellino" on September 14 and 15, 1943. He and another combat historian to the battalion's "bivouac area near Naples to do some interviews." They had briefed the battalion commander about their mission. Starr wrote, "[W]e, didn't need to say anything more." The commander "promptly ... [took them] in his office, sat ... [them] down and gave ... [them] a thirty-minute summary of the operation." The commander gathered records including a "'mass' of interviews, which he and others had made when the men trickled back," and made them available to Starr. The commander told them that "any man ... [they] wanted to see would be gotten." Starr found the interviews with the enlisted men to be "so complete and so much better than anything ... [they] could have elicited three months after the operation.... [A]t noon mess [they talked] to a number of the officers who participated. Everyone was very cooperative, and ... [they] got an engaging story as a result."[3] He thought the unit would submit reports later. But the unit was only thinking about it before their visit.

Then they went to Salerno to study the terrain. "If we were convinced beforehand that one would have difficulty in writing up an operation without seeing the terrain," Starr continued, "we now have the proof of actual experience." A bridge critical to one division was not on their map. From their visit to the battleground, they could "now see <u>why</u> the fighting took place as it did, why a little 'swell of ground' was geographically the place that the action would concentrate, and so on."[4]

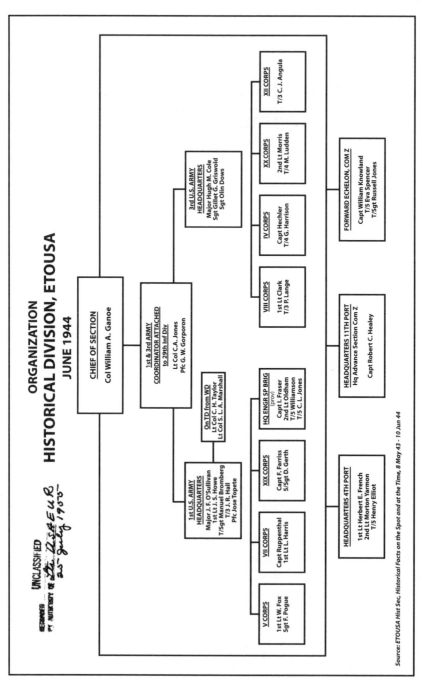

Organization, Historical Division, ETOUSA, June 1944. Note especially the names of: Lieutenant Colonel C. H. Taylor; Lieutenant Colonel S.L.A. Marshall; Major Hugh Cole; Sergeant Pogue; Captain Hechler and T/5 Eva Spencer. (Source: Occupations Forces in Europe Series, Historical Division, European Command, Karlsruhe, Germany, 1951)

Starr mentioned his conclusions based on "geographical exploration"; combat historians needed a good understanding of the action, maps, and aerial photographs before the terrain visit. Their compasses served them well. It was extremely useful to have a soldier who participated in the action with them and dependable transportation must be assured. Thanks to one of the colonels, they secured independent transport from 5th Army. A "general idea of the terrain," he advised, "could come from a 'few days of good weather.'" A month was needed to study it in detail. He thought two officers should work together on "terrain reconnaissance."

Chester Gibbs Starr, Jr. (Courtesy University of Michigan)

Starr wrote it was "impossible to write finished studies in the field." They were too cold during the day "to think very straight at night. But," he added, "it is advisable to whip out something on the spot when one can still check doubtful points. Before the impressions go out of … our heads … we plan to set down a terrain appreciation of some length, with an eye to an eventual operational monograph." Then they would "pull together all the threads … accumulated and fashion … [a] pamphlet." Starr included a draft two-page outline of the pamphlet that became part of the *American Forces In Action* series.[5]

The pamphlet was published in November 1944. The Chief Historian of the Army at that time was Dr. Walter Wright. He described it as "a great improvement over *Bizerte*."[6] Wright added, "It provided vastly more detailed information, specific and not generalized…. The units in action obviously consist of human beings and not vague abstractions." He believed some of the narratives were "overwritten … to achieve atmosphere," which Wright "deplored." "To discover or create a fitting style for our pamphlets," stated Wright, "will perhaps be difficult … 'but we must ... start with a style which is simple and unvarnished, even at the risk of being pedestrian.'"[7]

At the end of December 1943, Starr wrote to Kemper about the progress a team member was making on another operation. At first, the project was "slow going," because the soldier had to be "introduced to the peculiarities of military records...." But he now was "well initiated into aberrations of coordinates, times, false rumors, and all the rest." Since the unit had returned to the front, interviews would be done later. Starr posed several questions to Kemper about the Salerno pamphlet and two stories.[8] The letter was part of the "Orientation Material for Theater Historians." The Washington Historical Branch considered it to be excellent advice on how to conduct a U.S. Army combat historical program.

On January 8, 1944, an historical section was established in the Headquarters, Assistant Chief of Staff, G-2. Assistant Adjutant General Colonel H. V. Roberts outlined the section's purpose and duties:

1. [I]nsure that adequate material is forwarded to the War Department so that a history of U.S. Army Forces can be written;
2. coordinate all "historical activities" and offer "technical advice and assistance...;"
3. coordinate with The Adjutant General assuring subordinate U.S. units observe standing War Department and theater regulations about submitting operations reports, records and special historical studies;
4. stipulate ways to manage the "selection, preservation and forwarding of records of historical value of other than tactical organizations;"
5. assign personnel as needed to Army Headquarters facilitating the creation of special historical studies wanted by the War Department;
6. [p]repare such reports, histories, or historical studies as may be prescribed by the Theater Commander.[9]

As in the ETO, a network of historical personnel was established. Field army and air force commanders were assigned specific personnel to handle historical duties. In units below division, these historical activities were performed by personnel as an extra duty. Historical teams had "sufficient freedom of action in the discretion of commanders concerned, in order to obtain first-hand information and eye-witness accounts." There were "suggestions on the preparation of reports and histories."[10] The memorandum was in the "Orientation Material for Theater Historians." This unquestionably recognized and supported the work of historical teams.

Until September 1944, the Historical Section was assigned to Headquarters Company, Fifth Army. It worked "unobtrusively [resulting in] a wide freedom of operation." The section was aligned under the chief of staff and generally received support and cooperation from the Fifth Army's staff. But direct contact with the commander was "limited." Support came from historical officers and those charged with historical-related duties. In return, section personnel offered them assistance and advice, such as preparing historical reports and unit histories. Other assistance included "liaison visits" to units.[11]

The Historical Section concentrated on the divisions. Although the Fifth Army Historical Section was "technically" under the theater historian, "for all practical purposes it operated independently." The section did revert to theater control in the end, but not before completing its work. While the section's relations with the U.S. Navy were "haphazard," there was a "good working arrangement." Relations with the British were "difficult because of the disorganized state of their historical activities."[12]

The historical teams in the Mediterranean theater generally had command support. The importance placed upon the Historical Section to produce a history of the Fifth Army is seen in Lieutenant General Mark W. Clark's Foreword to Part I, From Activation to the Fall of Naples, 5 January–6 October 1943 written on October 27, 1944:

> Field conditions do not encourage the writing of history. To my knowledge this is the first attempt to set down the history of an American army while it is still engaged in active operations. Nevertheless, I have considered it desirable to secure an authentic story of the action of this army as we proceeded. A trained group of officers and men have been steadily occupied since our arrival in Italy, studying the terrain and operations, going over records, interviewing commanders and staff while events were still fresh. Though anything written as soon after the battle must necessarily be incomplete, I feel that the Fifth Army history possess an immediacy and freshness which cannot be said later. Above all, it is complete, straightforward study story, as far as we know it, which gives due credit to the units of all nations which have served in Fifth Army. The world knows the names Salerno, Cassino, Anzio and Futa; this history should explain why these names are glorious in military annuals.[13]

U.S. troops march up to join in the attack on the Germans on the Salerno shore. Coast Guard manned landing craft that brought them ashore are visible in the background. As the troops move forward, they pass a fellow soldier returning from the battle—on a stretcher. (Courtesy NARA)

The *Fifth Army History* began as an after action report. It was published shortly after the war in Italy. The history documented operations with information on command problems and on tactical details of units. The appendices included personnel and ammunition figures and lists; operations orders; and directives, along with maps, charts, and statistics.[14] The combat historians had collected all that together with photographs, operation plans, journals, and supplementary records. By October 1945 five other volumes were in various stages of development.[15]

Further evidence of command support was the status of the historical program in October 1945, which Salmon (previously mentioned in Chapter 5) described. In addition to the three published volumes of the *Fifth Army History*, there were three more being printed in Italy. Another was completed but not yet approved by Lieutenant General Clark. As the section prepared to close, it sent two more histories to the Washington Historical Branch. Three administrative history volumes were in various stages of completion. Meanwhile, nine officers, including Salmon, worked on projects to be finished between January 1945 and January 1946. Salmon made copies of all unit histories. He would take them to Washington to finish the theater histories.[16]

Starr's November 25, 1945, report to the Washington Historical Branch on its activities during the Italian campaign is key to understanding how the Fifth Army Historical Section was structured and operated. He explained the section's functions, its personnel, general methods of operations, its relationship with other organizations, and his own conclusions and observations. Starr listed the section's functions as being:

1. managing historical records;
2. preparing accounts of the campaign, by phases;
3. preparing monographs on the operations of smaller units;
4. forming an artistic record of the Italian campaign;
5. preparing a pictorial history of the Fifth Army based on Signal Corps photographs;
6. furnishing information to the commander, his staff, and units;
7. advising all units interested in preparing their own history for publication.[17]

The section was located with the rear echelon. It was briefly with the forward echelon. Towards the end of the war, the section "was forced to live with the Public Relations Section outside the headquarters." Starr believed the section's location had a direct impact on its operation. That sounds similar to the ETO Historical Section's experience.

Half of the section was housed in buildings and the other half in large storage tents. Besides typewriters, desk and chairs, the equipment was "improvised." Among the equipment were maps, photomaps, a case for the artists' work and "wooden boxes for records." Due to the voluminous records and frequent movement, there were no "lock boxes for classified material, which was under constant guard."

Eventually the section had a "field safe for Top Secret documents. Drafting tables were rudimentary. With tentage and personal baggage the Section normally had four to five 2½-ton truckloads."

Frequently the historians had no "independent transportation and relied upon the quartermaster car company pool." That was "generally adequate." The table of organization for the I&HS allowed for a jeep, "but the experience with vehicles was not entirely happy." There was no full-time driver, maintenance was problematic, and restricting vehicles to "genuinely official business was conducive to disaffection, especially among the officers."[18] These problems also resembled those confronting combat historians in the ETO.

Personnel usually included: 6 officers: 1 Army historian, 1 artist, and 4 writers; and 14 enlisted men: 1 chief clerk, 3 writers and research men, 4 artists, 3 draftsmen, 2 typists, and 1 records clerk and typist. He considered the staffing to be "barely adequate" since the "normal workweek was seven days a week, 8:30 to 5:30."[19]

As in the ETO, qualified manpower often was elusive. The Washington Branch sent 5 officers and 2 enlisted men, "the backbone of the writing staff." Competent replacements were "impossible from theater resources." Starr thought the "ideal field historian" was an officer interested in the work, one with military experience, young, adaptable, and trained as an historian "with a broad outlook and facile pen." It was easier to replace an artist than an historian. The writers' education ranged from a high school education up a doctorate. In peacetime, the draftsmen were commercial artists. The ability of the typists was exceptional. Starr attributed that to the section's esprit de corps.[20]

When the 7th I&HS was attached to Fifth Army the section's personnel were "transferred to the new unit on paper." Consequently, "the Headquarters Commandant tended to consider the 7th I.H.S. as a separate unit and not an integral part of Army Headquarters." The combat historian tried to overcome this. He made his "main points: that he remained a member of the Army staff, attending staff conferences and entitled to all staff privileges; and that the Section was considered part of the Army Headquarters."[21]

Starr stated the Washington Historical Branch initially provided most of the writers. He reported "a fair amount of direct communication at the outset, and relations long remained informal." Starr received just two "official directives." One related to the submission of periodic reports and the other to the submission of "all history to be printed for review and approval." But, he added, "relations were not entirely harmonious." Information from the branch was "very scant." This caused the section to feel as if it was "working in a far, remote corner." Their pamphlets were "extensively revised in Washington, sometimes almost rewritten … which a trained historian of independent standing could only consider an expressed mark of distrust in his ability." Personnel did not think the branch always understood field conditions. "Despite these difficulties," Starr claimed, the section "received essential cooperation from the Historical Branch in all matters relating to its work; above all it was left free to carry out its projects as it saw best." Those were the "important things, and the irritation caused by butchered pamphlets and uncomprehending letters was mitigated by a genuine interest in forwarding the historical program."[22]

One of Starr's conclusions was there must be "flexibility" in the historical program. But there must also be:

> greater common agreement on the general outlines of the program; the historians of the Army must know what they want to do (or are expected to) if we are to avoid the hodgepodge results which are becoming evident in the historical work of World War I. The Historical Branch ... must make up its mind definitely as to the general type of product it desires—subject to the condition that it does take its stand primarily on the basis of the field evidence, not on abstract theory of what might be desirable. Writing history in wartime is difficult; we must gear our plans to its difficulties and possibilities.[23]

Starr surmised that "Compromise [between the] scholarly and the military ways [was required] on either side: the graduate scholar must not let the form of presentation become more important than the substance; and the army must yield somewhat to the individualistic temperament of the personnel it utilizes."[24]

Starr made a case for contemporary history. He considered the "experience of World War I had indicated that if combat history were to be available within a reasonable time after the war it must be done with or shortly after the event; the Army Historian proceeded on the assumption that his personnel would disperse very shortly after the war." Popular histories could be "printed in the field." Those "accounts might evoke valuable comments [from the participants who] can still remember them easily."[25]

Starr commented on a historical section's organization and structure. It should be "an integral staff section ... not an ad hoc organization or a separate unit." To get cooperation the section should "not be attached and detached at the pleasure of a higher headquarters." The table of organization for an I&HS was founded on "a concept of historical teams ... not used at all in Fifth Army and apparently nowhere else as planned...." The concept was "incompatible with [the historical] functions" he had outlined.

Starr cautioned a "tie-up with public relations ... [which] gives false impressions to the ordinary staff officer and may even lead to suppression of truly historical activities." He supposed "establish[ing] ... field operating teams was 'an artificial scheme ... wasteful of manpower.'" The Historical Section did not use teams, but the units that did use them could better "report on their usefulness."[26] Some of Starr's comments echoed those of his ETO counterparts.

Starr judged a historical section needed only a "Historian and an Executive Officer as commissioned overhead." The historian acting as "administrator and 'front' for the section should best be a Regular Army colonel [with] considerable experience and wide acquaintance as Historian." He must have "military experience, field grade, interest in the historical program, and determination.... One of his principal functions, too little fulfilled in Fifth Army should be to participate in all important conferences and keep fully acquainted with Army policy and plans through close contact with the army commander and the chief of staff."[27]

He reasoned that field historical work "should be concentrated at army head-quarters, and historians should operate from that point as a base. On a lower-level historians will not have sufficient breadth of view and freedom of action. Especially it seems inadvisable to waste historical personnel by assigning them to divisions. At that level he will be given other duties."[28]

Starr wrote there should be limited supervision of the section from above. Personnel "must be treated as individuals and given broad assignments, to be carried out as they see best. The purely formal aspects of army discipline and life will have to be mitigated for persons of the training and temperament necessary in a historical section."

More interviewing would require allocated vehicles. If there were assigned artists, "they might well be added to the historical section.... Any finished historical work, to be effective, must be published." The fact that it might be revised in the future "need not discourage immediate publication." Some of Starr's observations, conclusions and lessons learned foreshadowed the character of the Army's future combat history program.[29]

The Historical Section was especially productive. It published a 1,500-page history based on an "exhaustive study of approximately 7 tons of records...." The combat historians completed three pamphlets for the *American Forces In Action* series based on "terrain reconnaissance" and written records. They placed increased emphasis on monographs. These were "detailed studies of smaller units for a brief period of time, designed to give a clear picture of the action of the unit." The monographs "relied heavily upon interviews." The artists produced paintings, either painted on the front or in the rear. The section prepared one of the volumes in a pictorial history. Starr thought it was of "scant value."[30] In November 1944, he issued a revised style sheet as guidance for the Fifth Army history.[31]

Starr, and other World War II combat historians, wrote history based on interviews, narrative reports, maps, charts and collected documents. Marshall was also an advisor. The interviews were typed as reports from notes and memory. Hechler tried to "persuade the commanding general to keep a transcript of telephone conversations, 'the stuff of history,'" to the chagrin and opposition of the commander's stenographer. From Hechler's account, collecting documents was not the "major operation...."[32] Hechler, Ganoe and Starr reported there were artists in the area. Hechler did not take photographs but "encourage[ed] the press photographers from the news media to share photos...."[33] Starr participated in producing a pictorial history.

Products differed between historical units and theaters. Resembling World War I, each U.S. Army commander controlled the I&HS as he saw fit. So, missions varied between the units. As products altered, so did their quality and quantity. The 1st

I&HS prepared operational reports and studies such as "Narrative of the Operations of the 27th Division on Okinawa," "The XXIV Corps In The Battle of Okinawa," "Army Tanks in the Battle for Saipan," and "Army Amphibian Tractor and Tank Battalions in the Battle of Saipan."

The 4th I&HS, 9th Army wrote "Operations IV, Offensive in November."[34] Starr's Fifth Army 7th I&HS wrote monographs and collected, art, photographs, and records. In addition to the multi-volume history of the Fifth Army, Starr's historians completed historical and operational reports. Among them were: "19 Days from the Apennines to the Alps: The Story of the Po Valley Campaign;" "Road to Rome;" "We Were All New Once;" and "The Advance on Rome, 11 May–June 1944."[35]

The 10th I&HS, Headquarters, Eighth Army historians included their observations, explanations for actions, analysis, and sometimes offered a historical perspective. A report from Tunisia from March 20 to April 19, 1943, read:

> Air bombing is important in driving an enemy out of a prepared defense. At Mareth it preceded the artillery preparation. The modern tendency is to provide all-purpose batteries. If the air preparations is [sic] a separate phase of an attack, enemy batteries will concentrate against the planes. It is not surprising that the Allies lost heavily, as the artillery preparation did not start until the air preparation was over.[36]

Another comment was "Numerous reports indicate that German divisions have no fixed T/Os. This writer noted this fact in 1941." And "The changing of front line units after a severe battle was practiced in the first World War."[37] So, these combat historians were not only recording the operation but offering their own interpretations and analyses.

The 10th I&HS also prepared a 14-page report with maps and charts of the battle of Panay Island. The report outlined the situation and defense preparations before the American landing. It highlighted the battle's progress after the landing and activities following the Japanese surrender. The report included observations and a tactical critique. A supplement included an interrogation of a Japanese officer along with his biography. The 10th I&HS also produced a staff study of the operation.[38]

As products varied, so did their quality and quantity. Subsequently, coverage of the war fluctuated from theater to theater. The ETO historical program was the most effective. History Sections faced problems such as alignment within a command; uncooperative or indifferent commands; inaccessible classified documents; and personnel turnover (redeployment before projects were completed). The latter caused what Hechler called a "crisis spirit." Administrative and transportation issues sometimes plagued the mission. Contributing factors were the late establishment of the Washington Historical Branch and the delayed start in organizing historical teams.

The qualifications of individual historians ranged from high school graduates to professional historians like Ganoe, Starr, Pogue, Hechler, Cole, Martin Blumenson (who served with the Third and Seventh Armies) and Roland G. Ruppenthal (who was assigned to VII Corps and the Third Army in four campaigns). Some earned decorations for their work. Ganoe, T/5 Spencer, and Starr were recipients of the Bronze Star as were Major Albert L. Hatch and T/4 Henry J. Webb, members of the 4th I&HS.[39] Hechler was awarded a Bronze Star and 5 battle stars. Pogue earned a Bronze Star and a Croix de Guerre. Among Marshall's awards were the Legion of Merit, the Bronze Star with oak-leaf cluster, the Combat Infantry Badge, and the Legion of Honor.[40]

The World War II combat historian was in the rear but also on the front lines with a notebook in one hand and a carbine in the other hand. Whether by Marshall's bringing up the rear of a battalion onto Makin Island and popping out of a billet in Sibret, France, as shells exploded on the road; Pogue's typing "on a little camp desk under an apple tree" and discussing the Crusades with a chaplain; Starr's terrain reconnaissance; and Hechler's command of a four-man historical team interviewing soldiers at the Remagen Bridge, and searching through secret documents, they captured the U.S. Army's "history on the spot and at the time."[41]

They were ever-ready to collect information supplementing records required by Army Regulation 345-105 *Military Records: Historical Records and Histories of Organizations*. Their secondary mission was writing operational narratives for immediate use and War Department publication. Combat historians blanketed the battlefields and worked with historical officers at all echelons. Ganoe remarked combat historians were "obtaining on the ground and at the time those happenings and statements that may be lost or distorted later."[42] Starr said, "If we were convinced beforehand that one would have difficulty in writing up an operation without seeing the terrain, we now have the proof of actual experience."[43] And Marshall later wrote to Hechler: "[T]he combat historians always carried guns, shot the enemy and were shot at, captured prisoners, and were with the infantry within the range of small-arms fire."[44]

CHAPTER 10

Post-World War II
Army Military History Doctrine

After the war Marshall wrote about the "mad scramble and bail-out that was called redeployment." He tried to keep the European combat historians on active duty because their projects needed completion. Marshall even contacted a congressman to intervene. Consequently, Secretary of War Stimson cabled Army Chief of Staff General Dwight D. Eisenhower's Chief of Operations, Lieutenant General Harold R. Bull: "If we allow officers to stay on as volunteers, provided they have essential work to do, and approve the discharge of enlisted personnel having points to come home, and their retention overseas as civilian employees with civil service rating, provided they are willing, will that satisfy your mad historian?"[1]

The "mad historian" kept enough personnel on duty to ensure the "sources for the European section of *The United States Army in World War II* were compiled." Pogue remained on duty as a civilian. Hechler stayed until 1946. Tons of classified records, collected by the ETO combat historians, were sent to the United States. The historical teams used them as they began to write.[2]

Hechler joined Marshall after V-E Day to interview German POWs. He stayed until 1946. In the end, the program expanded and ultimately 250 senior German officers flowed through the Historical Section. From this work, the Washington Historical Branch produced 620 studies.[3]

Cole stated that "within eight months of V-E Day" the ETO Historical Section "had collected, catalogued, and shipped to Washington thirty-four tons of original records, containing nearly all of the documentary story of the units which took part in combat." He maintained the British and the U.S. had about:

> 1,500 tons of German military records, some of more value than others. Fortunately, the operational records which have fallen into our hands come from the higher German headquarters and thus provide a causal connective tissue for the skeletal arrangement of facts derived from our own combat intelligence ... most of Hitler's orders re operations on the Western Front in 1944 and '45 may be found in the War Diaries of the field commands, complete with the statement of the reasoning behind the order. Thus, we are able to reconstruct in detail the ... [way] Hitler personally intervened to gather the forces and prepare the plans for the Ardennes counteroffensive.[4]

While certain records such as those at lower levels of command were missing, Cole said they could "mend and make do."[5] In 1954, Kent Greenfield wrote: "The Army alone produced 17,120 tons of records, enough to fill 188 miles of filing cases set end to end." He and others used them to begin writing the official history of World War II.[6]

The ETO Historical Section ceased operation in January 1946.[7] At least three Information and Historical Services remained on active duty. In July 1946, the 1st I&HS had 14 personnel. The 2nd I&HS redeployed to the United States and served on active duty until 1949. Various historical teams and historical units were activated and inactivated in 1945 and 1946. Twenty-six teams were formed in the Organized Reserve Corps. The history and public affairs missions were separated. The history unit focused on preparing special reports and conducting interviews instead of producing final monographs. The reports supplied the Office of the Center of Military History (OCMH) (the Historical Division being re-designated in March 1950) with "raw data and also served as a data base for immediate analysis within the theater."[8]

Greenfield thought Cole and other combat historians working for the Historical Division "had observed how the records had been generated and were, therefore, better able to evaluate their importance. These historians were personally interested in making a final report on the great events in which they themselves had played a part.... The mass of records," wrote Greenfield, "that survive a modern war is so overwhelming as to make it increasingly doubtful that its history can be written successfully *except* by that generation which created the records and knows how to use them selectively. We were, in short, convinced that unless the history of the war was written promptly, it could not be written either correctly or adequately. We had to face up to the problems of writing contemporary history."[9]

"In the case of more remote periods," wrote Greenfield, "such gaps are bridged by conjecture or closed by painful and elaborate research, or left gaping.... What I have said ... is not to be ... construed as an argument for 'official' history. To me it means only that when the job cannot be done unless the historians are employed by an agency of the government, official history can, under the right conditions of professional control, be honest history."[10]

A further justification Greenfield gave for writing contemporary history was using oral evidence. He described it as "indispensable, but ... highly perishable ... particularly for the history of recent warfare, in which oral and fragmentary orders have so largely taken the place of written orders." The oral interview technique was used:

> extensively by historical officers [in World War II] ... proved to be a highly effective means of penetrating 'the *fog* of battle' which has always baffled historians of combat. And it became the foundation for ... *American Forces In Action*, published by the War Department ... which

surprised professional critics by their completeness and accuracy…. [T]he record of many crucial decisions in battle … [was] written on air."[11]

Greenfield stated, "The rule of two independent witnesses … becomes particularly important. But without such evidence, the written records, though overwhelming massive, confront historians with gaps." Marshall's group interview technique could be used to validate written statements.[12]

General Eisenhower supported the effort to write an official history of World War II. On November 20, 1947, Eisenhower issued this order: "The history of the Army in World War II, now in preparation, must, without reservation, tell the complete story of the Army's participation…. The foregoing directive will be interpreted in the most liberal sense with no reservation as to whether … the evidence of history places the Army in a favorable light."[13] Cole believed Eisenhower's directive meant the history should "pull no punches…. We expect our final product will be criticized, as is all contemporary history, on the ground that it lacks perspective. But we believe that the dust churned up by Patton's tanks does less to distort perspective than the dust raised by the archivist as he thumbs through records a half century old."[14]

Eisenhower's backing and that of others for an official narrative history of World War II was in striking contrast to the former Secretary of War Newton Baker's position on writing an official narrative history of World War I. This was a revolutionary new direction rippling across the writing of military history. When officers reviewing draft chapters written by other historians asked Greenfield how they knew "all this," he replied they "had learned it from the records…."[15] And who had collected those records? None other than combat historians!

T/O&E 20-17, Historical Service Organization, dated February 11, 1949, officially structured what we now call the Military History Detachment (MHD). It established three types of teams.

1. A Team, manned with 2 historians (a lieutenant colonel and a major) and 1 noncommissioned officer, 1 stenographer and a driver supported theater operations through the theater historian and the theater communications zone. A Team supervised one or more B teams.
2. B Team with 1 officer historian (major), 1 stenographer, and a driver, supported a corps.
3. C Team with a captain (the commander), a stenographer and a driver, supported a division with the same B Team organization.

The unit to which the team was attached supplied administrative and communication support.[16]

The teams' functions were: "Observes action; interviews commanders, staff members, and other personnel; furnishes information obtained for subsequent use in Department of the Army history; and provides material for immediate use in preparing experimental data on battlefield tactics, techniques, and material."[17] Like the World War II combat historian, part of the post-war combat historian's mission was providing contemporary historical support.

A field manual, Military History, was drafted if not published after World War II. The objectives of the U.S. Army's historical program were to: (1) "assemble material for and to prepare a comprehensive and accurate history of the Army; (2) gather material on new developments in tactics, organization, equipment, and technique, for prompt disseminations to interested agencies of the Army; and (3) provide material for recording the achievements of component units of the Army."[18]

Mission accomplishment depended upon detailed and accurate information collected "at the time the events occur, from those who are engaged in the activities concerned, and it must be supported by documents which will make clear what happened, why, how, and with what result." Writing historical narratives and studies usually would be the responsibility of a theater of operation's headquarters or the War Department's Historical Division. Historical officers would assist in ensuring that the information on which those narratives and studies were based was collected. Information would come from operational historical reports, supporting documentation and "supplementary material, prepared by historical officers, based on interviews, personal observation, or other appropriate sources, to amplify or illustrate the required reports."[19] That was a broad mission, distinct from what combat historians did in World War I. It also differed from the World War II combat historians who wrote studies and short monographs.

Historical personnel were aligned under the unit commander to which they were attached or assigned and acted as his "agents" in historical matters. This was a major improvement in alignment. Members of the smaller historical service units remained under the command of the army historical officer. Since it was the responsibility of the army historian (defined as a special staff officer and advisor to the commander and his staff on all historical matters) "to cover decisive actions in the entire army zone, he was free to change the assignment of combat historians under his direction as the action" warranted.

Teams of combat historians were attached to the historical section of armies. The combat historian was not to interfere with unit operations. It was the responsibility of unit commanders to cooperate with the teams. The combat historian's duties were:

1. collecting and organizing interview material about campaigns, battles, small unit actions, including preparations and operations;
2. collecting photographs, maps, plans, sketches, and other material supplementing interviews relating to battle areas, troop dispositions, and actions;
3. advising, if required, historians at lower echelons, or officers detailed to maintain historical records about the regulatory requirements of keeping historically significant combat and logistical records.

The core function was conducting interviews. Interviews and any germane information the combat historian collected were forwarded to higher headquarters. The army historian in sending the combat historian to forward units provided him with "as much preliminary briefing as possible and with a list of the main points on [needed] information…." The division historian assisted the combat historian with background information.[20]

The combat historian's pre-interview preparation included examining the terrain and learning about the units involved in the action (as Starr had emphasized); talking to the commanders before an action to learn their battle plans; and studying the unit's standard operation procedures and becoming familiar "with the habits of the commander" in deploying soldiers. The combat historian concentrated on units critical to the action. Usually, interviews occur after units "have come out of line and gone into reserve. *Only rarely will it be possible to interview officers and men while they are in battle* [Italics added]." The combat historian arranged for interviews with unit commanders. He contacted the units, explained the mission, collected interview background information, and got support for moving forward. If reports of interviews were incomplete, then combat historians revisited units for additional information.[21]

Comat historians recorded and maintained diverse historical records including: (1) war diaries; (2) the organization's "daily chronological record" of activities, "prefaced by a narrative over-all summary…"; (3) activities reports; (4) a "detailed monthly summary" of non-tactical actions; (5) supporting documents like an annex to the war diary and the activities report; (6) interviews; (7) peacetime narratives; and (8) graphic materials such as photographs, maps and sketches and observations.

The field manual explained the historian's responsibilities. His "cardinal virtue … is objectivity, or freedom from bias or special interest." He must uncover the truth, record it and "indicate to the future reader what his prejudices and assumptions are…." He must use his judgment to reach conclusions supported by the evidence. "The straddler makes no useful contribution…." The historian was justified only in "refraining from judgment" when the evidence was simply not there. (This would be challenged during the next major conflict.) And writing "done under severe pressure" must be "clear, direct, idiomatic, and coherently organized." The manual continued by stating "Although the historical officer does not actually participate either in combat or logistical operations, he is frequently in an excellent position to make significant observations of his own concerning the action."[22] Marshall certainly would have disagreed. As we have seen World War II combat historians sometimes were on the battlefield in while performing their duties.

Research was an "aggressive search for information of historical importance." "The military historian's job is to go out and get it [information] wherever it is to be found." Qualitative information was more important than quantitative. Research must be "intelligent…." Historians yet to come "must be able to study and analyze the information … to understand decisions made and actions taken." The "principle of the leading problem" would guide the historian in concentrating on the major problems confronted on the battlefield.

The historian must "study orders ... [attend] ... staff and command conferences, and ... [query] ..." planners and decision makers. The historian "grasp[s]" the "critical problems" leading to further investigation "through documents, interviews, or personal observations." The historian must not leave gaps "for the future historian to try to fill after the evidence has been lost or dispersed." He must understand the particular "theory underlying the kind of operation he is ... [covering]...." The historian then knows what to ask; how to evaluate answers; ask more questions and find other knowledgeable, reliable witnesses and information verifying statements.

Personal biases must be considered. "[A] soldier who criticizes strongly the actions of an adjacent Marine unit is suspect; an infantryman who blasts the tankers is probably prejudiced...." An officer relieved of command was unable to give an impartial account of the action leading to his dismissal. The historian must analytically evaluate all statements. Generalizations and vague statements, like communication was "poor" or there were "heavy losses" must be more specific.[23]

Appendix 1, "Practical Suggestions For Combat Historians," was based on the experiences of World War II combat historians. Post-World War II combat historians were urged to consider their own situations. Everything was included from how to develop a form heading for the interview reports, pre-interview preparation work; and observing the terrain to notetaking; hunting for people who "by their position, retentive memory, and cooperative spirit" were "the richest sources of information," and avoiding "generalizations ... the bane of a good interview." Combat historians were told "Under rare circumstances, it may even be possible to observe the engagement itself [remembering that] a dead historian can't make interviews, and the mission of the historical officer is to see that an accurate account of the operation is prepared rather than win the war singlehanded."[24] Again some World War II combat historians would disagree.

A "Check List For Combat Interviews and War Diaries" included points considered to be "essential to a complete account of a given direction." They were divided into sections on strategy, logistics, operations, ship to shore movements, statistics, terrain and weather, armor, artillery, the enemy, and air cooperation. The combat historian was more interested in how a given "plan of attack was executed rather than just obtaining, like the war diarist, information on the plan...." The combat historian was to include a "general description of terrain, vegetation, and weather..." because that affected troop movement; determine how aware the troops were of the terrain; know whether there was more than one name for physical features; and know if any "important reconnaissance" was made.

The combat historian must also record the "number and accurate nomenclature of tanks and combat vehicles" used in an engagement. "Cite any special and wholesale modifications made on combat vehicles because of conditions existing in the particular operation (e.g., hedgerow cutters);" record the type of fire and types of projectiles; and pay attention to how "poor maps, dense jungle" and other factors affected the artillery's location of targets.

Other tasks included to record the enemy's order of battle and the names of commanders; give the "estimated rate of fire" of enemy forces in relation to friendly forces; establish how the enemy used "roadblocks, mines and booby traps"; give a detailed description of "enemy tactics of combined arms, offensive and defensive … [l]ist air support, measures taken for air–ground liaison … and how 'air intelligence' decisively affected decisions on ground tactical plans or courses of action."[25]

Records and Reports: Command Report was issued on October 3, 1950. Apparently, this was a revision of AR 345-105. The command report replaced the after action report, activities report, narrative report, and the war diary. The unit commander used the monthly command report to record, review, and evaluate the command's activities. The command report could include recommended changes in doctrine, organization, training, tactics, technique, administration, and equipment resulting from lessons learned. The focus was on contemporary use.

Furthermore, the command report would "serve as a basis for planning, aid to instruction, and facilitate historical research." Combat command and operations would be summarized in the "complete, impartial, and factual" report. Along with annexes, the command report would "include data concerning personnel, intelligence, operations, and logistics." The commander would incorporate the rationale used in decision making and the favorable or unfavorable outcome. Auxiliary documents would incorporate a daily journal with important actions, orders, a summary of major activities, maps, and diagrams. Copies of orders, periodic reports and other annexes were examples of documents. Change 1 to AR 345-105 in August 1951, made OCMH the proponent for the command report rather than the heretofore Assistant Chief of Staff, G-3.[26]

In the post-World War II years, many of the I&HS were deactivated. Twenty-six history teams in the Organized Reserve Corps were formed and historians focused on writing contemporary, narrative history of WWII, as supported by Eisenhower. T/O&E 20-17, Historical Service Organization formed what we know as MHDs and defined their duties. Field manual *Military History* described the objectives of the U.S. Army's historical program; it detailed the combat historian's duties, designating conducting interviews as the primary function, and defined the alignment of historical personnel. *Records and Reports: Command Report* replaced the after action report, activities report, narrative report, and the war diary. This was the combat historian's guidance for the next conflict.

The Korean War

In June 1950, the Korean War erupted setting off the first hot conflict of the Cold War. Six months later on December 22, 1950, President Harry S. Truman wrote to President of the American Historical Association Dr. Samuel Eliot Morrison (who had been involved in developing the Navy's historical program) (*see also* Chapter 3) that in the "critical effort which the free nations of the world are now making to peace, the work of American Historians is of the utmost importance." Truman was concerned in "keep[ing] the record clear, so that all the world may know the truth about what we have done and what we are continuing to do to build a peaceful and prosperous family of nations." He was "directing that a Federal historical program be instituted, with a primary purpose of recording the activities which the Federal Government is undertaking to meet the menace of communist aggression."[1]

Truman thought the effort needed the association's help. On January 29, 1951, Truman wrote to the Director, Bureau of the Budget, Frederick J. Lawton instructing him to "establish a Federal history program for all the agencies engaged in emergency activities." The Bureau of the Budget was to direct the program with

A 105 mm howitzer in action against the Communist-led North Korean invaders, somewhere in Korea, June 22, 1950. (Courtesy CMH)

"individual agencies" preparing studies. The studies "should concentrate upon the objective analysis of the problems confronted, how they are met, and the reasons underlying policy and administrative decisions."[2] This echoed Roosevelt's letter of March 1942 (see Chapter 3).

The old units in the Organized Reserve Corps were disbanded. Under TO&E 20-17, the U.S. Army created 2 A teams, 6 B teams, and 4 C teams; 1 A team and 3 B teams were deployed to Europe. The other 8 teams went to Korea. The Eighth Army historian in Korea had requested the activation of historical detachments to help in producing operational reports. Each detachment was to collect historical information on the command to which it was assigned or attached; "observe action; interview commanders, staff members and other personnel; furnish information for subsequent use in Department of the Army histories; and provide material for immediate use in preparing experimental data on battlefield tactics, techniques, and material."[3]

One A detachment, 3 B detachments, and 4 C detachments were to support the Eighth Army historian. The seven-manned A detachment was a quasi-administrative headquarters for the other detachments. The three-manned B detachments were to serve as research and liaison teams for corps and the logistical command. The three-manned C detachments were to work with the divisions.[4]

Due to a scarcity of trained personnel and the need to coordinate activities, the Eighth Army Historical Service Detachment was organized on April 1, 1951. It consisted of 1 A team, 5 B teams, and 2 C teams. The A team coordinated activities and handled administrative details for the 7 teams under it. The B teams (4th, 7th) and one C (6th) team were assigned to temporary duty with I Corps.[5]

The detachments reached Korea between March and June 1951. They were assigned to Eighth Army Special Troops and came under the operational control of Headquarters Eighth Army's historian Lieutenant Colonel Elbert L. Nelson. Within the headquarters the History Section was in The Adjutant General Section. In July 1950, it was aligned under the chief of staff.[6] The 10th I&HS was attached to Headquarters Eighth Army.[7]

Initially, the 1st Historical Detachment, Type A, at Taegu attempted to administer the actions of the other seven through correspondence. When this proved unmanageable the detachment was aligned in January 1952 under the Eighth Army historian. It recorded small unit actions. Detachment commanders selected actions and activities they considered significant and reconstructed them in some detail through interviews, terrain reconnaissance, and researching unit records.[8]

S. L. A. Marshall (see Chapter 4) was among those conducting interviews, sometimes with front line units. Recalled to duty, Marshall earned promotion to brigadier general in the Army Reserve. He once again used his after action interview technique and trained Korean War combat historians in the practice. He continued his desire to convey "personal impressions and observations as a military analyst" to the public.[9]

Frederick Lawton, right, speaking with President Harry S. Truman. (Courtesy Wikipedia)

Marshall served for a short time in 1950 as an operations officer for the Operations Research Office, an Army think tank. He interviewed soldiers two to three weeks following an action.[10] From his Korean War experience, he later wrote *Pork Chop Hill, The River and the Gauntlet,* and *The Critique of Tactics and Weapons in Korea.* At one time Marshall said he was a "research scientist, still subject to orders and charged as a committee-of-one with analyzing infantry operations."[11]

World War II and Korean War combat historian Billy Mossman wrote *Ebb & Flow: U.S. Army in the Korean War.* He said that in January 1953, as part of a "move to achieve centralized administration, personnel economy, and theater level control, Headquarters, Army Forces Far East (AFFE) … activated the 8086th Army Unit, Military History Detachment…" in Seoul. The 8086th was "to absorb the personnel and equipment of the eight separate historical detachments, which the Eighth Army inactivated at the same time." The 8086th was assigned to AFFE and aligned under the operational control of the chief of the AFFE Military History Section.[12]

A new system of historical coverage was formed. It consisted of a five-manned headquarters detachment to handle administration. Seven historical teams, each with a major and a sergeant, were assigned to this headquarters.[13] Mossman wrote that documenting small unit actions and activities continued to be an "important feature of the detachment's operations…. [B]ut under specific assignments from the AFFE historian, detachment officers also undertook broader projects, especially in the areas of personnel and logistical activities, to support the preparation of a campaign history." Unfortunately, this management style hampered the combat historians' ability to conduct interviews and saddled them with more staff duties.[14]

The eight detachments covered the actions of one army, three corps, and six divisions. Several major commands and corps had staff historians; some divisions had part-time historical officers. The army activated qualified U.S. Army Reserve officers to command the detachments. But there were not enough so the army resorted to other means. OCMH provided two weeks of orientation or training before the combat historians were deployed. Harry Middleton, a journalist by profession, described the training as "quite effective." He was assigned as the commander of the 5th Historical Detachment for two months and then was reassigned to Eighth Army's Historical Office.[15]

Evidently not everyone received that orientation. Many were unsure how they were assigned to a military history detachment. Korean War combat historian Bevin Alexander thought his education at a military college and an Army Reserve commission explained it. He received no training before deployment. Alexander said he "had just been wrenched out of civilian life and had been sent right straight to Korea." He commanded the 5th Historical Detachment.[16]

Some training occurred at mobilization stations. It was in the form of preparing reports and other products. The 1st Historical Detachment (type A) was activated at Fort Bragg, North Carolina, on October 9, 1950. The detachment assisted in compiling a V Corps command report for 1950 and outlined how the staff should do the next report. The 2nd Historical Detachment (type B), also activated at Fort Bragg that day, assisted the 1st Historical Detachment. The 6th Historical Detachment (type C) was activated on October 9, 1950, at Camp Atterbury, Indiana. The unit worked on a post diary, a brochure, a summary of daily activities, and assisted with combat training of the 28th Division. The 3d Historical Detachment (type B) was activated at Fort Hood, Texas, on October 12, 1950. Training

"Withdrawal From KAT'O-RI, 1950" by Master Sergeant Henrietta Snowden. (Courtesy Army Art Collection, CMH)

included research leading to a draft of the 2nd Armored Division's activities for 1950, a study of training, and the Enlisted Reserve Corps.

The 7th Historical Detachment (type B) was activated at Fort George G. Meade, Maryland, on November 15, 1950. The soldiers attended a meeting at the Historical Section, Headquarters Second Army. The Second Army historian told them about their future assignment to Korea. He said their training at Fort Meade was to research and document the preparedness of the Enlisted Reserve Corps and personnel of Second Army units before deployment. The soldiers collected reports and made official visits to staff sections of Headquarters Second Army Reserve including the Recruiting Office and Reception Center. The prepared report was delivered to the Historian on December 21, 1950. That completed the three-week training program. The 8th Historical Detachment, also activated that day at Fort Meade, received the same orientation.[17]

Some training happened after deployment. From February 15 to March 31, 1951, the 7th Historical Detachment conducted interviews in Tokyo. The detachment wrote after action reports of I Corps units and on the destruction of the Han River bridges. The 5th Historical Detachment (type C), was activated at Fort Campbell, Kentucky on October 1, 1950. It spent four months at Yokohama with the EUSAK (Eighth United States Army in Korea) historian. The soldiers received training on interviewing and preparing command reports.[18]

Korean War field historian Edward Cochley was stationed with the historian Eighth Army Headquarters in Yokohama. He gave detachments three days of "so called training." before deployment. It was interviewing wounded soldiers at the Tokyo General Hospital. He said, "There was never any instruction given. We just winged it as we went. The biggest problem was finding people who [would] talk to us.... [We] sent them on, with our best wishes. Hoped they could do the job over there. Apparently, they did because there are some pretty good reports there."[19]

Bevin Alexander explained how the detachments operated. The 23-year-old and youngest MHD commander recalled:

> ... bizarre orders ... that said [cover] points in Korea deemed necessary and that was the standing order.... In other words, we could decide where we went in Korea or what we did in Korea. The only control we got was this 1st Historical Detachment.... And ostensibly, we also got some control from 8th Army Historical Section, back in Yokohama, but that was ostensibly zero. The detachment control back in Taegu never came up to the front.... So, we were basically on our own. But we were responsible officers and ... we wanted to do what was right. So, we organized ourselves and divided ourselves between the corps; two of us went to each one of the corps.[20]

Alexander, who served with the 10th Corps, added: "[W]e could go to any headquarters, we could talk to any general, and we could sit in on any ... of these sessions. I went right straight in and sat down with all the senior officers. They were perfectly welcoming, and they understood my job." Due to road conditions, he explained, the first summer the historians used telephones. "We worked it out ... by these ridiculous little phone lines that we had across the front in those days.[21]

How did they know what actions to cover? "[W]e went right into the planning sessions," he remembered. "They told us what was getting ready to be planned and the actions that were [coming].... The G-3 of 2nd Division called and told me. He said, 'all of this is getting to happen. You ought to be up on the hill....'"[22]

The first battle Alexander covered was Bloody Ridge, a short but fierce battle beginning in late summer and early fall of 1951 and ending on September 5 when the North Koreans abandoned the ridge. He "got to be very close to these guys who were the assault guys." Alexander and his fellow combat historians took it upon themselves to

Bevin Alexander. Graduation portrait, The Citadel, Charleston, South Carolina, 1949. (Courtesy Bevin Alexander)

try to record actions that had occurred before they arrived in theater so they would not be "lost ... while there were men still there able to report it."[23]

How close did Alexander get to the action? "[W]hen the actual assault came out," he recounted, "I went up that day as it was going on.... I sat there and watched it and stayed right with it. One of them, a colonel, got killed just a hundred feet from me ... I stayed with the 2nd Division all the way through Bloody Ridge....We were on the front lines the whole time....We would interview the people afterwards and create a battle study. And it was ... flat authentic, because we got the exact comments by the GIs, all the officers involved." There was no "second guessing." At one point the enemy tried to hit his jeep. He said, "You never knew whether you were going to be shot at or not."[24]

Alexander thought not being on the front lines was:

> ... ridiculous.... That was the only way to do it.... I don't see how you can possibly report on war unless you are actually up there. You've got to be there.... We saw it all. And we got shelled and we ... lived in really rotten conditions.... And that to me made us all the more accurate as to what we were doing because we knew precisely what was happening and we knew why it was happening. And we knew the up side and down sides of it.[25]

When not on the front lines the detachment had a rear area in a government building in Seoul.

Three interconnected hills southwest of the Punchbowl, a Chinese key staging area, became known as Bloody Ridge. (Courtesy CMH)

What about group interviews? Alexander admired Marshall. "[He] was a writer—a pretty dynamic writer. Not all that accurate it turns out, but … quite a dramatic writer." Alexander described Marshall's technique as "brilliant." He did not receive "any instructions directly from Marshall," but rather got advice from the other combat historians. Recalling a group interview, he said they sat:

> around in a great big circle … [with] sixty or seventy guys…. I started asking them questions. And we had this kind of a back and forth little town meeting at which we discussed exactly what happened. I got beautiful quotes on what these guys were actually doing … point by point—what the GI was doing, not what the officers were doing, but what the GI saw, what they saw, how they saw it…. See a GI looks at a battle a hell of lot differently than a general looks at a battle. They see it from the point of view of looking at the dirt, you see. And so, they have a wholly different viewpoint. And sometimes it's more accurate than what the generals have. They know exactly what was taking place. And these details are what made our study so important … because we actually saw and said how things developed, whether the bazooka fired and hit … something and achieved anything or whether it bounced off…. I mean all kind of stuff like that we were reporting.[26]

The company commander was there too. A group interview could last an hour-and-a-half.[27]

Alexander typically did not conduct group interviews, but rather one-on-one interviews "by the boatloads. Normally [we] … start[ed] at the top and … [went] down to the bottom…. We went straight down to the units, because the units were perfectly happy to see us and were quite welcoming." They tried to interview the soldiers as quickly as possible after combat actions. Some were two days later.

Bevin Alexander stands beside an 8-inch howitzer on the front line in First (or I) Corps, Western Front, April 1952. (Courtesy Bevin Alexander)

Sergeant Gene Smykowski, 5th Historical Detachment clerk, at a forward artillery fire-direction center in First (or I) Corps on the Western Front, April 1952. (Courtesy Bevin Alexander)

The soldiers would be pulled back in reserve; the interviews took place right behind the line. They could get interviews as "easy as pie."[28]

He said, "all the studies were done that way." They were primarily of combat operations. But there were some service studies like grave registration. The studies reported the facts without making judgments. He thought they were "very good studies. They were absolutely topflight, original research and I'm very proud of what we did."[29]

Asked if he collected records, Alexander replied, "No, we didn't, because they were basically classified records.... I don't remember ever actually taking one of the documents because we didn't need those documents. See, we were the original source material to begin with.... So, we didn't need anything more than just the fact that this [action] had taken place." If anyone wanted to know what authorized an action, "you could always go back to Army or Division or whatever, and there would be an order.... There was no reason to include that in our studies." He did say the historians collected maps and photographs and took some of the photographs themselves. Alexander considered he had a "wonderful opportunity of actually recording how wars are actually fought."[30]

In May 1952, Alexander, and fellow historical detachment commander Major William J. Fox (previously mentioned in Chapter 7 when he was a Lieutenant), were at the Pusan harbor. Fox was planning to prepare a study on the recent POW uprising on Koje-do Island. Alexander was gathering information on Soviet weapons used by the Communist forces in Korea. Some of these weapons were stored at Masan, a few miles west of Pusan.[31]

Alexander redeployed from Pusan. He received three battle stars and the Commendation Medal for his service as a combat historian. Alexander's combat experiences greatly influenced one of his many books, *Korea: The First War We Lost.*[32]

Lieutenant Bevin Alexander at the 3rd Infantry Division front west of Chorwon, February 1952. (Courtesy Bevin Alexander)

Cochley recalled conducting interviews and writing after action reports:

> ... not any big picture, but just what happened.... We ... talked to other people. We talked to artillery people too. We tried to find out how many rounds had been expended and how much—what the food was like. If they had food. If it got to the front. But it was mainly about the battle action that had taken place and the results and what had happened.... I think most of the men we saw were in route back home.... There were two interviewed that died the ... next day. They were pretty badly beat up.... I was a stenographer.... I would just write down the questions and the answers.... I would write down in ... long hand and type it. And we would submit it to our 8th Army chief—in the section there in Yokohama.... They were read and approved and sent on.[33]

World War II and Korean War combat historian Russell Gugeler (*see* Chapter 6) wrote *Combat Actions in Korea.* Like Alexander, he told of being close to the battlefield. His son recalled an almost comical anecdote Gugeler told him. He was:

> typing up a daily report. And just as he finished the report, a large caliber round entered one end of his ... tent; both ends were open. It entered one end, hit the typewriter, carried the typewriter out the other end of the tent and embedded it in a tree. Dad, of course, was more than a little miffed because not only did he have to redo the report—he no longer had a typewriter on which to do it.... He was remarkably unflappable....[34]

Historical detachment commanders, from left: Pierce W. Briscoe, William J. Fox, and Bevin Alexander, with driver Private Donald L. Ruby and clerk Corporal Harry L. Knapp at Eighth Army Rear in Taegu as they are about to leave for the front in early June 1951. (Courtesy Bevin Alexander)

In the preface to *Combat Actions In Korea*, Gugeler wrote:

> This book is a collection of accounts describing the combat action of small Army units.... These are the units that engage in combat, suffer the casualties, and make up the fighting strength.... The author has tried to describe combat as individuals have experienced it, or at least as it has appeared from the company command post. In so doing, much detail has been included that does not find its way into more barren official records. The details and the little incidents of combat were furnished by surviving members of the squads and companies during painstaking interviews and discussions soon after the fighting was over.... Sometimes there are obvious gaps because important information was lost with the men who died in the battle.... No attempt has been made to mention everything that is either good or bad about the conduct of the battles described.... Neither has there been any attempt to place blame, since no one can claim that, in the same circumstances, he could have done better.[35]

The detachments prepared reports commonly consisting of a preface, narrative, summaries of interviews (after action interviews), sketches, and sometimes photographs. Captain Martin Blumenson of the 4th Historical Detachment prepared "Withdrawal from Taejon on 20 July 1950." This was a 30-page study with a preface and four interview summaries. [36]

Russell Gugeler. (Courtesy Gugeler's son)

Blumenson, an Army Reserve officer, was a professional military historian having earned master's degrees from Bucknell and Harvard Universities. In World War II he served at one time with Patton's Third Army (*see* Chapter 9). Blumenson later worked at OCMH and became a prolific author. His works include *Patton: The Man Behind the Legend, 1885–1945*; *The Patton Papers, 1940–1945*; and *Salerno to Cassino.*[37]

There were shorter studies. "Action at Chinju on 31 July 1950" had a preface, two interview summaries and a sketch prepared by Blumenson. He wrote: "The two interviews here submitted may have value as supplementary information on an early action of the Korean campaign. They may shed light on such questions as morale, training, and discipline. The intention has been to preserve fragments of information rather than to present a complete story." At the end of one interview he stated, "This action showed the lack of training for night fighting of the individual soldier."[38] This type of commentary was atypical.

"Action on Heartbreak Ridge" is an example of a more extensive study. Four combat historians (Major Edward Williamson, Major Pierce Briscoe, Captain Martin Blumenson and 1st Lieutenant John Mewha) prepared it. The study has a preface, an overall straight forward narrative, summaries of eight small unit actions, 55 interview summaries, an ammunition expenditures special report, casualty report, extracts from various records (e.g., journal, intelligence report), an after action report, an operations report, a radio message, sketches, maps, aerial photographs, and a pictorial supplement. In the preface, there is a recommendation that the Heartbreak Ridge operations be "considered in connection with the After-Action narrative (Historical report) of Bloody Ridge" because "as an unrelated action, Heartbreak Ridge loses much of its meaning." Comparing both actions would show "such similarities as the employment of units, the broader influence in effect, and the enemy resistance." This was uncommon for historical studies.

The four historians noted the interviewees were not always the "key personnel" but were readily available. So, they used command reports "much more than … usual." The four cautioned, "Because the narratives of the Command Reports are inaccurate in many instances, it is recommended that the information set forth in this report be verified by the pertinent journals, operations orders, and other primary source material."[39]

The 8086th prepared studies such as "Evacuation of Refugees and Civilians from Seoul, June 1950 and December 1950 to January 1951." The Military History Section asked the 8086th for the study. It called for a narrative with "appropriate illustrations and maps so that it could be used for a briefing of the CG, Eighth Army." Although the "bulk of the material was coming from command reports which would be readily available to future researchers…, much of the important detail was … obtained from more obscure sources, which unless preserved in some permanent form, could be easily become lost entirely." That was true of the refugee routes. The assistant adjutant general's statement on the comprehensiveness of the study was included. Another statement indicated its future use as lessons learned.[40] The study had two chapters, each with a narrative recounting the events, citations and supporting documents. Fourteen illustrations were included. The study indicates the type of work a detachment did, the Eighth Army Military History Section's review, and the routing process.

The detachments intended for these basic products to support the final preparation of a definitive campaign history. Blumenson stated they "only coincidentally provided information for use in analyzing

Captain Martin Blumenson. (Courtesy Bevin Alexander)

mation for use in analyzing tactics, techniques, and material." The emphasis was on recording what happened in an action and usually not any evaluation of the action.[41] That was distinct from what some World War II combat historians did.

The Combat Information Branch, Office, Chief, Army Field Forces (AFF) received copies of the studies on short-term loan from OCMH. The branch's mission was to review and extract information from command reports and other sources and disseminate combat data using AFF "Dissemination of Combat Information" letters and AFF training bulletins. According to the branch, "Studies prepared by historical detachments in Korea are utilized principally for action accounts in Army Field Forces Training Bulletins and are normally more adaptable to this purpose than Command Report narratives." As an example, the 7th Historical Detachment wrote three of four sections of *AFF Bulletin Number 5* dated August 14, 1952.[42]

Copies were sent to the unit involved, to the army, and to the theater, with the original going to OCMH. A representative from OCMH, who in May 1951 visited the Far East Command, advised the studies did not have to be submitted as polished products since they were seen as basic or raw material to be redeveloped by OCMH.[43] OCMH had created a Current Branch. It later began writing the Korean War volumes.[44] OCMH did not make this a directive as it had not officially established the methodology historical detachments were to use in producing the studies nor had it made known the intentions of Chief of Military History Major General Orlando Ward. He wanted stories of small unit combat actions directed at the private and non-commissioned officer level to portray what they might experience in combat.[45]

The assignment in April 1952 of a new chief of the Eighth Army Military History Section (MHS) upset any attempts to follow that policy. Reviews became more formalized and complex. First, the given unit evaluated the study. Then there were reviews by the next higher commander, the 1st Historical Detachment, the Eighth Army MHS and an Eighth Army staff section, usually the G-3. The required format and mechanics changed too. The study had to be typed with no pen corrections, paragraphs had to end on a page, and each new page had to begin with a new paragraph. No formal directive from OCMH supported the Eighth Army historian's position. Consequently, completing a narrative was extended from two to three weeks to more than six weeks. The result was a five-step approval process and, albeit perhaps inadvertently, some censorship. This micromanagement impeded combat historian field operations.[46]

Beginning in June 1952, the Eighth Army MHS published newsletters intended to disseminate information and improve program efficiency. The first one focused on the command report. It offered help in assembling the report, processing recommendations, the report's usage, news of available training, programs in various units, and OCMH's view of it as a "good operational report." Other news included the release of a new TO&E, staff visits made by the chief, EUSAK MHS to corps and divisions; conferences; a staff visit to 1st Battalion, 35th Infantry associated with a historical detachment's after-action interview; and personnel changes such as the redeployment of 1st Lieutenant Alexander from the 5th Historical Detachment to Continental United States (CONUS) on July 17, 1952.[47]

Another newsletter had details on the reorganization of the historical detachments. The eight T/O&E historical detachments, "presently located in Seoul … under operational control of MHS, EUSAK, may shortly be reorganized into one provisional military history detachment and may revert to operational control of FECOM [Far East Command]. These detachments prepare after-action interviews and provide on-the-spot historical coverage of EUSAK activities."[48]

A notice appearing in that newsletter reveals just how the different historical entities interacted as well as the historical detachments' productivity. Projects are listed "including after action interviews and orders of battle forwarded to FECOM." There were 96 completed projects "ranging … from a few to over 500 pages." The Eighth Army MHS was "preparing a synopsis and cross-indexing contents to show area, units involved, military topics covered, and combat arm or technical service represented." The newsletter contained a catalogue of the special projects with subject, date of action, and the existence of the MHS file copy. Some of the entries were:

- "Dismantling and Destruction of Han River Bridges at Seoul" (January 1– 4, 1951, action);
- "Withdrawal from WONJU" (January 6–7, 1951);
- "Chosin Reservoir" (November 24–30, 1951);
- "Innovations in the Medical & Dental services" (September 19– 20, 1951);
- "Operation SWING" (April 4–13, 1951);
- "Guerilla Attack on Hospital Train" (August 24,1950);
- "Heartbreak Ridge" (September–October 1951);
- "Study of Action 'The Mechanical Flame Thrower in Action' at YONGDAE" (August 24, 1951).

Among the five monographs were "Inter-Allied Cooperation," "Enemy Tactics" and "Logistical Problems."[49] This illustrates the wide range of topics the detachments covered and wrote about.

On March 8, 1952, a new T/O&E for MHDs defined their mission as collecting field information to "supplement and amplify the factual account of events as recorded by organizations in the course of operations." MHDs were to complement the written record through interviews and to prepare any required narratives or monographs. This expanded the Korean War combat historian's mission.

The T/O&E provided for more than one MHD per division. Command and control called for assigning MHDs to a theater commander under operational control of the theater historian and attachment to subordinate units as required. The MHD was to have an historian (major), an E-4 stenographer and a light truck driver. This was an obvious personnel cut.[50]

On April 4, 1952, the Far East Command Military History Section issued a bulletin on historical detachments and combat interviews. Chief of Military History Major General Ward stated: "The primary mission of historical teams within a theater is to collect and assist the theater in completion of the historical mission as assigned by the Department of the Army." Historical detachments were to prepare Department of the Army monographs and studies. If feasible, they were to "interview and gather detailed information … [about] critical, important, and revealing tactical operations; and … command decisions respecting these operations, if possible, to do so."[51]

The bulletin outlined the importance of interviews and provided interview techniques. Interviews were "especially important in the preparation of histories of small-unit actions, for which documentary evidence is usually fragmentary or entirely lacking…. Only rarely will it be possible to interview officers and men while they are in the line." The historian should explain that he was not a newspaperman or representative of the Inspector General or higher headquarters. He was "interested in the action only from the standpoint of writing accurate history that others may have the benefit of experiences of those concerned." The historian sought the "best evidence" and "[made] every attempt to determine the truth."

The bulletin advised limiting interviews to six hours or less. Larger groups were hard to control; people tended to "talk more frankly in small groups." Single person interviews took more time to "check [for] ... accuracy" and ensure dependability. The historian was responsible for "not damage[ing] unit integrity and the command structure by stirring up acrimonious disputes.... If a group interview results in a controversy between participants, it should be brought to a close at once in a tactful manner."[52]

Note-taking during the interview was contingent on the interviewees. "If it did not make the interviewee uncomfortable, then the historian may take notes in order to get witnesses's remarks in detail and to preserve exact statements for possible later use in direct quotations." Rough notes were acceptable. The historian should

UN correspondents confer at the Armistice Conference site, Kaesong, Korea, prior to start of the morning's meeting. Mr. Yong, New China news agency, stands in the left foreground. Father O'Conner, National News Catholic news service, stands in the right foreground. (Courtesy NARA)

"evaluate the <u>best evidence</u>.... But he should not judge an action. Yet, he must try to determine the facts. The facts would uncover conclusions and clarify problematic operations." The bulletin included instructions on the report's format, number of copies to be submitted, accompanying documents, and forwarding instructions.

A nine-page "Checklist for Historical Interviews" was an enclosure. Historians were urged to read it "concentrate[ing] on those points ... they can obtain information." The sections were: strategic, logistics, operations, statistical, terrain and weather, armor, artillery, and the enemy. There were five to 15 points under each.[53] The detachments operated under this directive until inactivated on January 24, 1953.[54] The war ended with an armistice on July 27, 1953.

Men of Battery C, 936th Field Artillery Battalion, U.S. Eighth Army, fire the 100,001st and 100,002nd shell at Chinese Communist position near Choriwon, Korea. October 10, 1951. (Courtesy CMH)

CHAPTER 12

The Vietnam War

In 1953, OCMH issued *The Military Historian in the Field.* It was a comprehensive manual about "duties and responsibilities in historical matters...." The document specified the "histories, monographs, and studies" the chief of military history considered appropriate or was instructed to do. It was "flexible and selective with respect to past events as well as current and anticipated operations and activities."[1] The field historian was "assigned to a military history detachment." The staff historian monitored and supervised the MHD. He ensured the MHD understood the mission and that provisions made along the chain of command effected mission accomplishment.

Chapter 3 detailed the MHD's organization, assignment, mission, operation, and liaison. MHDs were assigned to theaters and "under the operational control of the Theater Historian." Staff historians recommended MHD alignment. The MHD had one officer and one enlisted man. The latter was the light truck driver. The MHD commander was expected to work without direct and continuous supervision. He did not have to be a professional historian,

> ... but must be thoroughly familiar with the laws of evidence; he should have civilian experience in historical research or related activities; must be able to observe and write factually and with simple clarity what has been seen or what has taken place, based on research of records and/or personal interviews; detailed knowledge of organization and operations of combat area or services on which information is to be obtained is essential.[2]

MHDs had four missions (1) collect source material OCMH needed for histories, (2) produce monographs on operations, battles, activities, and problems, (3) create monographs on small unit actions and battles, and (4) supplement historical sections.

The command report was an "operational report giving a periodical narrative summary of events" from the commander's viewpoint, along with supporting documents for military histories. The MHDs' monographs, combat interview reports, or historical narratives reinforced the command report. The field historian determined the command report's parameters; in addition, he directed the detachment's work.

The historian must know the "mission, the plans, the objectives, and the enemy" and details affecting actions, like terrain and supplies, and should deploy as needed to best understand the action. That might mean going into forward areas and "wherever necessary to get a clear picture." Knowing "first-hand conditions" was invaluable in interviews with commanders.

The Military Historian in the Field detailed the necessity of starting to write early, thereby uncovering "gaps and inadequacies." It was important to establish liaisons with other historians. The historian must "sell himself," which sounded like Marshall and Hechler. Realizing contact with the commander was rare, the G-2 and G-3 were the "best sources of information" as were the regimental S-2 or S-3. Battalion commanders, company commanders, platoon leaders and platoon sergeants could offer their own perspectives on an action. Giving a copy of the written story, or photographs, would make the historian "more welcome next time." Historians appreciated "having the 'big picture' explained to them." The military historian must get the who, what, when, where, why, and how of an event.

The six appendices included a checklist for the command report and a checklist for interviews. The command report incorporated significant activities, the commander's recommendations, and subject matter survey information. Among the topics in the interview checklist were identifying individuals, units, organization, and key individuals; physical features (terrain and weather, culture, and fortifications); intelligence; directives; operations; and results.[3]

The March 1953, *Combat Operations: Command Report Regulation* (Special Regulation 525-43-1) gave further guidance on the command report. The report's purpose basically remained the same. The regulation distinguished between theater, combat zone, and communications zones to those required to submit the report. Units down to evacuation and surgical hospitals had to tender a report. There were even more specifics on how to prepare it.[4]

In 1959, OCMH published a more extensive version of *The Military Historian in the Field*. It resembled the pre-Korean War manual and may have been a revision. It concentrated on the command report, unit journals, interviews, observations, graphic materials, historical properties, and historical records. The "emphasis ... [was] on the [field] work ... of military historians in armies, corps, divisions, and in large administrative and logistical headquarters." This update also was intended to help "personnel who though not trained historians may be detailed in units lacking assigned historical personnel to compile historical reports...."[5] A less exhaustive section outlined the organization of historical personnel. There was no mention of a war diarist or photographer in the historical section of an army headquarters; the army headquarters structure was the same. The MHD commanding officer's duties remained the same. The organization, assignment, and central mission of the MHD were like the 1959 and 1953 manuals, although the former did not include a separate chapter on the MHD.

While MHDs helped "bridge the gap created by faulty records, their contribution to military history ... [was] not their only value." They were of "immediate value to current military history operations through their capability of uncovering, recording, and disseminating battlefield expedients and improvisations." Their "detailed accounts of tactical operations provide material for immediate use in preparing data on tactics, techniques, and material" as proven in World War II and in Korea.[6] Marshall certainly made the case for contemporary use of his studies. Yet Mossman said the Korean War studies "only coincidentally provided information for use in analyzing tactics, techniques, and material."[7] What doctrine might follow and its effect on the mission and approach of combat historians in the Vietnam War remained to be seen.

America's involvement in Vietnam began in 1950. Army advisers of the U.S. Military Assistance Advisory Group (MAAG), Indochina, assisted France's war against the Viet Minh, the "Communist-dominated revolutionary movement" led by Ho Chi Minh. As America's immersion in Vietnam increased, U.S. Army staff called for special studies. OCMH began its first historical project in 1962. This was a monograph on French operations through 1954 and the evolution of United States military assistance. That resulted in a 1963 classified monograph, "The United States Policy Toward Vietnam Since 1945."[8]

In October 1962, the Department of the Army released AR 870-5, Historical Activities: Military History Responsibilities, Policies, and Procedures. It was a more extensive doctrine than *The Military Historian in the Field*. The chief of military history was to specify the procedures for field historical operations. Operations were "those additional historical activities generated by combat operations in overseas theaters," defined as a "command responsibility." The command report remained "the basic historical summary of combat operations, supplemented as required by special studies, interviews, notes, journals, maps, photographs, and historical properties. Staff and operational historical assistance … [was to] be provided to overseas commanders engaged in combat operations … to meet the additional requirements for field historical operations."[9]

A MHD was assigned to each command level. The two-manned MHD remained the same, but the requirement for a "professionally trained officer historian" was new. The MHD served the organization's commander in a staff and operational capacity, including execution or supervision of selected functions:

1. preparing and maintaining journals and journals;
2. preparing the Command Report;
3. conducting interviews of commanders, staff officers, and others;
4. recording observations concerning weather, morale, fatigue, physical condition, etc.;
5. collecting and forwarding significant documents;
6. collecting, classifying, marking, and reporting historical properties;
7. preparing special historical monographs and historical studies;
8. preparing sketches;
9. collecting photographs and maps.[10]

These were broadened functions from those identified for the combat historian in the pre-Korean War manual and in the 1953 and 1959 releases of *The Military Historian in the Field*. AR 870-5 was the "first consolidated governance of all of the service's historical activities."[11]

It became clear to OCMH that MHDs were needed to help document the expanding war. The office recommended that U.S. Army Pacific Command (USARPAC) activate two MHDs "forthwith." Consequently, MHDs were activated on July 19, 1963. Their mission was to collect "information in the field to supplement and amplify the factual account of events as recorded by organizations in the course of operations." That was the same mission stated in the February 20, 1959, T/O&E. The manpower was unchanged with one officer (major) and an enlisted man as an administrative specialist (E-5), replacing the stenographer (E-4). Little differed in the authorized equipment except for the magnetic tape recorder, a ground-breaking development. Two types of MHDs were formed: (1) the traditional MHD assigned to divisions, brigades, and combat support units and (2) a larger MHD attached to corps and a higher command.[12]

The USARPAC historian recommended the enlisted man in the traditional MHD be increased to E-6, thereby ensuring the unit had skilled administrative non-commissioned officers. On October 16, 1963, the 1st MHD and 2nd MHD, Headquarters, USARPAC, became authorized units, minus the approved enlisted men.

Concern over historical coverage mounted. Korean War combat historian Lieutenant Colonel John Mewha, who commanded the 1st MHD, made a "fact-finding trip" beginning on October 23, 1963. He reported the historical program in Vietnam was "nil." OCMH had learned from its work on historical studies and monographs there were sobering problems with reports at the small unit and operational levels, exactly the type of warfare in Korea and Vietnam. Difficulties stemmed from the insignificant emphasis placed on historical documentation; failure to record actions; and the loss of organizational records—all problems MHDs faced. OCMH and USARPAC had made several efforts to upgrade historical reporting. In January 1965, USARPAC required unit command reports. Not without some problems, OCMH received copies. In June, USARPAC was authorized to activate two more MHDS. The 3d MHD was activated on June 27, 1965 and destined for deployment to Vietnam.[13]

In December 1964, Chief of Military History Brigadier General Hal Pattison established historical teams for the U.S. Army in Vietnam (USARV). He had two objectives.

1. Get approval from the Joint Chiefs of Staff (JCS) to "organize and support a historical team for operations in Vietnam." The team would be charged with "covering all operational aspects of U.S. Army activities." The team would

have access to all records needed to prepare "an accurate, objective account of the Army's role...."

2. Get the JCS to direct CINPAC [Commander in Chief Pacific Fleet Headquarters] to "establish a joint historical team in Vietnam ... available to the Department of the Army."

Meanwhile on December 8, 1964, the Military History Section, USARPAC informed OCMH that the Military Assistance Command, Vietnam (MACV) had approved the establishment of an operational historical section. In the spring of 1965, Army Vice Chief of Staff General Creighton W. Abrams talked to Pattison voicing his own concern over the lack of "broad-based field historical coverage." In July and August, Abrams declared he wanted a series of volumes on the U.S. Army's role in Vietnam like the volumes produced on World War II.[14]

Then in July 1965, President Lyndon B. Johnson revealed plans for the U.S. Army's burgeoning role in Vietnam. Obviously, that meant sizeable deployments of soldiers. And in July there was a major development in the U.S. Army's Vietnam history program and in deploying MHDs. The army formed Headquarters, USARV, under the command of General William C. Westmoreland. Before that MACV, a joint command, was aligned under the JCS History Offices' chain of command. Now OCMH had access to a separate U.S. Army headquarters.[15]

Chief of Military History Brigadier General Hal Pattison. (Courtesy CMH)

General Creighton Abrams, July 27, 1966. (Courtesy The Military Memorial Museum)

On July 20, 1965, the history office was organized within Headquarters, USARV. Major Albert Froede, commander of the 2nd MHD stationed at Headquarters USARPAC, arrived on temporary duty to establish the history program. He reported to Assistant Chief of Staff, G-3 Colonel William Potts. Froede introduced reporting methods, collected historical material, and emphasized maintaining good records. He "drafted the first historical regulation.... Froede contacted major subordinate units on historical matters, encouraging them to ... [keep] good records and [ensure] accurate reporting procedures." He made staff visits across the USARV headquarters. He was key in fostering interest in the history program. His observations along with those from USARPAC's staff visits revealed the sad state of recordkeeping. The MHDs would have to deal with this as part of their mission.[16]

Responding to a request from Abrams, OCMH prepared a study outlining Westmoreland's responsibilities for field historical operations. It included using MHDs as defined in AR 870-5.

MHDs were to complete reports for "historical research and future reference, have free access to ... [relevant] records, and submit 'historically adequate unit histories.'" OCMH requested one of its historians visit Vietnam and that three MHDs be deployed to Southeast Asia. It also advised "planning guidance on ... assign[ing] ... MHDs...." OCMH submitted the study to Abrams.[17]

On August 18, 1965, U.S. Army Chief of Staff General Harold Keith Johnson expressed his ideas on the importance of the army's military history effort in Vietnam. Westmoreland agreed. He "described the personnel structure for History Detachments in USARV as planned since the military personnel had been programmed but had as yet not arrived. Until arrival, officers on temporary duty were performing the functions of the MHD." Westmoreland explained "the plans for MHD assignment with the 3d MHD at USARV, the 4th to be deployed from USARPAC when ready and five additional MHDs". Those plans called for eight MHDs.[18]

Westmoreland's letter to USARV deputy commanding general underscored the importance of the history program; it meant staffing the historical office effectually; guaranteeing military history resources were sufficient; accentuating the importance of "recording the factual and complete history of the U.S. Army effort in Vietnam"; helping the USARPAC military history staff to retrieve documents and records needed for interviews; and coordinating the U.S. Army Reserve's military history program with Headquarters USARPAC and "input for the USARPAC annual historical summary."[19] Westmoreland's support was critical to the success of the MHDs and the military history program at large.

Pattison kept Abrams abreast of history program developments. He contacted commanders of deploying units guaranteeing they realized the worth of the military history program. He offered them OCMH's assistance. Pattison explained the value of record keeping, historical summaries, and command reports.

OCMH tried to train officers before their assignment. The office used a systematic series of "liaison visits and correspondence with the detachments in the field." But the "personnel system in Vietnam," wrote Dr. Wright (*see* Chapter 9), "frequently resulted in officers receiving assignments without prior training. The judicious selection of enlisted men with historical backgrounds to fill the clerk positions helped to ameliorate this problem, as did periodic visits by OCMH historians." Wright continued: "A far more significant issue was the tactical deployment of the detachments themselves. Policy called for each corps, division, separate brigade, armored cavalry regiment, or equivalent headquarters to have one detachment attached to it. Each major commander was therefore able to determine the tasks the detachment carried out and to place it anywhere he chose within his headquarters."[20] That sounds like the same situation previous combat historians faced. And like them, several military historians in Vietnam were assigned to Operations (G-3) and "used merely as additional personnel." Other historians simply were snubbed. "A lucky few," Wright stated, "received command support and worked through the command's chiefs of staff. Depending on these variables, the quality of the product ranged from excellent to poor…. [A] detachment could be anywhere from two to eleven persons. As in World War II, much depended on the initiative of the detachment commander."[21]

In December 1966, Brigadier General (Retired) Marshall and Lieutenant Colonel David Hackworth (Regular Army) deployed to Vietnam on a 90-day mission. Army

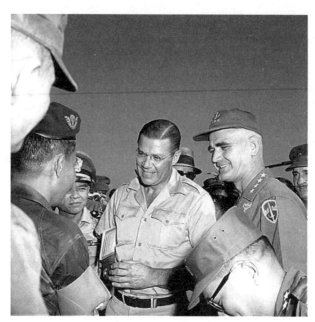

Secretary of Defense Robert S. McNamara and General William C. Westmoreland, Vietnam Assistance Command Commander, talk with General Tee on condition of the war in Vietnam. General Tee is (I) Corp Commander in the Danang Area, August 1965. (Courtesy NARA)

Chief of Staff General Johnson wrote the Foreword to their Department of the Army Pamphlet (525-2) *Military Operations, Vietnam Primer: Lessons Learned: A critique of U.S. Army tactics and command practices in the small combat unit digested from historical research of main fighting operations from May 1966 to February 1967.* The primer was published in April 1967. Johnson described the pair: "[O]ne as a private citizen with vast experience in analyzing combat operations, the other, a Regular Army officer representing the U.S. Army's Chief of Military History." The Chief of Staff then explained their mission.

> Their collaborative task was to train combat historians in the technique of the postcombat interview. [While] … conducting six schools for officers selected for this duty in Vietnam, they put into practice the principles they advocated, and from their group interrogation of the men who had done the fighting, they were able to reconstruct most of the combat actions of the preceding six months [May 1966 to February 1967], including all but one of the major operations. The present work emerged from this material. Brigadier General S. L. A. Marshall, Retired, longtime friend of the Army, and Lieutenant Colonel David Hackworth, veteran of a year's combat in Vietnam as a brigade executive and infantry battalion commander, have pooled their experience and observations to produce an *operational analysis* [Italics added] that may help American soldiers live longer and perform better in combat.[22]

Marshall and Hackworth began with "The Post-Action Critique," writing:

A Sky Trooper from the 1st Cavalry Division (Airmobile) keeps track of the time he has left on his "short time" helmet, while participating in Operation *Pershing*, near Bong Son, 1968. (Courtesy NARA)

> All of the lessons and discussion presented in this brief document are the distillate of after action group interviews with upwards of a hundred rifle companies and many patrols and platoons that have engaged independently in Vietnam. Every action was reconstructed in the fullest possible detail, including the logistical and intelligence data, employment of weapons, timing and placement of battle losses in the unit, location of wounds, etc.
>
> What is said herein of the enemy derives in whole from what officers and men who have fought him in battle learned and reported out of their experience…. The document … is in itself evidence of the great store of information about the Viet Cong that can be tapped by talking with men of our combat line, all of which knowledge lies waste unless someone makes the effort.[23]

The average interview for company actions was "three and one-half hours." It took the pair "seven to eight hours of steady interrogation … to reconstruct a fight" lasting that long. They wrote interviews needed to take place quickly after a fight. "[Any] combat unit commander can do this same thing … until he knows all that happened to them [his men] during the fire fight." This required no distinctive skill; "so long as exact chronology is maintained in developing the story of the action, and so long as his men feel confident that he seeks nothing from them but the … the whole truth…. Every division and every independent brigade in Vietnam," they continued, "has at least one combat historian [who] … is charged with conducting this kind of research; he can also assist and advise any unit commander who would like to know how to do it on his own."[24]

The group interview tells the commander what his men did "under fire." There was a bonus. "Just as the critique is a powerful stimulant of unit morale, having all the warming effect of a good cocktail on an empty stomach, and even as it strengthens each soldier's appreciation of his fellows, it enables troops to understand…" the demands on the commander. From that the men "will go all the better for him the next time out and he will have a much clearer view of his human resources…." The critique reveals blunders and heroic actions, leading to "an improved awards system based on a standard of justice…." So, there were benefits from interviews beyond documenting the fight.[25] Marshall had expressed this view in World War II.

Marshall and Hackworth's next section was "The Core of The Problem." They thought the principal challenge to routing the North Vietnam Army and the greatest difficulty to defeating the Viet Cong were "joined in the tactical task of eliminating their fortified areas with maximum economy of force." The enemies were "hit-and-run guerrilla[s]." They used their camouflaged "fortified base camps and semi fortified villages to deceive American forces." Marshall and Hackworth added self-assuredly: "Yet there is no such camp or armed village in Vietnam today that is beyond the reach of U.S. forces…. When the fortified bases go, the infrastructure withers, and thus weakened, finally dies."[26] Remember, the pamphlet was published in 1967. Marshall and Hackworth, like many Americans, were optimistic about an American, South Vietnamese and allied nation victory in this early stage of the Vietnam War. However, anti-war protests had already begun in the U.S. Eventually, it was the North Vietnamese who claimed victory in April 1975.

They described the enemies' fortified base camp and semi fortified village, which included various outer shapes, foxholes, bunkers, trenches, living quarters, kitchen, and "tunnels connect[ing] the bunkers and earthworks…." All this aided the enemy to "to pop up, disappear, then fire again from another angle, a jack in-the-box kind of maneuvering that doubles the effect of their numbers…. But until bombardment has blown down most of the foliage any maneuver into the complex by infantry skirmishers is a deepening puzzle…."[27] The duo referenced "three ground units of the 1st Air Cavalry Division [which] fought through an action of this kind in early December 1966 and took heavy losses."[28] They were *analyzing* the fight.

Next Marshall and Hackworth wrote about the 14 lessons learned:

Lesson One—The Direct Assault
Lesson Two—Warning and Movement
Lesson Three—Doubling Security
Lesson Four—Contending With Jungle
Lesson Five—Rates of Fire
Lesson Six—Communications

Lesson Seven—Security on the Trail
Lesson Eight—The Company in Movement
Lesson Nine—Ruses, Decoys, and Ambushes
Lesson Ten—Field Intelligence
Lesson Eleven—The Defensive Perimeter
Lesson Twelve—Policing the Battlefield
Lesson Thirteen—Training
Lesson Fourteen—The Strange Enemy

In Lesson One—The Direct Assault, the historians advised against company-sized direct assaults. Prior "artillery and/or air strikes" were needed due to the enemy's fortifications. They wrote that when a rifle company unwarily attacks a stronger enemy "position ... at least 50 percent of the time" the consequences are: (1) undermining "its ... fighting formations ... through immediate losses in its frontal element;" (2) focusing "on the problem of extracting its casualties under fire;" and (3) reducing "its direct pressure against the enemy...and disorganiza[tion]...." Impetuosity impedes "effective aggressiveness...."[29]

Marshall and Hackworth suggested alternative tactics. The "rifle platoon or company" must keep its forces covert given the particular "environment." It should "continue desultory fire from its forward weapons, or seek the enemy rear when favored by terrain, weather, and light." In the event the "environment and weather" support this intrusion, "artillery fires should concentrate on the rear, while tactical air targets on the enemy camp." If not, the position should be aborted early.[30] Evidence shows that the "most effective way to deal with the enemy ... is to zap him with the heaviest artillery and tactical air ordnance, not to maneuver against him with infantry only."[31]

In Lesson Two—Warning and Movement, Marshall and Hackworth described how the enemy moved. "Any direct fire out of a village serves warning.... A sudden volley ... out of the hamlet ... or any location must prompt caution and reconsideration rather than ... immediate forward extension in the assault.... [H]is surprises are staged most often by his choosing a position that we would rate impractical or untenable." Then they explained two preventive strategies.[32]

In Lesson Three—Doubling Security, the historians noted that more than 100 U.S. Army rifle companies and platoons had engaged the enemy since May 1, 1966. The greatest, recurrent source of "surprise, disorganization of the unit under fire, and heavy initial losses has been excessive haste in the advance overland and outright carelessness about security...." They urged more judgment and common sense. "It is not common sense to run chances by making haste when one is rushing straight to an entrapment."[33]

In Lesson Four—Contending With Jungle, Marshall and Hackworth began by defining "jungle." Why? They thought the term was misused. "Men fresh from a

FOR OFFICIAL USE ONLY

MILITARY OPERATIONS

DA PAM 525-2

VIETNAM PRIMER

LESSONS LEARNED

HEADQUARTERS, DEPARTMENT OF THE ARMY
FOR OFFICIAL USE ONLY

DECLASSIFIED Authority
NND 994025

Department of the Army Pamphlet (525-2) *Military Operations, Vietnam Primer: Lessons Learned:* A critique of U.S. Army tactics and command practices in the small combat unit digested from historical research of main fighting operations from May 1966 to February 1967. (Courtesy NARA)

fight say something like this, 'We engaged them in impossibly dense jungle.'" But, reading a "detailed description, or a firsthand visit to the premises [which the pair evidently did], reveals ... it was merely the thickest bush or heaviest tropical forest that they had yet seen." They defined the jungle to be when "the condition of the forest ... [limited] ... forward movement ... to 300–500 meters per hour, and [when] to make this limited progress troops must in part hack their way through." Marshall and Hackworth advised the ways troops should advance. The historians ended this lesson on a "positive note" explaining that "the jungle as to its natural dangers—is not the fearsome environment that the imagination tends to make it."[34]

In Lesson Five—Rates of Fire, the historians discussed the rates of fire by American soldiers in sundry situations. "Within the rifle company, during engagement prolonged for several hours the rate will run 80 percent or more." They analyzed "effectiveness over distance" and the effectiveness of weapons. The two men found that "The M-16 has proved itself an ideal weapon for jungle warfare." But "the

Infantry advancing at X-RAY. *Seven Firefights In Vietnam.* (Courtesy CMH)

fragmentation hand grenade, a workhorse in the infantryman's arsenal of weapons in Korea, is of limited value in jungle fighting." They recommended "jungle hand grenade courses" for soldiers. "The old byword that was once synonymous with the art of grenade throwing, 'Fire in the Hole,' should be brought back in use to warn all that a grenade has been dispatched and cover must be sought."[35]

In Lesson Six—Communications, Marshall and Hackworth wrote there had been to date (1966) no "radio failure or a break in communications" to prevent the successful outcome of an action. However, there was "a serious gap … in the flow of critical information during … combat…." They said this was especially true at the "rut platoon and company level." Too many people at various command levels used the same radio frequency. That inhibited getting through a full message. Resorting to brief messages cost needed information details. Their answer: "[E]xcept for rare and unusual circumstances all commanders should follow established radio procedures and not 'come up' on the radio of the next subordinate unit." Commanders must report the facts as they see them on the battlefield. If they don't know the situation, they must say just that![36]

In Lesson Seven—Security On The Trail, the pair detailed how the nature of jungle warfare mandated the role and nature of trails. "Command must keep itself informed

Soldiers laying down covering fire with M60, *Seven Firefights In Vietnam*. (Courtesy CMH)

AN/PRC-25 radio. (Courtesy CMH)

of where its patrols have moved recently and must safeguard its upcoming patrol against the danger of becoming trapped from having beaten over the same old route."[37]

In Lesson Eight—The Company In Movement, the men examined how the diverse Vietnam landscape and population concentrations affected unit formations and movements. The historians recommended that security, control, and concentration of firepower without undue loss of time and personnel dictated the best formation. They included sketches of some formations.[38]

In Lesson Nine—Ruses, Decoys, and Ambushes, Marshall and Hackworth began with two generalizations: (1) The enemy's "bag of tricks" was intended to generate "illusions," ensnaring American forces. (2) "The unit commander must 'keep his guard up,' listen to his men, and learn all the available information as to the enemy's location." The historians thought combat in 1966 and 1967 showed "the average U.S. soldier … in Vietnam has a sharper scouting sense and is more alert to signs of the enemy than the man of Korea or World War II." They quoted from an after action combat interview of a 25th Division patrol in early 1967 to demonstrate how American soldiers learned the enemy's ruses and decoys.[39]

Soldier crossing a stream. (DA PAM (525-2) *Military Operations, Vietnam Primer: Lessons Learned*, page 26)

In Lesson Ten—Field Intelligence, Marshall and Hackworth gave several examples of combat maneuvers in Vietnam. These showed the importance of reliable, timely, field intelligence. They discussed intelligence flow and collection. Plus, they listed and critiqued informational sources. "Special Force teams ... have developed [their own] sophisticated search and surveillance systems...." The men recommended that tactical unit commanders learn from those teams.[40]

They used adverse and winning combat actions in Lesson Eleven—The Defensive Perimeter, to demonstrate how "procedures used in forming the defensive perimeter vary greatly along with their effectiveness from unit to unit." They examined adaptations to the three-man foxhole, trip flares and additional anti-intrusion devices, including the Claymore. Marshall and Hackworth considered "the company perimeter as the basic defensive element, careful tying-in of weapons, and alertness will beat him every time."[41]

In Lesson Twelve—Policing the Battlefield, the historians said that age-old axiom was especially true in Vietnam: soldiers carried too much, which weighed them down. Out of exhaustion soldiers lessened the load by tossing items onto the battlefield. The enemy used that "litter" to his benefit. "Any discarded C-ration tin can be

Searching an abandoned village. (DA PAM (525-2) *Military Operations, Vietnam Primer: Lessons Learned*, page 32)

Foxhole line along defense perimeter. (DA PAM (525-2) *Military Operations, Vietnam Primer: Lessons Learned*, page 45)

transformed into a booby trap. The enemy is good at such tricks...." Marshall and Hackworth knew that "while policing the field there is importance on counting the number of enemy killed." They urged an examination and awareness of the two oftentimes conflicting requirements.[42]

In Lesson Thirteen—Training, the duo counseled leaders to "accept the old but absolute maxim: 'The more sweat on the training field, the less blood on the battlefield.'" A vigilant leader ensures his men are so well trained that "even under the pressure of fear and sudden danger each soldier, automatically, will do the right thing."[43]

In Lesson Fourteen—The Strange Enemy, Marshall and Hackworth wrote: "A more bizarre, eccentric foe than the one in Vietnam is not to be met, and it is best that troops be told of his peculiar ways lest they be unnerved by learning of them for the first time during combat.... Getting to know them better is a large part of the game."[44]

From the fall of 1969 to the summer of 1970, Sergeant Robert K. Wright, Jr., a history degree graduate from the College of the Holy Cross, was the noncommissioned officer in charge (NCO-IC) for the 18th MHD. The 18th was attached to the 25th Infantry Division. The division's mission was to "cover an arc of the perimeter between Saigon and Cambodia." The MHD was aligned under the division's chief of staff. This was a meaningful change. A captain, or sometimes a major, commanded the MHD; a specialist E-5 was the stenographer. Wright said, "the majors were not

Laden soldiers pushing through elephant grass near Dak To. *Seven Firefights In Vietnam.* (Courtesy CMH)

interested in the job and they spent their time up at headquarters and they and I in succession had a deal. They let me run the detachment and they stayed up at headquarters and kept headquarters off my back."[45]

The 18th MHD "worked in a little shed, like hutch … adjacent to …[their] office hutch." The mission was to document the 25th Infantry Division's history. Within the detachment's enlisted structure was a four-man combat art team. The team "visually captured the impressions of the war" from a soldier's viewpoint. The command group insisted on that. The "division museum forward" collected and logged artifacts, which were sent to Schofield Barracks, Hawaii. The "office proper" consisted of a clerk, driver, typist, and Wright, who "usually had one or two other writers." Wright said the writers typically "had at least a bachelor's degree in history or in a related field. We had a couple of guys who had MA degrees…."[46]

In August 1966, the USARV Command Historian was Lieutenant Colonel Donald F. Harrison. He required units to prepare Operational Report Lessons Learned (ORLL). Wright explained the ORLL was the "narrative war-time command report." ORLLs were quarterly, later semi-annual, comprehensive reports on a unit's activities. Typically, ORLLs contained information on "operations, logistical activities, significant personnel events, changes in command, and lessons learned."[47]

Although preparing ORRLs was not the MHDs primary responsibility, they frequently were given that duty. In the 25th Infantry Division it was the G-3's job, but the task was assigned to the 18th MHD. The ORLL was due "72 hours after the close of the reporting period. And this was a document," Wright said, "that normally ran 150 to 200 pages. Therefore, causing me to go into a 72-hour no-sleep mode once a quarter." Ordinarily one person wrote the ORLL. That person used daily divisional situation reports and other sources. Wright said, "at different times ... [he] would do the writing for a couple of weeks to give ... [the main writer] a break...." They all discussed the ORLL as it was being written. Wright added:

> And we had a big map.... And we would track evolving operations. Plus, usually the major [Ralph Ballway] attended ... morning and evening updates. So he would come back and feed us information about what was being seen as important up at headquarters.... And we would try to build the narrative a week at a time. And then we would type the stencils and then the stencils would go up to the SGS [Secretary to the General Staff], who would review them and he was an English major and considered himself the ultimate copy editor. So he would screw with the stuff and we would have to re-do it. And then we would get the blessing of the chief of staff so that we could get the narrative piece of the report out of the way without having to try to type 100 pages in the last couple hours.

Wright said this way he and other MHD members kept abreast of operations. That was especially true since the division was in a "small unit action mode."[48]

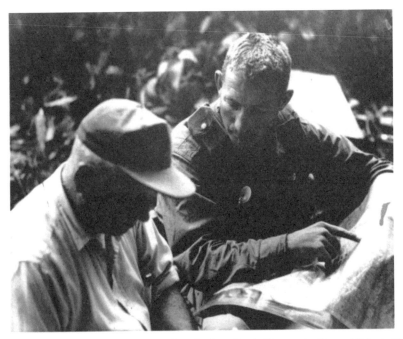

Colonel David Hackworth being interviewed on the front line in Vietnam by General S. L. A. Marshall following the Battle of Dak To in 1967. (Courtesy "Lt. Col Hackworth is a legend...now, that is.—We Are The Mighty.")

The 18th MHD examined daily situation reports (SITREPS) and intelligence summaries (INTSUMS). The unit had access to all company, battalion, brigade, and division documents. Plus, the detachment operated with the 25th Administration Company, acquiring diverse personnel statistics. The 18th collected these and other sources, along "with anything else … [it] might have catalogued or picked up as being important materials…." The 18th stored them in five-drawer classified safes, with a "grenade taped to the top of each one in the event … the base camp … [was] 'overrun.' Somebody would be responsible for torching the records."[49]

Wright said the ORLL program's success was due to the attentiveness of the MHD's personnel. "It became for us more than just merely accomplishing a report. It became a way for us to structure our efforts. And I found it a very useful mode, even though it had not been something that had been done *per se* in World War II or Korea. It sort of evolved to us that we took that to be an important mission."[50]

Wright explained the 18th MHD had "another sort of unique function." He was placed on the division's IG team, journeying "on all the IG inspections…. [He] was the inspector for historical documents." Wright reviewed the records. He certified each unit saved them in accordance with army "records keeping regulations." In addition, he examined the contents of the records. He took "time with the action officers who were responsible for filling out … the daily journals, to point out … that 'routine operations' is not an acceptable log entry."

Another task was taking photographs. "We did not particularly do a good job," he claimed. "We collected for a specific purpose but everything else was thrown into a heap that was used as source material by the artist. In retrospect," Wright added, "that was one of the big failings that I learned later and spent a lot of time correcting."[51]

One of the key duties OCMH assigned to MHDs was scrutinizing combat operations as they happened. Then they prepared thorough narrative reports grounded specifically on soldiers' reflections and on oral interviews. The MHDs used the interview techniques developed during World War II. These narratives, known as Combat After Action Interview Reports (CAAIRs), provided vital information. They enhanced the standard staff journals and radio logs. The CAAIRs were intended to assist future historians.

In the CAAIR, the MHD earmarked "things that were significant … ensuring that we gave detailed coverage to those. So, this would be important after-action reports…." When they found out there was "a big action … going down, we would jump on it and get out there and do a separate report, trying to get into the operation *as it was happening* [italics added]. We didn't have a whole lot of mobility, we only had one jeep. But we got fairly proficient at hitchhiking helicopter rides and stuff like that."[52]

In April 1970, Major Ballway assigned Sergeant Wright and Specialist Henry Welsh to cover Operation *Renegade Woods*. The campaign (May 1 to June 30, 1970) concentrated on the allied infiltration into Cambodia. The objective was to cut off enemy communication lines, overrun the sanctuary areas and seize the Central Office for South Vietnam (COSVN). COSVN was the control center for military operations against III Corps tactical zone (III CTZ), an Army of the Republic of Vietnam group responsible for Saigon and 11 adjacent provinces.[53] Wright described the operation as "a battalion-sized action, composite battalion, built up of companies from different maneuver battalions that spent about four days ... in sequential action with two different main force battalions. And the only big duke out we had between the time I got there and when we went into Cambodia."[54]

Wright and Welsh began working on the Renegade Woods CAAIR. First, they contacted the division's ranger company and cavalry squadron "as soon as the first radio reports of the original engagement reached the division headquarters." Wright did most of the labor for the CAAIR, such as preparing the maps and overlays. When Ballway and other detachment personnel were free from additional duties, they helped. Ranger Company Commander Captain Paul Schierholz let the MHD copy several of his personal photographs for the CAAIR. The division commander agreed to using "a photographic reconnaissance OV-1 Mohawk aircraft to gain specific overhead imagery."[55]

Wright detailed the mission:

> We had a ... security company guarding the radio-relay point [established in February 1966 by the 121st Signal Battalion] up on the peak of the only significant terrain feature in the whole division AO [Area of Operation]. So we were up on top of that. And periodically it would come under probe and then we would do a retaliatory sweep because that had been a Viet-Minh and then Viet-Cong stronghold since 1944. There were all kinds of caves and tunnels, and we did periodic operations called Rock Crushers.... Henry and I really covered that one in great detail using the SLA Marshall technique. And, in fact I had a copy that I wish I had kept of the checklist he had helped the US Army Vietnam historian develop for how to do the oral interviewing.[56]

The 18th MHD examined the SITREPS and INTSUMS. The 18th had access to documents from the company up to the division level. Plus, the detachment operated with the 25th Administration Company, acquiring personnel statistics. The research took extensive man hours to execute the oral history interviews. The 18th tried to record the different observations about the actions. "Ground combat troops' views ... [were] balanced by aviators' and a 'joint' flavor came through the cooperation of the forward air controllers of the 19th Tactical Air Support Squadron...."[57]

Wright said he did "between 150 to 200 interviews for a variety of the after-action reports.... as well as if ... I needed to find out something to use in the ORLLs or if we got tasked to come up with a special study...." He had a "a reel-to-reel tape recorder that weighed about 40 pounds, require[ing] a generator to operate." So, he explained, "I used it as a door jam because it was just impractical.... I used spiral notebooks and speed wrote.... [L]ater we were smart in the history program and fielded the cassette recorder which you … can schlepp around with you." Wright stated he "religiously used the recording because that always gives you proof that what you heard is what the guy actually said."[58]

Wright said the MHD conducted "both individual … and group interviews [at least 40]…." He worked a lot:

> on what kicked off this Renegade Woods operation…. [A] … double ranger team was inserted and got into a hot LZ [landing zone], went through a hellish firefight and finally pulled out after suffering several killed in action. When they ran out of ammunition, in a very heroic rescue mission, 1UH-1 came in and pulled them all out, despite having what the flight engineers later said was damage that should have prevented it from being able to fly. The guys had been down to throwing rocks, simulating hand grenades, and throwing rocks to try to keep the enemy from rushing them.

Wright described what he considered "a little bit I think innovative."

> SLA Marshall had been a big proponent of group interviews…. What I stumbled upon was the notion … when I had the luxury, I would individually interview the participants. Then I would sit down and review my notes. Then pull them all back together and do one more

"9th Infantry Division GI" by Michael Crook. (Courtesy of the Army Art Collection, CMH)

Vietnam paradrop. (Courtesy NARA)

[group] interview.... But I got the individual stories first ... because that gives you the ability that you can't do in traditional history, which is go back and cross-examine a witness. So that is how I would reconcile apparent conflicts.[59]

Major Alexander S. Cochran was the commanding officer of the 13th Military History Detachment, Headquarters, I Field Force Vietnam. He conducted a CAAIR on the Ambush at the Dak Po, January 21–22, 1969. The command-and-control headquarters was Company A, 1st Battalion (Mechanized), 50th Infantry, 173d Airborne Brigade. This group interview of six soldiers ranged from Commanding Officer, 1/50 Infantry (Mechanized) Major James R. Woodall down to Private First-Class Richard Snyder, the M60 Machine Gunner. Like Sergeant Wright, Major Cochran included background information on the operation. He described Route 19 as "one of the most important supply routes in II Corps Tactical Zone." Enemy forces had tried unsuccessfully to "mine the road and blow the pipeline." The 173rd Airborne Brigade's mission was to "secure the section of Route 19 from An Khe Pass to the 4th Infantry Division's area of operations.... About 10 kilometers west of An Khe is a north–south stream called the Dak Po."[60]

Cochran detailed the operation's concept and execution. The commanding officer decided "to place an ambush in the Dak Po on the night of January 21, 1969. The 2nd Platoon was given this mission, and a 14-man patrol was selected from the unit." Cochran listed the platoon's weaponry and described the communications

SP4 Tinney, PFC Allmon, and PFC Perez being inserted. Operation *Renegade Woods*. (Courtesy CMH)

system. Then he laid out the execution plan and the reasoning behind the patrol leaders' decisions. Cochran listed five lessons learned:

1. Sweep of the Kill Zone.;
2. Responsiveness of Artillery Fire;
3. Placement of 81mm Mortar;
4. Cross Training in Artillery FO Procedures;
5. Use of Drugs by NVA [North Vietnamese Army] Soldiers.

He concluded the CAAIR with:

HISTORIAN'S COMMENTS AND ANALYSIS:

The two principal reasons for the lack of a significant body count in this ambush were the amount of time required to obtain illumination so that the patrol leader could estimate the situation and the inability to sweep the contact area immediately after the ambush. All ambush patrol members interviewed specifically mentioned these two shortcomings.[61]

On June 21, 1968, Sergeant Dennis Smith with the 18th MHD conducted a series of combat after action interviews with eight soldiers from the 1st Battalion, 27th Infantry, 25th Infantry Division. The interviews were about an Eagle Flight operation on June 19 and 20, 1968. The interviews covered "Platoon heliborne assaults within a battalion area, seeking targets of opportunity." The area of operations was northeast of Saigon. Smith used 18 endnotes to clarify phrases like "Eagle Flight ... the Vietnam-era term for air mobile insertion" and the "Radio call sign for the leader of 2nd Platoon, Company C."[62]

Commander, 44th Military History Detachment, 199th Infantry Brigade, First Lieutenant James G. Lindsay conducted an exit interview on June 24, 1969, with Major Dennis Hightower, Brigade S-2. They discussed the Separate Brigade S-2 in Vietnam, its activities, problems, and operations. The 44th was the Regular Army's sole MHD.[63]

MHDs conducted end-of-tour interviews. For example, Major Charles C. Pritchett, commander of the 20th Military History Detachment, interviewed infantry officer Captain Joseph W. Kinzer, Advisory Team 163 Liaison Officer, 3d Airborne Brigade, Airborne Division. Kinzer was the senior advisor to the battalion. He had served in country for about a year and was scheduled to redeploy in 10 to 15 days. Questions ranged from his arrival in country; his duties; and the battalion advisory team's organization to operations; logistical problems; weapons teams; and battalion training programs, such as how to use the M-16 rifle.[64]

MHDs conducted research too. The 19th MHD had the task of researching information for the writing of the 9th Infantry Division's history. Exit interviews with redeploying strategic personnel were indispensable sources. Major Robert L. Keeley, commander of the 19th MHD, interviewed Lieutenant Colonel Douglas S. Smith, Battalion (Mechanized), 47th Infantry commanding officer. The taped 43-page interview examined problems of "static position occupied by mechanized battalion, rules of engagement, training, sniper program, ARVN units, administration, and logistics."[65]

Vietnam War combat historians forwarded the taped interviews along with supporting documents to OCMH. The OCMH used them in writing the official history of the war. As 1966 ended, the office had a rough blueprint for a history of the U.S. Army in Vietnam expanding over several volumes. In the 1970s, OCMH dedicated serious resources to the task. By 1996, five volumes had been published.[66]

MHDs provided historical support to the Vietnam advisory effort. On April 13, 1970, Command Historian Lieutenant Colonel Wegner wrote to the Secretary of the General Staff, U.S. Army Vietnam Headquarters about the status of the historical program. He reported that the 17th MHD had the mission of covering advisory teams in III Corps' tactical zone (III CTZ). MHDs documented redeployment too. Wegner looked forward to the arrival of Major Jasper Hunter who assumed command of the 27th MHD. Wegner wrote: "He is OCM-trained." Assigning the 27th MHD to II CTZ, Wegner stated "will complete the arrangement of one MHD per CTZ and will establish a posture adequate to furnish present and future historical support to the advisory effort." He assigned his XO (executive officer) to provide "advice and assistance on maintenance and preservation of records."[67]

Some USARC command historians, like Major Godwin P. McLaughlin, used newsletters to communicate with MHDs. His December 22, 1971, newsletter referred to the inactivation of five MHDs. That action resulted in "the realignment of responsibility…", changes to operating procedures and "changes to policy or procedure…. As a result, there is a definite need for increased coordination between detachments." Each MHD was responsible for providing historical services to its supported unit. That did not mean preparing ORLLs and after action reports. He added, "It is expected, however, that each detachment will respond enthusiastically to requests for historical services." The MHD was to: "organize reliable historical information on specific subjects to assist in staff planning, preparation of studies and execution of programs"; conduct "historical research and furnish … information in response to … inquiries … fall[ing] within the unit/headquarters' responsibility. Examples … would be historical information needed for briefings or reports, statistical or factual data available in historical files and needed for studies and assistance to the unit in maintaining its organizational history file…." Another duty was to … "[guarantee] that … necessary documents … [were] retired…." Records management was "paramount." And MHD personnel were to "continue corresponding with … [their] present pen-pal[s] until … receive[ing] the change from this office or from OCMH." He thought "the OCMH pen-pal is invaluable in assisting you and … [did not]expect a month to go by that you don't correspond."[68]

A U.S. Army soldier directs a UH-1 helicopter approaching to pick up injured after a paradrop in South Vietnam. October 1966. (Courtesy NARA)

On February 11, 1972, McLaughlin used another newsletter to explain that "with the continuing but accelerated drawdown of US Army forces throughout RVN [the Republic of Vietnam], it is necessary that we intensify our efforts along several lines...." He announced some mission changes. For example, the 46th MHD assumed the 23nd MHD's mission "for field historical operations involving engineer, military police and signal activities throughout RVN." McLaughlin stated the drawdown and probable shortened tours of duty made it "increasingly difficult to plan on end-of-tour interviews. For the next few months," he explained, "I desire that you select knowledgeable individuals at all levels and interview them immediately. While not an end-of-tour interview, the approach and format should be similar." He instructed the MHDs to focus on guaranteeing that historically significant records were "correctly retired." That meant an "adequate plan for files...." He told the historians to "continue to collect documents when there is doubt as to their preservation, but too often MHDs are being used as a retirement system which must be phased out." McLaughlin urged them to coordinate with unit and staff historians "to ensure that they will be able to pick up the slack when they are required to operate without the advice and assistance of an MHD." He concluded by instructing the combat historians to "identify current and anticipated problem areas in your weekly reports and address yourself to actions needed for their solution."[69] These and similar newsletters document the mission and duties of combat historians in the final stages of the Vietnam War.

Afterword

Without combat historians, it would be extremely difficult to record battlefield operations, strategy, and tactics. If not for the combat historian, those actions and lessons learned would be lost to posterity. Army Chief of Staff General Johnson evidently knew that. He told Marshall and Hackworth that their four-month 1968 mission in Vietnam was: "… improving the collection of basic data on U.S. fought battles in Vietnam for a future, official Army history of the war …" Hackworth wrote in *About Face* that Marshall "… set up a system that will use my postcombat interrogation techniques … SLAM would teach the after-action reporting techniques he'd pioneered during World War II to selected U.S. Army officers in all divisions and separate brigades in theater."[1] Hackworth said the police-style system was sound. "[T]he interviewer was the crucial element, because a good one could capitalize on the tiniest scraps of information to get to the crux of a story." Their task "was simply to train our students, all officers from the Army's Military History Detachments already in place in Vietnam, in a method of after-action scrutiny. They were the ones to draw conclusions from their own battles while collecting their historical data and make fallout 'lessons learned' available to their commands to prevent the same mistakes being repeated in future engagements."[2] Their *Vietnam Primer* was used in MHD curriculum development. It was "basically [14] … 'lessons learned'".[3]

The current authors were Department of the Army civilian historians for the U.S. Army Reserve Command first at Fort McPherson, Georgia and then at Fort Bragg, North Carolina. While at Fort McPherson, one of our responsibilities was training Military History Detachments. In 2008, the U.S. Army Training and Doctrine Command (TRADOC) accredited the Combat Historian School. Usually, the MHDs were staffed by an officer and two to five enlisted personnel. In many cases, the MHDs were awaiting deployment. The school's curriculum was grounded on the experiences of U.S. Army combat historians from World War I through the Vietnam War and beyond and on administrative doctrine. That is evident when examining the curriculum:

- studying background history and the role of U.S. Army combat historians;
- orientation to equipment (i.e., computers, software programs, audio and visual recording devices, smart phones);

- cultivating good working relationships and rapport with the command group being examined and documented;
- individual interview techniques;
- group interview techniques;
- terrain/battlefield analysis;
- collection and appraisal of paper and digital data messages reports, journals, photographs, maps, sketches, war diaries, operation and battle plans;
- collecting and cataloging artifacts;
- writing the command report;
- writing narratives;
- role playing and practice interviews;
- logistics—getting there, doing the job, getting back.

The liveliest curriculum element was the role playing and practice interviews. These were conducted on American Civil War battlefield parks. We remember climbing the steep Kennesaw Mountain Battlefield Park—one of us more exhausted and winded than the other. The June 27, 1864, battle was part of the Atlanta Campaign. It was one of the most critical frontal assault of Union forces against fortified Confederate positions during the war. We wore wool U.S. Army Civil War style uniforms and carried replica equipment in the broiling, humid Georgia mountains. Jason even participated in replicating the storming of the Confederate trenches. At the end of the day, we gathered for a debriefing to compare notes and make further assessments. We discussed and analyzed why the battle ended in the Union army's tactical defeat. Compact thickets, steep and stony slopes, and poor knowledge about the terrain were factors—so like Vietnam. But strategically the battle was unsuccessful in stopping Sherman's advance on Atlanta.

For several days, we trampled the extensive Chickamauga battlefield, living in a stark, remote U.S. Army National Guard training center's World War II-era barracks. Before setting foot on the ground, the instructors and soldier-students researched the battle and scrutinized the terrain from battle maps. And like the Kennesaw Mountain practical exercise, we studied the background and role of a soldier engaged in the battle. After the daily briefing, we conducted interview drills at pre-selected sites. The students interviewed the instructors. The MHD soldiers had learned and applied many of the practices of their predecessors such as Arthur Conger, Ken Hechler, Forrest Pogue, Bevin Alexander, Russell Gugeler, S. L. A. Marshall, and Robert Wright.

Today's MHD course, grew from the original Combat Historian School. The U.S. Army Reserve Command sponsors the course. It is taught at the Army Reserve Readiness Training Center, (ARRTC), Fort Knox, Kentucky. CMH and ARRTC are charged with the training, "which is battle-focused and uses ... standards from Army doctrine and real-world experiences from subject matter experts (SMEs) ...

[who] have been in a contingency." The course uses "a hands-on systematic approach" to teach "[military] personnel from all … service branches … [and] Department of Defense … civilians … the critical skills required to perform their duties as a Combat Historian."[4]

Since the Vietnam War, MHDs have continued to train, deploy, gather historical information, and ascertain lessons learned. Former Commander of the 305th MHD Major David Hanselman wrote in "*The Tip of the History Spear: Capturing the Combat History of the Army in Current Operations*," the MHD's mission "is to deploy into theaters of combat … to collect historical data from Army units in the field…. Together, this compilation becomes the official historical archives of the Army at war. What separates the MHD from other historians in theater is that MHD members are soldiers first, nearly all of them [Army] Reserve and National Guard soldiers, and they deploy into the combat arena and into harm's way to conduct their missions."[5]

The 305th MHD illustrates how more recent combat (field) historians have implemented and improved upon the techniques of their predecessors. Weeks following the September 11, 2001, terrorist attacks on America, the 305th, newly designated as an MHD, was activated and "participated in Operation *Noble Eagle* and Pentagon recovery operations." For five months in 2003, the 305th deployed to Iraq. The unit assisted in Hurricane Katrina relief actions. The 305th was gathering data on the home front as well as on the battlefield.[6]

The unit was reactivated in July 2007. Hanselman recalled that he and two other MHD soldiers, Master Sergeant Richard Gribenas and Sergeant Julie Wiegand, "with less than thirty-days notice" deployed "to Afghanistan as part of Combined Joint Task Force-82, Operation *Enduring Freedom* 06-08. The deployment," he wrote, "would be the first coverage by an MHD in Afghanistan in over three years, so the mission was not only to conduct the traditional collection mission, but also to establish conditions for follow-on detachments to provide continuous coverage in the Afghanistan Area of Operations…."[7]

The three combat-tested soldiers had just two weeks "notice to put their personal affairs in order and report to their home station." One week was spent at the Army Reserve center preparing equipment for overseas shipment. The other week was at the Fort Benning, Georgia, mobilization station. After a week in Germany the soldiers "arrived in Afghanistan on 10 September 2007, and without any sleep, conducted their first mission—documenting the 11 September 2001 ceremonies at Bagram Air Field."[8] This sounds like the experience of some earlier combat historians.

Hanselman contrasted their situation to that of historians in Afghanistan. There were five MHDs plus three or four other historians in Iraq. Meanwhile "the 305th comprised the only history coverage in … Afghanistan. Historically," he explained, "the number of history detachments required in a region was dependent upon the number of troops deployed in that area. Whereas the Iraqi theater had approximately

150,000 troops, Afghanistan only fielded about 30,000 soldiers. This ratio made the number of MHDs appear comparable, but … the two theaters of combat could not be compared so easily…."[9] He was offering his perspective and analysis. Sounds familiar.

Hanselman described how better Iraqi transportation resources meant mobility of larger units stationed at a single forward operating base. Consequently, a MHD could visit that base "and cover an entire battalion." On the other hand, Afghanistan's limited transportation assets handicapped the mobility of forces particularly in "a combat zone that was geographically the most challenging theater of combat in recent times." He described "mountain ridges rising up to over 14,000 feet [that] bordered isolated valleys under constant threat of enemy attack with few roads and sparse population centers."[10] This is reminiscent of Marshall and Hackworth writing about ground conditions in their *Vietnam Primer*.

These and other conditions in Afghanistan, including climate, meant that "combat operations … centered on company and platoon operations, with the battalions and brigades … providing support to locally planned operations." So, the 305th MHD "had to cover down to the company and platoon level." Remember, Russell Gugeler wrote about small unit actions in Korea. The *Vietnam Primer* discussed it too. Since there were no other in-theater history personnel, Hanselman had to also serve as the U.S. Army theater historian. "This additional task," he penned, "required the commander and his two NCOs to participate in senior level planning, briefings, and tasks at their home base of Bagram. All of this was in addition to being responsible for an area over sixty-five percent larger than any other MHD deployed."[11]

Hanselman recounted the MHD being "imbedded … with the 173d Airborne Brigade Combat Team … in the most contested regions of Afghanistan." The MHD interviewed the brigade leaders and key staff at a forward operating base. The brigade's high-ranking personnel "welcomed the history team into their ranks and showed great enthusiasm for its efforts to document the operations of the 173d."[12] Combat historians before them talked about the need for command support.

And like their predecessors, the 305th saw combat action. The unit:

> … participated in the pivotal operation, *Rock Avalanche*, in the Korengal Valley, while visiting the 2nd Battalion, 503rd Parachute Infantry. Major Hanselman and Master Sergeant Gribenas were both cited for direct combat with the enemy (Hanselman's second such recognition) when they were conducting interviews at the Korengal Outpost, …home to Battle Company, 2-503 Parachute Infantry. The outpost came under direct attack by enemy personnel, and the two historians were compelled to serve as combat soldiers before being able to resume their interviews after the enemy had been suppressed and wounded personnel had been evacuated.[13]

We recall Bevin Alexander on the Korean War battlefield when the soldier beside him was killed. As Marshall wrote to Hechler: "[T]he combat historians always carried guns, shot the enemy and were shot at, captured prisoners, and were with the infantry within the range of small-arms fire."[14]

Hanselman reported, "the 305th MHD traveled to thirty-one different bases, collecting 379 interviews totaling over 325 hours of first-person histories. Over 8,500 photographs and 3,000 documents were collected to add to the historic archives of the U.S. Army."[15] These archives, and those collected by MHDs following in the footsteps of the 305th, and combat historians before them provide the historical data from which lessons learn emerge. They built upon the battlefield experiences and information collection techniques of combat historians recorded here from World War I to the Vietnam War.

Acronyms and Abbreviations

AAR	After Action Report/Review
AEF	American Expeditionary Force
AFF	Army Field Forces
AFFE	Headquarters, Army far East (Korean War)
AFHQ	Army Field Headquarters
AO	Area of Operations
AR 345-105	Army regulation governing command reports
AR 870-5	Army Regulation for Historical Activities: Military History Responsibilities, Policies and Procedures
ARVN	Army, Republic of Vietnam
ASF	Army Service of Supply
CAAIRs	Combat After Action Interview Reports
CALL	Center for Army Lessons Learned
CG	Commanding General
C-in-C	Commander in Chief
CINPAC	U.S. Commander in Chief, Pacific
CMH	Center for Military History
Com Z	Communications Zone (aka CZ)
CONUS	Continental United States (refers to the United States of America)
COSSAC	Chief of Staff, Supreme Allied Commander
COSVN	Central Office for South Vietnam

CPA	Central Pacific Area
C-Ration	A canned field ration (meal) of the U.S. Army
CTZ	Corps Tactical Zone
D.C.	District of Columbia (aka Washington D.C.)
D-Day	Debarkation Day (June 6, 1944, the invasion of Normandy)
ETO	European Theater of Operations
ETOUSA	European Theater of Operations United States Army
EUCOM	European Command
EUSAK	Eighth U.S. Army Korea
FE/Com Z	Forward Element/ Communications Zone
FECOM	Far East Command (Korea)
G-1	Army General Staff, Personnel and Administration
G-2	Army General Staff, Intelligence and Security
G-3	Army General Staff, Operations
G-4	Army General Staff, Logistics
G-5	Army General Staff, Plans
G-6	Army General Staff, Signal (Communications and Information Technology)
G-7	Army General Staff, Training
G-8	Army General Staff, Finance and Contracts
G-9	Army General Staff, Civil Affairs
GHQ	General Headquarters
GI	Government Issue (vernacular term for United States soldier)
I&HS	Information and Historical Service
IG	Inspector General
INTSUMS	Intelligence Summaries
JCS	Joint Chiefs of Staff
LCVP	Landing Craft Vehicle Personnel (U.S. Navy designation for small amphibious assault)

LST	Landing Ship Tank, (U.S. Navy designation for a ship carrying large vehicles for amphibious assault)
LZ	Landing Zone
MAAG	U.S. Military Assistance Advisory Group (Vietnam)
MACV	Military Assistance Command, Vietnam
MHD	Military History Detachment
MHS	Military Historical Section
NARA	National Archives and Records Administration
NCO-IC	Noncommissioned officer in charge (enlisted person)
Non-Com	Noncommissioned officer (Enlisted rank vs officer rank)
NVA	North Vietnamese Army
OCMH	Office of the Center for Military History
OPD	Operations Division
ORLL	Operational Report Lessons Learned
PRO	Public Relations Officer
PW	Prisoner of War (also POW)
S-2	Intel and Security (manages security clearances for unit personnel)
S-3	The command responsible for planning and coordination during combat
SGT	Sergeant
SHAEF	Supreme Headquarters, Allied Expeditionary Force
SITREPS	Situation Reports
SLAM	Samuel Lyman Atwood Marshall
SOP	Standard Operating Procedures
T/O	Theater of Operations (Geographic area in a war zone)
T/O&E	Table of Organization and Equipment
USARC	United States Army Reserve Command
USARPAC	U.S. Army Pacific Command (Vietnam war)

USARV	U.S. Army in Vietnam
V-E Day	Victory in Europe Day
Viet Minh	Army of North Vietnam in the 1950s and early 1960s
V-J Day	Victory over Japan (end of World War II)
WAC	Women's Army Corps

Selected Military History Detachment Lineage & Honors

20th Military History Detachment

Constituted 28 October 1966 in the Regular Army as the 20th Military History Detachment

Activated 1 December 1966 at Fort George G. Meade, Maryland

Inactivated 26 January 1967 at Fort George G. Meade, Maryland

Activated 8 January 1968 at Fort George G. Meade, Maryland

Inactivated 30 April 1972 in Vietnam

Withdrawn 18 May 2006 from the Regular Army and allotted to the Army Reserve

Activated 17 September 2008 at Chattanooga, Tennessee

Campaign Participation Credit

Vietnam

Tet Counteroffensive

Counteroffensive, Phase IV

Counteroffensive, Phase V

Counteroffensive, Phase VI

Tet 69/Counteroffensive

Summer–Fall 1969

Winter–Spring 1970

Sanctuary Counteroffensive

Counteroffensive, Phase VII

Consolidation I Consolidation II

Cease-Fire

Decorations

Meritorious Unit Commendation (Army), Streamer embroidered IRAQ 2011

23d Military History Detachment

Constituted 23 March 1966 in the Regular Army as the 23d Military History Detachment

Activated 20 May 1966 at Fort George G. Meade, Maryland

Inactivated 20 March 1972 in Vietnam

Withdrawn 18 May 2006 from the Regular Army and allotted to the Army Reserve

Activated 8 August 2007 at Chattanooga, Tennessee

Campaign Participation Credit
Vietnam

Counteroffensive, Phase II

Counteroffensive, Phase III

Tet Counteroffensive

Counteroffensive, Phase IV

Counteroffensive, Phase V

Counteroffensive, Phase VI

Tet 69/Counteroffensive

Summer–Fall 1969

Winter–Spring 1970

Sanctuary Counteroffensive

Counteroffensive, Phase VII

Consolidation I Consolidation II

Decorations

Meritorious Unit Commendation (Army), Streamer embroidered VIETNAM 1966–1967

Meritorious Unit Commendation (Army), Streamer embroidered VIETNAM 1967–1968

Meritorious Unit Commendation (Army), Streamer embroidered IRAQ 2011

46th Military History Detachment

Constituted 28 October 1966 in the Regular Army as the 46th Military History Detachment

Activated 1 December 1966 at Fort George G. Meade, Maryland

Inactivated 26 January 1967 at Fort George G. Meade, Maryland

Activated 8 January 1968 at Fort George G. Meade, Maryland

Inactivated 30 April 1972 in Vietnam

Withdrawn 16 September 1998 from the Regular Army and allotted to the Army Reserve; concurrently activated at North Little Rock, Arkansas

Ordered into active military service 1 October 2001 at North Little Rock, Arkansas; released 30 June 2002 from active military service and reverted to reserve status

Campaign Participation Credit
Vietnam

Tet Counteroffensive;

Counteroffensive, Phase IV;

Counteroffensive, Phase V;

Counteroffensive, Phase VI;

Tet 69/Counteroffensive;

Summer-Fall 1969;

Winter-Spring 1970;

Sanctuary Counteroffensive;

Counteroffensive, Phase VII;

Consolidation I;

Consolidation II;

Cease-Fire

Decorations

Meritorious Unit Commendation (Army) for VIETNAM 1968

Meritorious Unit Commendation (Army) for VIETNAM 1968–1971

Endnotes

Preface

1 The others were Lesson 1: Choose your battles; Lesson 2: Timing is essential; Lesson 3: Know yourself, know your enemy; Lesson 4: Have a unique plan; Lesson 5: Disguise your plans; Lesson 6: The best way to win is not to fight at all; Lesson 7: Change represents opportunity; Lesson 8: Success breeds success; Lesson 9: No one profits from prolonged warfare.

2 Sun Tzu, *The Art of War*, translated by Thomas Cleary, Shambhala Publications, 1988, Boston and London, 93.

3 Colonel David H. Hackworth and Julie Sherman, *About Face*, Simon and Schuster, NY, New York, 1989, 548.

4 Noel Barber, *A Sinister Twilight: The Fall of Singapore 1942,* Houghton Mifflin Company, Boston, Massachusetts, 1968, 36.

5 James D. Hornfischer, *Neptune's Inferno—The U.S. Navy at Guadalcanal*, Bantam Books; Random House, 2011), 436.

6 David Alan Johnson, "The Long Lance Torpedo at Guadalcanal," warfarehistorynetwork.com/barroom-brawl-off-guadalcanal/.

7 Hornfischer, *Neptune's Inferno—The U.S. Navy at Guadalcanal,* 392.

8 Hackworth, *About Face*, 554.

Chapter 1

1 Robert Wright, Jr. "Clio in Combat: The Evolution of the Military History Detachment," *The Army Historian*, No. 6, Winter 1985, 1.

2 Stetson Conn, *Historical Work in the United States Army, 1862–1954* (Washington, D.C.: CMH, 1980), 1-7 and Bell Wiley, *Historical Program Of the U.S. Army 1939 To Present [1945]*, HMC, 2-3.7 AB.A, 2, 17.

3 Ibid, 14–15.

4 Ibid, 17–18 and Royce L. Thompson, Establishment of the War Department's Historical Program for World War II, August 1947, Chapter I, 3, Historical Research Collection (HRC) 314.72, U.S. Army Center of Military History (CMH).

5 "Robert Matteson Johnson," Robert Matteson Johnston – Wikiwand.

6 Conn, *Historical Work in the United States Army, 1862–1954,* 17.

7 Ibid.

8 Ibid.

9   Ibid and Thompson, Establishment of the War Department's Historical Program for World War II, Chapter I, 3–4.
10 Thompson, Establishment of the War Department's Historical Program for World War II, Chapter I, 3–4.
11 Conn, *Historical Work in the United States Army, 1862–1954,* 24.
12 Ibid, 23–24.
13 Ibid, 24.
14 "The USS Leviathan," The USS Leviathan | Cheney Historical Museum (cheneymuseum.org).
15 Ibid, 17 and Wiley, *Historical Program Of The U.S. Army, 1939 To Present [1945],* 2.
16 Conn, *Historical Work in the United States Army, 1862–1954,* 25 and "Arthur L. Conger," Arthur L. Conger—Wikipedia.
17 Ibid.
18 Ibid.
19 Ibid.
20 Ibid, 25.
21 Ibid, 25–26.
22 Ibid, 26–27.
23 Conn, *Historical Work in the United States Army, 1862–1954,* 27–28.
24 Ibid.

Chapter 2

1   Thompson, Establishment of the War Department Historical Formation for World War II, Documentation, no date, HRC 314.72, CMH.
2   Ibid, 29.
3   Ibid.
4   Ibid.
5   Ibid, 31. BG Spalding retired in 1939. In WWII, he was recalled to the War College faculty. He is one of the few officers who served as a general in both world wars. He retired again in 1945. Spalding's awards included the Distinguished Service Medal and Legion of Merit. See Oliver Lyman Spalding, Jr., Brigadier General, United States Army, http://www.arlingtoncemetery.net/ospauldingjr.htm.
6   Thompson, Establishment of the War Department Historical Formation, 30–31.
7   Ibid, 32.
8   Ibid.
9   Ibid, 33–34.
10 Ibid, 35.
11 Ibid.
12 Ibid, 35–36.
13 Conn, *Historical Work in the United States Army, 1862–1954,* 37.
14 Ibid, 39.
15 Ibid, 36–36
16 Ibid, 36, 37, 39.
17 Ibid, 40.
18 Ibid, 49.
19 Ibid.
20 Ibid.
21 Ibid, 46–67.

22 Ibid, 62, 64.

23 Ibid, 64.

24 Ibid, 68.

25 Ibid, 64, 68 and Wiley, *"Historical Program of the U.S. Army 1939 To the Present [1945]*, 2.

26 Terrence J. Gough, "The U.S. Army Center of Military History: A Brief History," Army *History*, Spring 1996.

27 Conn, *Historical Work in the United States Army, 1862–1954*, 71.

28 AR 345-105, *Military Records: Historical Records and Histories of Organizations*, 18 November 1929 and 22 November 1930.

29 Thompson, Establishment of the War Department's Historical Program for World War II, Chapter I, 9.

30 Ibid, Chapter I, 11.

31 Ibid, Chapter I, 12–13 and Wiley, *Historical Program Of the U.S. Army 1939 To Present [1945]*, 3.

32 Thompson, Establishment of the War Department's Historical Program for World War II, Chapter I, 13 and Wiley, *Historical Program of the U.S. Army 1939 To the Present [1945]*, 3.

Chapter 3

1 Thompson, Establishment of the War Department's Historical Program for World War II, Chapter III, 1 and Wiley, *Historical Program Of the U.S. Army 1939 To Present [1945]*, 3.

2 Franklin D. Roosevelt to Mr. Harold D. Smith, 4 March 1942, Thompson, Establishment of the War Department Historical Formation for World War II, Documentation and Thompson, Establishment of the War Department's Historical Program for World War II, Chapter III, 1.

3 Ibid.

4 Ibid.

5 Wiley, *Historical Program of the U.S. Army, 1939 to Present [1945]*, 3, 4 and Conn, *Historical Work in the United States Army, 1862–1954*, 79.

6 Thompson, Establishment of the War Department's Historical Program for World War II, Chapter III, 4, Chapter III, 4–8.

7 Ibid, Chapter III, 8–9.

8 Thompson, Establishment of the War Department's Historical Program for World War II, Chapter IV, 5.

9 Memorandum, Major Kent Roberts Greenfield, subject: Plans For The Historical Section of the Army Ground Forces, 16 November 1942, Thompson, Establishment of the War Department Historical Formation for World War II, Documentation; Thompson, Establishment of the War Department's Historical Program for World War II, Chapter IV, 8; and Conn, *Historical Work in the United States Army, 1862–1954*, 81.

10 Memorandum, Major Kent Roberts Greenfield, subject: Plans For The Historical Section of the Army Ground Forces, 16 November 1942, Thompson, Establishment of the War Department Historical Formation for World War II, Documentation.

11 Ibid.

12 Ibid.

13 Ibid.

14 Ibid and Thompson, Establishment of the War Department's Historical Program for World War II, Chapter IV, 9.

15 Thompson, Establishment of the War Department's Historical Program for World War II, Chapter IV, 9–10.

16 Memorandum, Brigadier General Robert A. McClure to Assistant Chief of Staff, G-2, subject: Historical Records, 18 November 1942, Thompson, Establishment of the War Department Historical Formation for World War II, Documentation and Thompson, Establishment of the War Department's Historical Program for World War II, Chapter IV, 11–12.

17 Memorandum, BG McClure to Assistant Chief of Staff, G-2, subject: Historical Records, 18 November 1942; Thompson, Establishment of the War Department Historical Formation for World War II, Documentation and Thompson, Establishment of the War Department's Historical Program for World War II, Chapter IV, 12.

18 Memorandum, Brigadier General Oliver L. Spaulding, subject: Historical records in theaters of operations overseas, 11 December 1942, Thompson, Establishment of the War Department Historical Formation for World War II, Documentation.

19 Thompson, Establishment of the War Department's Historical Program for World War II, Chapter IV, 13.

20 Memorandum, BG Spaulding, subject: Historical records in theaters of operations overseas, 11 December 1942, Thompson, Establishment of the War Department Historical Formation for World War II, Documentation.

21 Thompson, Establishment of the War Department's Historical Program for World War II, Chapter IV, 13; Wiley, *Historical Program of the U.S. Army, 1939 to Present [1945]*, 6–7; and Conn, *Historical Work in the United States Army, 1862–1954*, 76.

22 Memorandum, Major General Thomas T. Handy for the Deputy Chief of Staff, subject: Historical Records, 16 January 1943, Thompson, Establishment of the War Department Historical Formation for World War II, Documentation; Thompson, Establishment of the War Department's Historical Program for World War II, Chapter IV, 13–19 and Chapter V, p 1–2 and Wiley, *Historical Program of the U.S. Army, 1939 to Present [1945]*, 7. Thompson does cite an earlier "startling" plan in which Spaulding mentions publishing narratives after the war and that "'Methods and procedure for carding preparation for publication" could be "'under way even before the close of the war. . . .'" Thompson states: "Actually, this plan existed only on paper, as later events demonstrated." See Thompson, Establishment of the War Department's Historical Program for World War II, Chapter II, 3–4.

23 Memorandum, Major General Thomas T. Handy for the Deputy Chief of Staff, subject: Historical Records, 16 January 1943, Thompson, Establishment of the War Department Historical Formation for World War II, Documentation and Thompson, Establishment of the War Department's Historical Program for World War II, Chapter V, 3.

24 Thompson, Establishment of the War Department's Historical Program for World War II, Chapter V, 4–5.

25 Ibid, 5–6.

26 Letter, Colonel Otto Nelson to Colonel John Kemper, 17 March 1947, Thompson, Establishment of the War Department's Historical Program for World War II Documentation; Thompson, Establishment of the War Department's Historical Program for World War II, Chapter V, 7; and Wiley, *Historical Program of the U.S. Army, 1939 to Present [1945]*, 9.

27 Wiley, *Historical Program of the U.S. Army, 1939 to Present [1945]*, 9.

28 Letter, Colonel Otto Nelson to Colonel John Kemper, 17 March 1947, Thompson, Establishment of the War Department's Historical Program for World War II Documentation.

29 Thompson, Establishment of the War Department's Historical Program for World War II, Chapter V, 5–8. Morrison was the author of the 15-volume *History of United States Operations WWII* published between 1947 and 1962.

30 Ibid, Chapter V, 9.

31 Ibid, Chapter V, 10.

32 Wiley, *Historical Program of the U.S. Army, 1939 to Present [1945]*, 10.

33 Thompson, Establishment of the War Department Historical Formation for World War II, Documentation and Thompson, Establishment of the War Department's Historical Program for World War II, Chapter V, 12.

34 Royce L. Thompson, "History of the Historical Section, European Theater of Operations," Historical Section, European Theater of Operations, no date, 7, HRC 314.72, CMH and Bruce Siemon, "Focus on the Field," *Army History*, Winter 1991/92, 28. Ganoe also wrote *The English of Military Communications* published in 1918, *My Heart Remembers* published in 1950, and *MacArthur Close Up: Much Then and Some Now* published in 1962.

35 Ibid.

36 Ibid.

37 Thompson, Establishment of the War Department's Historical Program for World War II, Chapter V, 17–18.

38 Thompson, Establishment of the War Department's Historical Program for World War II, Chapter V, Chapter V, 21, 26.

39 Conn, *Historical Work in the United States Army, 1862–1954*, 85.

40 Wiley, *Historical Program of the U.S. Army, 1939 to Present [1945]*, 12 and Thompson, Establishment of the War Department's Historical Program for World War II, Chapter V, 12.

41 Thompson, Establishment of the War Department's Historical Program for World War II, Chapter V, 16.

42 Ibid, Chapter V, 20 and Wiley, *Historical Program of the U.S. Army, 1939 to Present [1945]*, 13.

43 Thompson, Establishment of the War Department's Historical Program for World War II, Chapter V, 22–27.

44 Ibid, Chapter V, 26, 30 and Wiley, *Historical Program of the U.S. Army, 1939 to Present [1945]*, 13.

45 Memorandum No. W345-21-43, MG I. H. Edwards, Chief of Staff, The Adjutant General's Office, War Department, subject: Military History of the Second World War, 3 August 1943. Historical Program, Record Group (RG) 498, Records of Headquarters, European Theater of Operations United States Army (ETOUSA) (World War II), National Archives and Records Administration (NARA).

46 Ibid; Conn, *Historical Work in the United States Army, 1862–1954*, 87; Thompson, Establishment of the War Department's Historical Program for World War II, Chapter VI, 30; and Wiley, *Historical Program of the U.S. Army, 1939 to Present [1945]*, 13–14.

47 Wiley, *Historical Program of the U.S. Army, 1939 to Present [1945]*, 14 and Conn, *Historical Work in the United States Army, 1862–1954*, 87–88.

48 Conn, *Historical Work in the United States Army, 1862–1954*, 91–92.

49 Wiley, *Historical Program Of the U.S. Army, 1939 to Present [1945]*, 18.

Chapter 4

1 Interview, Ken Hechler with Kathryn Roe Coker, 19 June 2009, USARHRC, USARC.

2 Wiley, *Historical Program of the U.S. Army 1939 to Present [1945]*, 31.

3 Interview, Hechler with Coker.

4 Quoted in Williams, *SLAM: The Influence of S.L.A. Marshall on the United States Army*, 23. Pogue was the author of a four volume history of General George C. Marshall and among other works the author of the *European Theater of Operations: The Supreme Command* in the U.S. Army in WWII series. His notes from the war were later published in *Pogue's War: Diaries of a WWII Combat Historian*.

5 Forrest Pogue, *Pogue's War Diaries of a WWII Combat Historian*, ix.

6   Ibid.
7   Major F. D. G. Williams, *SLAM The Influence of S.L.A. Marshall on the United States Army*, edited and introduced by Susan Canedy. Office of the Command Historian, United States Army Training and Doctrine Command, Fort Monroe, Virginia and Center of Military History United States Army Washington, D.C ., 1999, 5.
8   Ibid, 19.
9   S.L.A. Marshall, *Victory Island: The Battle of Kwajalein* with an Introduction by Joseph Dawson III, to the Bison Books printing (Lincoln: University of Nebraska Press, 2001,), viii–ix.
10 Major F.D.G. Williams, *SLAM: The Influence of S.L.A. Marshall on the United States Army* (Office of the Command Historian, US Army Training and Doctrine Command, Fort Monroe and Center of Military History, 1994), 5 and S.L.A. Marshall, *Bringing Up the Rear, A Memoir* (Presidio Press, San Rafael, California, 1979), xii.
11 Conn, *Historical Work in the United States Army, 1862–1954*, 91–92.
12 Marshall, *Bringing Up the Rear*, 94.
13 Bauer, Frederiksen and Anspacher, "The Army Historical Program In The European Theater, 8 May 1943–31 December 1950," 10.
14 Bauer, Frederiksen and Anspacher, "The Army Historical Program In The European Theater, 8 May 1943–31 December 1950," 10.
15 Colonel W.A. Ganoe, Schools, "Orientation Material for Theater Historians."
16 Memorandum, Colonel W.A. Ganoe to Colonel Shannon, G-1, Headquarters ETO, subject: Personnel Requirements, History Section, ETO, 19 February 1944, Manpower, RG 498, Box 5, Records of Headquarters, ETOUSA (World War II), NARA.
17 Ibid, 32.

Chapter 5

1   Conn, *Historical Work in the United States Army, 1862–1954*, 92–93.
2   Ibid, 93.
3   Letter, Lieutenant Colonel John Kemper to Colonel Paul Birdsall, September 16, 1943, in "Orientation Material for Theater Historians."
4   Ibid.
5   Letter, Lieutenant Colonel John Kemper to Colonel W.A. Ganoe, September 18, 1943, Organization of Writing of History, RG 498, Box 1, Records of Headquarters, ETOUSA (World War II), NARA.
6   Letter, Lieutenant Colonel John Kemper to Colonel Paul Birdsall, 16 September 1943, in "Orientation Material for Theater Historians." Wiley, *Historical Program of the U.S. Army*, 40-41.
7   Ibid.
8   Letter, Lieutenant Colonel John Kemper to Colonel Paul Birdsall, September 16, 1943, in "Orientation Material for Theater Historians."
9   Letter, Colonel W.A. Ganoe to Lieutenant Colonel John Kemper, October 11, 1943, Organization of Writing of History, RG 498, Box 1, Records of Headquarters, ETOUSA (World War II), NARA.
10 Ibid.
11 Bauer, Frederiksen and Anspacher, "The Army Historical Program In The European Theater, 8 May 1943–31 December 1950," 12.
12 Letter, Colonel W.A. Ganoe to Brigadier General Sir James E. Edmonds, 13 September 1943, Organization of Writing of History, RG 498, Box 1, Records of Headquarters, ETOUSA (World War II), NARA.

13 Ibid.
14 Conn, *Historical Work in the United States Army, 1862–1954*, 93.
15 Ibid, 13.
16 Wiley, *Historical Program of the U.S. Army, 1939 to Present [1945]*, 21–22.
17 Ibid, 21.
18 Letter, Lieutenant John Kemper to Colonel W.A. Ganoe, 29 March 1944, Organization of Writing of History, RG 498, Box 1, Records of Headquarters, United States Army (World War II), NARA.
19 Ibid.
20 Wiley, *Historical Program of the U.S. Army, 1939 to Present [1945]*, 21.
21 Ibid, 31–32.
22 Ibid, 21.
23 Memorandum No. W 220-44, Headquarters and Headquarters Detachment and Assignment Units, Information and Historical Service, 19 April 1944, RG 498, Box 6, Records of Headquarters, ETOUSA (World War II), NARA.
24 Ibid and Bauer, Frederiksen and Anspacher, "The Army Historical Program In The European Theater, 8 May 1943–31 December 1950," 15.
25 Bauer, Frederiksen and Anspacher, "The Army Historical Program In The European Theater, 8 May 1943–31 December 1950," 15.
26 Thompson, "History of the Historical Section, European Theater of Operations," 42.
27 Organizational Chart, Historical Section, First Army, TO&E 2 February–27 March 1944, RG 498, Box 5, Records of Headquarters, ETOUSA (WWII), NARA
28 Organizational Chart, Historical Section, Third Army, TO&E 2 February–27 March 1944, RG 498, Box 5, Records of Headquarters, ETOUSA (WWII), NARA.
29 Letter, Lieutenant Colonel Charles Taylor to Lieutenant Colonel John Kemper, July 1944, Organization of Writing of History, RG 498, Box 1, Records of Headquarters, ETOUSA (WW II), NARA.
30 T/O&E20-12S, 3 October 1944, War Department, Force Structure and Unit History Branch, CMH and Wiley, *Historical Program of the U.S. Army, 1939 to Present [1945]*, 22.
31 Thompson, "History of the Historical Section, ETO," Documentation Vol. I, (Parts 1 and 2).
32 Wiley, *Historical Program of the U.S. Army*, 22.

Chapter 6

1 Ibid, 16–17 and Conn, *Historical Work in the United States Army, 1862–1954*, 92–93.
2 Major Robert H. Fechtman "The Value of Historical Detachments," Student Monograph, Advanced Infantry Officer Course, Fort Benning, Georgia, December 13, 1952, 7 and Robert Wright, Jr., "Clio in Combat: The Evolution of the Military History Detachment," *The Army Historian*, Number 6, Winter 1985, 3.
3 Letter, Lieutenant Colonel S.L.A. Marshall to Lieutenant Colonel Charles Taylor, December 28, 1943, in "Orientation Material for Theater Historians."
4 Letter, Lieutenant Colonel S.L.A. Marshall to Lieutenant Colonel John Kemper, February 23, 1944, in "Orientation Material for Theater Historians."
5 Ibid.
6 Ibid.
7 Ibid.
8 Letter, Lieutenant Colonel S.L.A. Marshall to Lieutenant Colonel John Kemper, 7 December 1943, in "Orientation Material for Theater Historians."
9 Ibid.

10 Ibid.

11 Ibid.

12 Letter, Lieutenant Colonel S.L.A. Marshall to Major Charles Taylor, December 28, 1943, in "Orientation Material for Theater Historians."

13 Letter, Lieutenant Colonel S.L.A. Marshall to Major Charles Taylor, January 9, 1944, in "Orientation Material for Theater Historians."

14 Marshall, *Victory Island: The Battle of Kwajalein* with an Introduction by Joseph Dawson III, 1.

15 Letter, Lieutenant Colonel S.L.A. Marshall to Lieutenant Colonel John Kemper, 9 March 1944 in "Orientation Material for Theater Historians."

16 Marshall, *Victory Island: The Battle of Kwajalein* with an Introduction by Joseph Dawson III, 1.

17 Letter, Lieutenant Colonel S.L.A. Marshall to Major Charles Taylor, 19 December 1943, in "Orientation Material for Theater Historians."

18 Marshall, *Victory Island: The Battle of Kwajalein* with an Introduction by Joseph Dawson III, 108–115.

19 Letter, Lieutenant Colonel S.L.A. Marshall to Major Charles Taylor, December 19, 1943, in "Orientation Material for Theater Historians."

20 Letter, Major General Ralph C. Smith to Major General George V. Strong, 12 December 1944 in "Orientation Material for Theater Historians."

21 Williams, *Slam: The Influence of S. L.A. Marshall on the United States Army*, 24.

22 Letter, Lieutenant Colonel S.L.A. Marshall to Lieutenant Colonel John Kemper, February 23, 1944, in "Orientation Material for Theater Historians." It is interesting to note that Marshall thought "that for years to come, joint operations will be the outstanding fact of warfare."

23 Letter, Lieutenant Colonel Charles Taylor to Lieutenant Colonel John Kemper, 27 June 1944, Notes On Historical Program, RG 498, Box 1, Records of Headquarters, ETOUSA (World War II), NARA.

24 Memorandum, Lieutenant Colonel Charles Taylor to Colonel W.A. Ganoe, 5 June 1944, Notes On Historical Program, RG 498, Box 1, Records of Headquarters, ETOUSA (World War II), NARA.

25 Letter, Lieutenant Colonel John Kemper to Lieutenant Colonel Charles Taylor, 13 July 1944, Notes On Historical Program, RG 498, Box 1, Records of Headquarters, ETOUSA (World War II), NARA.

26 Letter, Lieutenant Colonel S.L.A. Marshall to Lieutenant Colonel John Kemper, 23 February 1944 in "Orientation Material for Theater Historians."

27 Extracts from correspondence of Lieutenant Colonel S.L.A. Marshall, Field Representative, Historical Branch, G-2, relative to writing historical accounts of the Makin and Kwajalein operations, in "Orientation Material for Theater Historians." It is uncertain as to whom Marshall sent this letter.

28 Letter, Lieutenant Colonel S.L.A. Marshall to Lieutenant Colonel John Kemper, 2 February 1944, Notes On Historical Program, RG 498, Box 1, Records of Headquarters, ETOUSA (World War II), NARA.

29 *History of the First Information and Historical Service From Activation until December 31, 1944*, RG 407, Box 16840, Records of the Adjutant General's Office, World War II Operations Reports, Information and Historical Service, NARA.

30 Greer, "Fort Shafter: Scholars in Khaki," 146–155.

31 Ibid and *History of the First Information and Historical Service From Activation until December 31, 1944*, RG 407, Box 16840, Records of the Adjutant General's Office, World War II Operations Reports, Information and Historical Service, NARA.

32 *History of the First Information and Historical Service From Activation until December 31, 1944,* RG 407, Box 16840, Records of the Adjutant General's Office, World War II Operations Reports, Information and Historical Service, NARA.

33 Ibid.

34 Roy E. Appleman, James M. Burns, Russell A. Gugeler, and John Stevens, *OKINAWA: THE LAST BATTLE (UNITED STATES ARMY IN WORLD WAR II: The War in the Pacific)*, CMH, 1948, x–xiii.

35 Ibid and Adjutant General, War Department to Commanding General USAF, Central Pacific Area, subject: Organization of Information and Historical Service in Central Pacific Area, 11 July 1944, Force Structure and Unit History Branch, CMH; T/O&E20-12S, 3 October 1944.

36 Unit History, 1st Information and Historical Service, 1945, RG 407, Box 16840, Records of the Adjutant General's Office, World War II Operations Reports, Information and Historical Service, NARA.

37 Ibid.

38 Major David Hanselman, "The Tip of the History Spear: Capturing the Combat History of the Army in Current Operations," The Tip of the History Spear: Capturing the Combat History of the Army in Current Operations—The Campaign for the National Museum of the United States Army (armyhistory.org).

39 Unit History, 1st Information and Historical Service, 1945, RG 407, Box 16840A.

40 AG 322, Adjutant General, War Department to Commanding General European Theater of Operations, subject: Organization of Information and Historical Service in Central Pacific Area, 11 July 1944, Force Structure and Unit History Branch, CMH.

41 Bauer, Frederiksen and Anspacher, "The Army Historical Program In The European Theater, 8 May 1943–31 December 1950," 16. Unfortunately, this source gave no specific dates for their activation and, except in the case of the 4tah I&HS, a search of primary sources was futile.

42 Report After Action, Ryukyus Campaign, 1st Information and Historical Service, Box 16840, RG 407, Records of the Adjutant General's Office, WW II Operations Reports, 1941–1948, Information and Historical Service, NARA.

43 Ibid.

44 Ibid.

45 Staff Study, Japanese Operation on Panay Island, 10th I&HS, Headquarters Eighth Army, CMH.

46 Ibid.

47 Staff Study of Japanese Operations on Mindanao Island, 10th Information and Historical Service, Box 16841, RG407, Records of The Adjutant General's Office, WWII Operations Reports, 1941–1948, Information and Historical Service, NARA.

Chapter 7

1 Theodore Bauer, Oliver Frederiksen and Ellinor Anspacher, "The Army Historical Program In The European Theater, 8 May 1943–31 December 1950," Occupations Forces in Europe Series, Historical Division, European Command, Karlsruhe, Germany, 1951, 1.

2 Ibid; Thompson, "History of the Historical Section, European Theater of Operations," 8; and Siemon, "Focus on the Field," 28.

3 Memorandum, Lieutenant Colonel Charles Taylor to Colonel W.A. Ganoe, 7 April 1944, Organization of Writing of History, RG 498, Box 1, Records of Headquarters, ETOUSA (World War II), NARA.

4 Memorandum, Colonel W.A. Ganoe to Chief of Section, Information and Censorship Section, Headquarters, EOUTSA, subject: Proposed Initial Plan for Producing the History of the E.T.O,

20 May 1943, Administration # 161, RG 498, Box 33, Records of Headquarters, ETOUSA (World War II), NARA.

5   Communication, Chief of Staff History and Address Section thru PRO, 28 May 1943, Administration #161, RG 498, Box 33, Records of Headquarters, ETOUSA (World War II), NARA.

6   Ibid.

7   Ibid.

8   Memorandum, Colonel W. A. Ganoe, 7 June 1943, Historical Program, RG 498, Box 5, Records of Headquarters, ETOUSA (World War II), NARA.

9   Notes On Importance And Possible Extension Of This Section, Colonel W.A. Ganoe, 27 May 1943, Administration #161, RG 498, Box 33, Records of Headquarters, ETOUSA (World War II), NARA. The record is not signed but has Ganoe's mark of getting information "on the ground and at the time."

10 Ibid.

11 Ibid.

12 Bauer, Frederiksen and Anspacher, "The Army Historical Program In The European Theater, 8 May 1943–31 December 1950," 2–4; Thompson, "History of the Historical Section, European Theater of Operations," 7–8 and Siemon, "Focus on the Field," 28.

13 Ibid.

14 Bauer, Frederiksen and Anspacher, "The Army Historical Program In The European Theater, 8 May 1943—31 December 1950," 4.

15 Royce L. Thompson, "History of the Historical Section, European Theater of Operations," Historical Section, European Theater of Operations, no date, 29, HRC 314.72, CMH.

16 Ibid.

17 Ibid, 30.

18 Statement-Theater Historian, Colonel W. A. Ganoe, no date, Information and Historical Units, Administration #161, RG 498, Box 33, Records of Headquarters, ETOUSA (World War II), NARA.

19 Ibid. 31.

20 Bauer, Frederiksen and Anspacher, "The Army Historical Program In The European Theater, 8 May 1943–31 December 1950," 6.

21 Letter, Colonel W. A. Ganoe to Major Charles Taylor, 13 August 1943 in Royce L. Thompson, "History of the Historical Section, ETO," Documentation Vol. I (Parts 1and 2), Historical Section, ETO, CMH and Thompson, "History of the Historical Section, European Theater of Operations, 14–15.

22 Ibid, 15.

23 Ibid, 16.

24 Ibid, 16–17.

25 Ibid.

26 Letter, Colonel W. A. Ganoe to Major Charles Taylor in "Orientation Material for Theater Historians."

27 Ibid.

28 Memorandum, Colonel W. A. Ganoe, subject: Functions Of History Section Regarding Pictures, 4 June 1943, Administration #161, RG 498, Box 33, Records of Headquarters, ETOUSA (World War II), NARA.

29 Colonel W.A. Ganoe, "Notes On Our Present Objective and Plans," in "Orientation Material for Theater Historians," 9 March 1944, 314.7 HRC2, CMH.

30 Ibid.

31 Ibid.

32 "Notes on the Methods of Production of the History of the E.T.O." in "Orientation Material for Theater Historians."

33 Research Procedures and Filing, History Section, no date, RG 498, Box 33, Records of Headquarters, ETOUSA (World War II), NARA.

34 Siemon, "Focus on the Field," 28 and Thompson, "History of the Historical Section, European Theater of Operations," 33.

35 Letter, Colonel W.A. Ganoe to Major General William S. Key, 11 October 1943, Organization of Writing of History, RG 498, Box 1, Records of Headquarters, ETOUSA (World War II), NARA.

36 Ibid.

37 Letter, Colonel W.A. Ganoe to Lieutenant Colonel John Kemper, 11 October 1943, Organization of Writing of History, RG 498, Box 1, Records of Headquarters, ETOUSA (World War II), NARA.

38 Memo, Major C.A. Jones to Colonel W.A. Ganoe, subject: Daily Activities, 27 October 1943; Memo, Major C.A. Jones to Colonel W.A. Ganoe, subject: Daily Activities, 28 October 1943; and Memo, Major C.A. Jones to Colonel W.A. Ganoe, subject: Activities, 1–3 November 1943 in Thompson, "History of the Historical Section, ETO," Documentation, Vol. 1 (Parts 1 and 2).

39 Siemon, "Focus on the Field," 28

40 Letter, Colonel W.A. Ganoe to Lieutenant Colonel John Kemper, 11 October 1943, Organization of Writing of History, RG 498, Box 1, Records of Headquarters, ETOUSA (World War II), NARA and Thompson, "History of the Historical Section, European Theater of Operations," 33.

41 Colonel W. A. Ganoe, Memorandum to Major General, subject: Record of Oral Material, in "Orientation Material for Theater Historians," no date, 314.7 HRC2, CMH.

42 Memorandum, Colonel W.A. Ganoe to Brigadier General George A. Davis, subject: Record of Oral Material, no date, Historical Program, Box 1, RG 498, Records of Headquarters, ETOUSA (World War II), ETO Historical Division, Miscellaneous Records of the Theater Historian, 1943–1946, NARA and Memorandum, Colonel W. A. Ganoe to Brigadier General Williston B. Palmer, subject: Record of Oral Material, no date, Administration #161 B, RG 498, Box 33, Records of Headquarters, ETOUSA (World War II), ETO Historical Division, Miscellaneous Records of the Theater Historian, 1943–1946, NARA.

43 Siemon, "Focus on the Field," 28–29.

44 Bauer, Frederiksen and Anspacher, "The Army Historical Program In The European Theater, 8 May 1943–31 December 1950," 8.

45 Ibid, 7.

46 Ibid and Siemon, "Focus on the Field," 29.

47 Letter, Colonel W. A. Ganoe to Lieutenant Colonel John Kemper, 11 October 1943, Organization of Writing of History, Box 1, RG 498, Records of Headquarters, ETOUSA (World War II), NARA.

48 AAF Regulation 20-8, Major General George E. Stratemeyer, Organization AAF Historical Division, 19 July 1943, RG 498, Box 1, Records of Headquarters ETOUSA (World War II), Organization of Writing of History, NARA and AAF Regulation No. 20-8, Headquarters, Army Air Forces, 23 August 1945, RG 498, Box 2, Records of Headquarters ETOUSA (World War II), History Division, Miscellaneous Records of Theater Historian, 1943–1946, NARA.

49 Letter, Lieutenant Colonel Charles Taylor to Lieutenant Colonel John Kemper, 27 June 1944, Notes On Historical Program, RG 498, Box 1, Records of Headquarters, ETOUSA (World War II), NARA.

50 Letter, Lieutenant Colonel John Kemper to Lieutenant Colonel Charles Taylor, 13 July 1944, Notes On Historical Program, RG 498, Box 1, Records of Headquarters, ETOUSA (World War II), NARA.

51 Memorandum w/enclosure, Colonel W.A. Ganoe to G-1, subject: Study and Plan for Future History Coverage, 9 November 1944, Notes on History Program, RG 498, Box 1, Records of Headquarters, ETOUSA (World War II), NARA.

52 Ibid.

53 Ibid.

54 Letter, Lieutenant Colonel S.L.A. Marshall to G-1, Headquarters, ETOUSA, subject: History Plan following termination of hostilities in the Theater, 13 December 1944, Post War Organization of Historical Section, RG 498, Box 1, Records of Headquarters, ETOUSA (World War II), NARA and S.L. A. Marshall, *Bringing Up the Rear, A Memoir* (Presidio Press, San Rafael, California, 1979), 135.

55 Organization and Procedure of Operational History Personnel, no date, Organization of Writing of History, RG 498, Box 1, Records of Headquarters, ETOUSA (World War II), NARA.

56 Bauer, Frederiksen and Anspacher, "The Army Historical Program In The European Theater, 8 May 1943–31 December 1950," 8–9; Siemon, "Focus on the Field," 29; Release No. 1837, Headquarters, ETO, no date; Memorandum, Colonel W.A. Ganoe to Assistant Chief of Staff, G-3, subject: Report and Personnel Forecast, & October 1943, Organization of Writing of History, RG 498, Box 1, Records of Headquarters, ETOUSA (World War II), NARA. Other WACs included: Pfc. B.L. Flaugh; Pfc. M.C. Sweeny, and Pfc. M.G. Shearer.

57 Enlistment in WAC, Box 1, Folder 5, Eva Spencer Ostenberg Papers, University of Texas at El Paso (UTEP), UTEP Library, Special Collections Department and Enlisted Record and Report Of Separation Honorable Discharge, Eva C. Spencer, November 1944, National Personnel Records Center, NARA.

58 Service in England, Box 1, Folder 6, Eva Spencer Ostenberg Papers, University of Texas at El Paso (UTEP), UTEP Library, Special Collections Department.

59 Letter William A. Ganoe to Eva Spencer, August 31, 1946, Box 26, Eva Spencer Ostenberg Papers, UTEP, UTEP Library, Special Collections Department.

60 Letter, Colonel W.A. Ganoe to Mr. Joe Spencer, January 3, 1945, Box 1, Folder 12, Eva Spencer Ostenberg Papers, UTEP, UTEP Library, Special Collections Department.

61 Marshall, *Bringing Up the Rear*, 135.

62 Letter, Eva Spencer to Parents, December 16, 1945, Box 19, Eva Spencer Ostenberg Papers, UTEP, UTEP Library, Special Collections Department.

63 Ibid.

64 Letter, Eva Spencer to Parents, 1944, Box 6, Eva Spencer Ostenberg Papers, UTEP, UTEP Library, Special Collections Department.

65 Patch for Historians in ETO, December 1945, Box 19, Eva Spencer Ostenberg Papers, UTEP, UTEP Library, Special Collections Department.

66 See UTEP, Finding Aids Special Collections Department 2-28-2020 Guide to MS305 Eva Spencer Osterberg papers. She passed away on July 30, 2002, at age 81.

67 "Forrest C. Pogue," National Museum of the United States Army (thenmusa.org) and Franklin D. Anderson, Preface to Forrest C. Pogue, *Pogue's War: Diaries of a WWII Combat Historian* (Lexington, Kentucky: The University Press of Kentucky, 2001), ix.

68 Anderson, Preface to Forrest C. Pogue, *Pogue's War: Diaries of a WWII Combat Historian,* xvii.

69 Bauer, Frederiksen and Anspacher, "The Army Historical Program In The European Theater, 8 May 1943–31 December 1950," 16.

70 After Action Report, 4th Information and Historical Service, September 1944 and Annual Report, 4th Information and Historical Service, 17 January 1945, RG 407, Box 16840, Records of the Adjutant General's Office, WW II Operations Reports, 1941–1948, Information and Historical Service, NARA.

71 Ibid.

72 CMH retains all these reports.

73 Ibid.

74 Ibid.

75 Ibid.

76 Marshall, *Bringing Up the Rear*, 80–81.

77 Williams, *SLAM: The Influence of S.L.A. Marshall on the United States Army*, 31–35.

78 Quoted in Williams, *SLAM: The Influence of S.L.A. Marshall on the United States Army*, 27.

79 Ibid, 27–28.

80 "S.L.A. Marshall's Men Against Fire," http://www.theppsc.org/Grossman/SLA_Marshall/Main.htm.

81 S.L.A. Marshall, *Victory Island: The Battle of Kwajalein* with an Introduction by Joseph Dawson III, vii–xi, 109.

82 Ibid, x.

83 Ibid, xiii–xiv.

84 Quoted in Williams, *SLAM: The Influence of S.L.A. Marshall on the United States Army*, 27.

85 Associated Press, "Ken Hechler, congressman who fought for miners and marched with Martin Luther King, dies at 102," December 12, 2016, https://www.chicagotribune.com/news/obituaries/la-na-ken-hechler-20161212-story.html and Ken Hechler, https://en.wikipedia.org/wiki/Ken_Hechler#cite_note-5.

86 Interview, Hechler with Johnson.

87 Kenneth Hechler, *The Enemy Side of the Hill, The 1945 Background on Interrogation of German Commanders,* 30 July 1949, Chapter, 1–2.

88 Ibid, Chapter I, 2.

89 Ibid.

90 Ibid, Chapter I, 3.

91 Ibid, Chapter I, 2–3.

92 Siemon, "Focus on the Field," 29

93 Interview, Hechler with Coker.

94 AG 314.7 OpH, Headquarters, European Theater of Operations, subject: Operation of Information and Historical Services, 6 April 1945, RG 498, Box 2, Records of Headquarters, ETOUSA (World War II), History Division, Miscellaneous Records of Theater Historian, 1943–1946, NARA.

95 Hechler, *The Enemy Side of the Hill*, Chapter, XVII, 11.

96 Ken Hechler, https://en.wikipedia.org/wiki/Ken_Hechler#cite_note-5.

97 Hechler, *The Enemy Side of the Hill*, Chapter, XVII, 11.

98 Associated Press, "Ken Hechler, congressman who fought for miners and marched with Martin Luther King, dies at 102," December 12, 2016, https://www.chicagotribune.com/news/obituaries/la-na-ken-hechler-20161212-story.html and Ken Hechler, https://en.wikipedia.org/wiki/Ken_Hechler#cite_note-5.

99 Memorandum, Colonel J.B.L. Lawrence, and Colonel W.A. Ganoe, subject: Supplementary S.O. for Information and Historical Units, June 13, 1944, Information and Historical Units, RG 498, Box 6, Records of Headquarters, ETOUSA, US. Army (WW II), NARA.

100 Wiley, *Historical Program of the U.S. Army, 1939 to Present [1945]*, 22.

101 Letter, Lieutenant Colonel John Kemper to Colonel W.A. Ganoe, 5 June 1944, RG 498, Box 6, Records of Headquarters, ETOUSA (WWII), NARA.

102 Siemon, "Focus on the Field," 29 and Richard Hunt, "The Military History Detachment in the Field," in Robert Coakley, *A Guide to the Study and Use of Military History* (CMH, Washington, D.C.: Government Printing Office, 1982 reprint), 313.

103 Bauer, Frederiksen and Anspacher, "The Army Historical Program In The European Theater, 8 May 1943–31 December 1950," 5.

104 Ibid, 6 and Siemon, "Focus on the Field," 29.

105 Bauer, Frederiksen and Anspacher, "The Army Historical Program In The European Theater, 8 May 1943–31 December 1950," 5.

106 "Suggestions," Colonel W.A. Ganoe, Spring 1944 in Thompson, "History of the Historical Section, ETO," Documentation Vol. 1 (Parts 1 and 2).

107 Ibid, Chapter I, 9.

108 Interview, Hechler with Coker.

109 Ibid.

110 Colonel W.A. Ganoe, History Sub-Section, G-3, Subject: Brief of the 10-minute talk before Commanders, 18 August 1943, Administration #161, RG 498, Box 33, Records of Headquarters, ETOUSA (WWII), NARA.

111 Release No. 1837, Headquarters, European Theater of Operations, History to be Given To The World-Straight from the Battlefront, no date, Administration #161, RG 498, Box 33, Records of Headquarters, ETOUSA (World War II), NARA.

112 Letter, Lieutenant Colonel John Kemper to Colonel W.A. Ganoe, 5 June 1944, Notes On Historical Program, RG 498, Box 1, Records of Headquarters, ETOUSA (World War II), NARA.

113 Letter, Lieutenant Colonel John Kemper to Lieutenant Colonel Charles Taylor, 13 July 1944, Notes On Historical Program, RG 498, Box 1, Records of Headquarters, ETOUSA (World War II), NARA.

114 Wiley, *Historical Program of the U.S. Army 1939 to Present [1945]*, 30. Efforts to obtain primary source documentation was unsuccessful.

115 Colonel W. A. Ganoe to Commander, First Army History team, 20 June 1944, First Army History Team, RG 498, Box 7, Records of Headquarters, ETOUSA (World War II), ETO Historical Division, Miscellaneous Records of the Theater Historian 1943–1946, NARA.

116 Letter, Commander of First Army history team to Colonel Ganoe, 21 June 1944, First Army History Team, RG 498, Box 7, Records of Headquarters, ETOUSA (World War II), ETO Historical Division, Miscellaneous Records of the Theater Historian, 1943–1946, NARA.

117 Letter, Colonel W.A. Ganoe to All History Teams of the European Theater, subject: Clarification of Objectives, 1 January 1945, RG 498, Box 2, Records of Headquarters, European Theater of Operations (World War II), History Division, Miscellaneous Records of Theater Historian, NARA.

118 Memorandum, Colonel W.A. Ganoe to All Historical Officers, subject: After Action Reports, 6 March 1945, RG 498, Box 2, Records of Headquarters, ETOUSA (World War II), History Division, Miscellaneous Records of the Theater Historian, 1943–1946, NARA.

119 Communication, Lieutenant Colonel S.L.A. Marshall to Adjutant General, subject: After Action Reports, 24 March 1945, RG 498, Box 2, Records of Headquarters, ETOUSA (World War II), History Division, Miscellaneous Records of the Theater Historian, 1943–1946, NARA.

120 AG 314.7 OpH, Headquarters, European Theater of Operations, subject: Operation of Information and Historical Services, 6 April 1945, RG 498, Box 2, Records of Headquarters, ETOUSA (WWII), NARA.

121 Staff Memo 46, Headquarters, U.S. Forces, European Theater, 19 September 1945, RG 498, Box 2, Records of Headquarters, ETOUSA (WWII), NARA.

122 Communication, Headquarters European Theater of Operations, 10 March 1945, RG 498, Box 2, Records of Headquarters, ETOUSA (World War II), History Division, Miscellaneous Records of Theater Historian, 1943–1946, NARA. Efforts to locate these studies were futile.

123 Letter, Adjutant General, subject: Historical Program in European Theater of Operations, 14 October 1944, Historical Program, RG 498, Box 2, Records of Headquarters, ETOUSA (World War II), History Division, Miscellaneous Records of Theater Historian, NARA.

124 Ibid.

125 Ibid.

126 Ibid.

127 Ibid.

128 Letter, Headquarters, European Theater of Operations, subject: Historical Program in European Theater of Operations, 26 February 1945, RG 498, Box 2, Records of Headquarters, ETOUSA (World War II), History Division, Miscellaneous Records of Theater Historian, NARA. The report has no author but Marshall refers to it in a 26 February 1945 message.

129 Wiley, *Historical Program of the U.S. Army 1939 to Present [1945]*, 30.

130 Hechler, *The Enemy Side of the Hill*, Chapter I, 8.

131 Ibid.

132 Memorandum, Colonel S.L.A. Marshall to Detachment Commanders of the First, Third and Ninth Armies, subject: Dispatch of Material, 1 February 1945, Directives to Writing Personnel, RG 498, Box 7, Records of Headquarters, ETOUSA (World War II), Historical Division, Miscellaneous Records of Theater Historian, NARA.

133 Memorandum, Colonel S.L.A. Marshall to All Detachment Commanders, subject: Coverage of Occupational Problems, 1 May 1945, Directives to Writing Personnel, RG 498 Box 7, Records of Headquarters, ETOUSA (WWII), NARA.

134 Memorandum for Theater Historian, subject: Memorandum of Lieutenant Colonel Gayle, 25 May 45, on "Proposals concerning the Form and Content of the Tactical History of the ETO," 28 May 1945, Directives to Writing Personnel, RG 498, Box 7, Records of Headquarters, ETOUSA (World War II), Historical Division, Miscellaneous Records of Theater Historian, NARA.

135 Memorandum, Colonel S.L.A. Marshall to All Detachment Commanders, subject: Completion of Historical Coverage of Military Operations in ETO, 29 May 1945, Directives to Writing Personnel, RG 498, Box 7, Records of Headquarters, ETOUSA (World War II), Historical Division, Miscellaneous Records of Theater Historian, NARA.

136 Letter, Lieutenant Colonel Hugh Cole to All Concerned, subject: Procedure, 1 July 1945, Directives to Writing Personnel, RG 498, Box 7, Records of Headquarters, ETOUSA (World War II), Historical Division, Miscellaneous Records of Theater Historian, NARA.

137 Hechler, *The Enemy Side of the Hill*, Chapter I, 8.

Chapter 8

1 Ken Hechler, *The Enemy Side of the Hill: The 1945 Background on Interrogation of German Commanders*, Washington Historical Branch, OCMH, 30 July 1949. Hechler wrote in the forward: "It is difficult to write very objectively about something like this which grips an individual in a way that he forgets about everything else in the world. Hindsight now enables the writer to comment critically on his own shortcomings at various stages of the project. But the account is personalized and subjective in the sense that proportionate weight is not given to the activities of others who worked along parallel lines; perhaps too much weight is given to the activities of the agencies which seemed to be working at cross purposes."

2 Hechler, *The Enemy Side of the Hill*, Foreword, 1.

3   Ibid, Chapter I, 4–7.

4   Ibid, Chapter I, 7.

5   Ibid, Chapter X, 3.

6   Ibid, Chapter I, 7.

7   Ibid, Chapter I, 9 and Chapter XIV, 1.

8   Ibid, Chapter XIV, 1.

9   Ibid, Chapter II, 1.

10   Interview, Dr. Kenneth Hechler with Mr. Niel M. Johnson, 29 November 1985, http://www. trumanlibrary.org/oralhist/hechler.htm and Hechler, *The Enemy Side of the Hill*, Chapter II, p 1–3. Dr. George N. Shuster, president of Hunter College and an expert on Central Europe chaired the commission n. Other members were Dr. Frank Graham, professor of economics at Princeton University; Dr. John Brown Mason at Stanford University and a member of the Foreign Economic Administration; LTC Oron J. Hale, G-2 and former professor of history at the University of Virginia and LTC J.J. Scanlon from the Army Service Forces Materiel Division.

11   Hechler, *The Enemy Side of the Hill*, Chapter II, 1–6.

12   Ibid, Chapter II, 6–11.

13   Ibid.

14   Ibid, Chapter, III, 1 and Interview, Hechler with Johnson.

15   Hechler, *The Enemy Side of the Hill*, Chapter III, 1–2, 8, Chapter VII, 4 and Interview, Hechler with Johnson.

16   Ibid, *The Enemy Side of the Hill*, Chapter, VII, 5 and Chapter X, 2.

17   Ibid, Chapter XIII, 2.

18   Ibid, Chapter, VII, 5 and Chapter X, 2.

19   Ibid, Chapter VI, 7. He used this technique in an interview with Kesselring in which he talked to him and then decided to ask seven questions about the Remagen Bridge.

20   Ibid, Chapter IV, 3.

21   Ibid, Chapter IV, 4, 6, and Chapter X, 1.

22   Ibid, Chapter IV, 5.

23   Ibid, Chapter VI, 4.

24   Ibid, Chapter V, 7; Chapter VII, 1, 4; and Chapter VII, 8.

25   Ibid, Chapter VII, 2 and "Publication Number: M1035 Publication Title: Guide to Foreign Military Studies, 1945-54 Date Published: 1954, Microsoft Word - M1035.doc (fold3.com).

26   Hechler, *The Enemy Side of the Hill*, Chapter VII, 2.

27   Ibid, Chapter VII, 3.

28   Ibid, Chapter X, 1.

29   Ibid, Chapter IX, 15 and Chapter X, 1.

30   Ibid, Chapter X, 6.

31   Interview, Hechler with Johnson. Hechler did state that the Historical Section's reactions to his first reports were "somewhat mixed. The Ardennes Section ... was enthusiastic."

32   Hechler, *The Enemy Side of the Hill*, Chapter, XIV, 1–14.

33   Ibid, Chapter XV, 1–7.

34   Ibid, Chapter XIII, 7.

35   Ibid, Chapter XVI, 1.

36   Ibid, Chapter XVI, 1–13.

37   Ibid, Chapter, XVII, 1–17.

38   Ibid, Chapter XIII, 1.

39   Hugh M. Cole, "Writing Contemporary Military History," *Military Affairs*, Vol. 12, No 3, Autumn 1948, 167.

40 Kent Roberts Greenfield, "For the Future: A Memory of the Present," *Johns Hopkins Magazine*, Nov 1959, 12, 13, 29, 31. Greenfield remained the chief historian until October 1958. He was the general editor of the *U.S. Army in WWII* series. By the time he retired in October 1958, 51 volumes had been published or were awaiting publication.

Chapter 9

1 "Chester G. Starr, Jr.," Memorial | Faculty History Project (umich.edu); Anonymous, "Chester G. Starr," *The Friday Review*, October 15, 1999 and Anonymous, "Chester G. Starr, noted historian, dies," University of Michigan, September 29, 1999. Among Starr's publications were: *A History of the Ancient World* and *Individual and Community, The Rise of the Polis, 800–500 B.C.* Perhaps his greatest work was *The Origins of Greek Civilization*.

2 Letter, Captain Chester Starr to Lieutenant Colonel John Kemper, 31 December 1943, in "Orientation Material for Theater Historians."

3 Letter, Captain Chester Starr to Lieutenant Colonel John Kemper, 31 December 1943, in "Orientation Material for Theater Historians."

4 Ibid.

5 Letter, Captain Chester Starr to Lieutenant Colonel John Kemper, 31 December 1943, in "Orientation Material for Theater Historians."

6 Wiley, *Historical Program Of The U.S. Army 1939 to Present [1945]*, 18.

7 Ibid.

8 Letter, Captain Chester Starr to Lieutenant Colonel John Kemper, 31 December 1943, in "Orientation." Material for Theater Historians."

9 Staff Memorandum Number 2, Colonel H.V. Roberts to Distribution W, subject: Historical Section, 8 January 1944 in "Orientation Material for Theater Historians."

10 Memorandum, Major A.B. King to each major command, each staff section, and AG records, subject: Historical Records and Histories of Organizations, 8 January 1944 in "Orientation Material for Theater Historians."

11 Report, Lieutenant Colonel Chester Starr, to Chief, Historical Division, War Department, subject: Report on the Activities of the Historian Section, Fifth Army during the Italian Campaign, 1943–1945, 25 November 1945, 228.01, HRC 314.7, CMH.

12 Ibid.

13 Lieutenant General Mark Clark, Foreword to Fifth Army, Part I, From Activation to the Fall of Naples, 5 January – 6 October 1943, RG 338, Box 45, Records of U.S. Army Command, Records of HQ Fifth Army Adjutant General, NARA.

14 These records are in RG 338: Records of U.S. Army Operational, Tactical, and Support Organizations (WWII and Thereafter), NARA.

15 General Status of Historical Program, MTOUSA, 3 October 1945, Mediterranean Theater of Operations Historical Program, RG 498, Box 5, Records of Headquarters, ETOUSA (World War II), ETO Historical Division, Miscellaneous Records of Theater Historian, Mediterranean Theater of Operations Historical Section, NARA. Mediterranean Theater of Operations records later became RG 492.

16 General Status of Historical Program, MTOUSA, 3 October 1945, Mediterranean Theater of Operations Historical Program, RG 498, Box 5, Records of Headquarters, ETOUSA (World War II), ETO Historical Division, Miscellaneous Records of Theater Historian, Mediterranean Theater of Operations Historical Section, NARA.

17 Report, Lieutenant Colonel Chester Starr, to Chief, Historical Division, War Department, subject: Report on the Activities of the Historian Section, Fifth Army during the Italian Campaign, 1943–1945, 25 November 1945, 228.01, HRC 314.7, CMH.
18 Ibid.
19 Ibid.
20 Ibid.
21 Ibid.
22 Ibid.
23 Ibid.
24 Ibid.
25 Ibid.
26 Ibid.
27 Ibid.
28 Ibid.
29 Ibid.
30 Ibid.
31 Memorandum No. 3, 7th Information and Historical Service, November 15, 1944, RG 407, Box 16840, Records of The Adjutant General's Office, WW II Operations Reports, 1941–1948, Information and Historical Service, NARA.
32 Interview, Hechler with Coker.
33 Ibid.
34 CMH retains all these reports.
35 These reports are in RG 338: Records of U.S. Army Operational, Tactical, and Support Organizations (WWII and Thereafter), NARA.
36 Monthly Reports, 10th I&HS, 20 March 1943 – 20 May 1944, Box 16840, RG 407, Records of the Adjutant General's Office, WW II Operations Reports, 1941–1948, Information and Historical Service, NARA.
37 Ibid.
38 Ibid.
39 Anonymous, "Chester G. Starr, noted historian, dies," University of Michigan News Service, April 25, 2007, and Annual Report, 4th Information and Historical Service, 17 January 1944, RG 407, Box 16840, Records of The Adjutant General's Office, WWII Operations Reports, 1941–1948, Information and Historical Services, NARA.
40 "Ken Hechler," Wikipedia, Ken Hechler – Wikipedia; "Forrest Pogue," Wikipedia, https://en.wikipedia.org/wiki/Forrest_Pogue; and Thomas Burdett, "Marshall, Samuel Lyman Atwood," Texas State Historical Association, https://www.tshaonline.org/handbook/entries/marshall-samuel-lyman-atwood.
41 Memorandum, Ganoe to Chief of Section, Information and Censorship Section, Headquarters, EOUTSA, subject: Proposed Initial Plan, 20 May 1943, RG 498, Box 33, Records of Headquarters, ETOUSA (World War II), NARA.
42 Memorandum, Colonel W.A. Ganoe, 7 June 1943, Historical Program, RG 498, Box 5, Records of Headquarters, ETOUSA (WWII), NARA.
43 Letter, Starr to Kemper, 31 December 1943.
44 Letter, S.L.A. Marshall to Dr. Ken Hechler, July 15, 1958, Hechler Personal Records.

Chapter 10

1   Marshall, *Bringing Up the Rear*, 145 and Quoted in Williams, *SLAM: The Influence of S.L.A. Marshall on the United States Army*, 34.

2   Marshall, *Bringing Up the Rear*, 164; Interview, Hechler with Coker; and Williams, *SLAM: The Influence of S.L.A. Marshall on the United States Army*, 34 – 35.

3   Marshall, *Bringing up the Rear*, 153–159 and Williams, *SLAM: The Influence of S.L.A. Marshall on the United States Army*, 35.

4   Hugh M. Cole, "Writing Contemporary Military History," *Military Affairs*, Vol. 12, No 3, Autumn 1948, 164, 166.

5   Ibid.

6   Kent Greenfield, *The Historian and the Army*, (Rutgers University Press; Rutgers College, New Jersey, 1954), 6; Terrence Gough, "The U.S. Army Center of Military History: A Brief History," *Army History*, Number 37, Spring 1996, 2 and Wiley, *Historical Program of the U.S. Army 1939 to Present [1945]*, 39. See pages 35 through 39 of Wiley for more details.

7   Thompson, "History of the Historical Section, European Theater of Operations," 148.

8   The Adjutant General Office, War Department, AG 322 (20 June 1946), AO-IWDGOT-M, subject: Redesignation, Constitution, Activation and Reorganization of Certain Units in the Pacific Theater, 1 July 1946, Force Structure and Unit History Branch, CMH; Wright, "Clio in Combat: The Evolution of the Military History Detachment, " 4 and Gough, "The U. S. Army Center of Military History: A Brief History," *Army History*, Number 37, Spring 1996, 3.

9   Greenfield, "For the Future: A Memory of the Present," *Johns Hopkins Magazine*, November 1959, 27–28.

10 Ibid.

11 Williams, *Slam: The Influence of S.L.A. on the United States Army*, 19.

12 Ibid.

13 Kent Greenfield, "For the Future: A Memory of the Present," *Johns Hopkins Magazine*, November 1959, 28.

14 Hugh M. Cole, "Writing Contemporary Military History," *Military Affairs*, Vol. 12, No 3, Autumn 1948, 164, 167.

15 Greenfield, "For the Future, 28, 31.

16 T/O&E 20–17; Robert Fetchman, "The Value of Historical Detachments," Student Monograph, Advanced Infantry Officers Course, Fort Benning, Georgia, 1952 and Wright, "Clio in Combat: The Evolution of the Military History Detachment," 4.

17 Ibid.

18 Field Manual 0-0 Military History, 1, no date, 228.01, HRC 314.7, CMH.

19 Ibid.

20 Ibid.

21 Ibid, 1–5.

22 Ibid, 5–13.

23 Ibid, 13–18.

24 Ibid, iii–iv.

25 Ibid.

26 Army Regulation 345-105, Records and Reports: Command Report, 3 October 1950, and Terrence Gough, "Military Historians and Lessons-Learned Activities In World War II, Korea, and Vietnam," 16, Histories Division, CMH, 2 June 1980.

Chapter 11

1   Harry S. Truman to Dr. Morrison, 22 December 1950, copy in 228.01, Historical Research Collection (HRC) 314.72, Center of Military History (CMH).

2   Ibid.

3   Wright, "Clio in Combat: The Evolution of the Military History Detachment," 4 and Gough, "Military Historians and Lessons Learned Activities in World War II, Korea, and Vietnam," 17.

4   1st Lieutenant Donald Grant and Captain Richard A. Hill, "A Chronology of the Historical Detachments in Korea, October 1950 to January 1954," iv, HMC-1 Collection 8-5.1A DO, CMH.

5   Grant and Hill, "A Chronology of the Historical Detachments in Korea, October 1950 to January 1954," iv.

6   James Ferguson, "The U.S. Army Historical Program In Vietnam, 1954–1968," 2–3, CMH and Bill Mossman, "The Military History Detachments in Korea," 28 April 1980, Terence Gough Collection, CMH; Fetchman, "The Value of Historical Detachments," 9–10; Wright, "Clio in Combat: The Evolution of the Military History Detachment," 4 and Hunt, "The Military History Detachment in the Field," 314.

7   This is apparent from an action report and special studies completed by the 10th Information and Historical Service. These are retained at CMH.

8   Mossman, "The Military History Detachments in Korea," 28 April 1980, Terence Gough Collection, CMH; Fetchman, "The Value of Historical Detachments," 9–10; Wright, "Clio in Combat: The Evolution of the Military History Detachment," 4 and Hunt, "The Military History Detachment in the Field," 314.

9   Marshall, *Victory Island: The Battle of Kwajalein* with an Introduction by Joseph Dawson III, xii–xiii. He retired from the Army Reserve in 1960 and died in 1977.

10   Marshall, *Bringing Up the Rear*, 179 and Williams, *SLAM: The Influence of S.L.A. Marshall on the United States Army*, 63. Marshall detailed his Korean War experience in chapters 17 and 18 of his memoir.

11   S.L. A. Marshall, *Pork Chop Hill, The American Fighting Man in Action, Korea, Spring 1953*, 1. and Williams, *SLAM: The Influence of S.L.A. Marshall on the United States Army*, 63.

12   Mossman, "The Military History Detachments in Korea" and Gough, "Military Historians and Lessons Learned Activities In World War II, Korea, and Vietnam," 18. The 8086th Army Unit, Military History Detachment was activated on 24 January 1953. See Grant and Hill, "A Chronology of the Historical Detachments in Korea, October 1950 to January 1954," 17.

13   Grant and Hill, "A Chronology of the Historical Detachments in Korea, October 1950 to January 1954," iv.

14   Grant and Hill, "A Chronology of the Historical Detachments in Korea, October 1950 to January 1954," iv; Mossman, "The Military History Detachments in Korea"; Wright, "Clio in Combat," 5; Hunt, "The Military History Detachment in the Field," 314 and Interview, Harry Middleton with Kathryn Roe Coker 30 October 2009, USARHRC, USARC.

15   Interview, Coker with Middleton.

16   Interview, Bevin Alexander with Kathryn Roe Coker, 6 April 2009, USARHRC, USARC.

17   Grant and Hill, "A Chronology of the Historical Detachments in Korea, October 1950 to January 1954," 2–11.

18   Ibid.

19   Interview, Mr. Edward D. Cochley with Mr. Frank R. Shirer, MISC-CMH-2000-001.

20   Interview, Alexander with Coker, 6 April 2009.

21   Ibid.

22 Ibid.
23 Ibid and CMH, *The Korean War: Years of Stalemate, July 1951– July 1953*, Washington, D.C., no date.
24 Interviews, Alexander with Coker, 6 April, and 6 May 2009.
25 Ibid.
26 Ibid.
27 Ibid.
28 Ibid.
29 Ibid.
30 Ibid.
31 Bevin Alexander, Korea," https://www.bevinalexander.com/korea/.
32 Interviews, Alexander with Coker, 6 April and 6 May 2009; "Bevin Alexander," https://www. bevinalexander.com/about.htm; and "Korea: The First War We Lost," https://www.bevinalexander. com/books/korea-first-war-we-lost.htm.
33 Interview, Cochley with Shirer.
34 Interview, Richard Gugeler with Kathryn Roe Coker, May 15, 2009, USARHRC, USARC. Russell Gugeler was also a veteran of World War II. He joined the OCMH then under Chief of Military History Major General Orlando Ward. He co-authored *Okinawa: The Last Battle*. He wrote a biography of Ward, entitled *Major General Orlando Ward: Life of a Leader*. Gugeler died in 1985.
35 Russell A. Gugeler, *COMBAT ACTIONS IN KOREA*, CMH, Washington, D.C.., 1987, v–vii
36 Captain Martin Blumenson, "Withdrawal from Taejon on 20 July 1950," Historical Manuscripts Collection, 8-5.1A, CMH.
37 "WWII Historian, Patton Expert Blumenson Dies," *Washington Post*, 17 April 2005, C 11.
38 Captain Martin Blumenson, "Action at Chinju on 31 July 1950," Historical Manuscripts Collection, 8-5.1A, CMH.
39 Major Edward Williamson, Major Pierce Briscoe, Captain Martin Blumenson and 1st Lieutenant John Mewha, "Action on Heartbreak Ridge," Historical Manuscripts Collection, 8-5.1A, CMH.
40 8086 Army Unit (AFFE) Military History Section, Headquarters, US Army Forces, Far East, Evacuation of Refugees and Civilians from Seoul, June 1950 and December 1950 to January 1951, Historical Manuscripts Collection, 8-5.1A, CMH.
41 Mossman, "The Military History Detachments in Korea" and Fetchman, "The Value of Historical Detachments," 1.
42 Fetchman, "The Value of Historical Detachments," 9.
43 Ibid, 15.
44 Ferguson, "The U.S. Army Historical Program In Vietnam, 1954–1968," 4.
45 Fetchman, "The Value of Historical Detachments,"15.
46 Ibid, p 15–16 and Hunt, "The Military History Detachment in the Field," 314–315.
47 EUSAK Military History Newsletter, Number 1, 25 June 1952, Historical Manuscripts Collection, 8-5.1A, CMH and EUSAK Military History Newsletter, Number 2, 30 September 1952, Historical Manuscripts Collection, 8-5.1A, CMH.
48 EUSAK Military History Newsletter, Number 2, 30 September 1952, Historical Manuscripts Collection, 8-5.1A, CMH.
49 EUSAK Military History Newsletter, Number 2, 30 September 1952, Historical Manuscripts Collection, 8-5.1A, CMH.
50 Department of the Army, T/O & E 20-17A, 8 March 1952.
51 Grant and Hill, "A Chronology of the Historical Detachments in Korea," 63.
52 Ibid.

53 Ibid.
54 Ibid, 72–76.

Chapter 12

1   Department of the Army, Office Center of Military History, *The Military Historian in the Field*, 1953, 1.
2   Ibid.
3   Ibid, 15–28, 33–35, 46.
4   Special Regulation 525-45-2 Combat Operations: Command Report, 24 March 1953.
5   OCMH, Department of the Army, *The Military Historian in the Field*, 1959, 1.
6   Ibid, 3–6.
7   Mossman, "The Military History Detachments in Korea."
8   Ferguson, "The U.S. Army Historical Program In Vietnam, 1954–1968," I-1–I-3; Ronald H. Spector, *United States Army in Vietnam, Advice and Support: The Early Years 1941–1960*, CMH, Washington, D.C., 1985, 97–105, 115–121; and Richard W. Stewart, *Deepening Involvement 1945–1965*, CMH, Washington, D.C., 2012, 7–11.
9   Department of the Army, AR 870-5, *Historical Activities: Military History Responsibilities, Policies, and Procedures*, October 1962.
10 Ibid.
11 Terrence J. Gough, "The U.S. Army Center of Military History: A Brief History," *Army History*, PB-20-96-2 (No.37), Washington, D.C., Spring 1996.
12 Ferguson, "The U.S. Army Historical Program In Vietnam, 1954–1968," II-1–I-3
13 Ibid, II-2–II-4.
14 Ibid, I-8–I-9.
15 Ibid.
16 Ibid, II-14–II-15.
17 Ibid.
18 Ibid, II-9–II-11.
19 Ibid, II-11.
20 Wright, "Clio in Combat," 4.
21 Ibid.
22 Department of the Army Pamphlet (525-2) *Military Operations, Vietnam Primer: Lessons Learned* (Headquarters, Department of the Army; Washington, D.C.), April 27, 1967, i.
23 Ibid, 1.
24 Ibid, 1–2.
25 Ibid, 2.
26 Ibid, 3.
27 Ibid, 4.
28 Ibid, 3–5.
29 Ibid, 7.
30 Ibid.
31 Ibid, 8.
32 Ibid.
33 Ibid, 11.
34 Ibid, 13–14.
35 Ibid, 15–16.
36 Ibid, 17.

37 Ibid, 19–23.
38 Ibid, 24–30.
39 Ibid, 31–38.
40 Ibid, 39–42.
41 Ibid, 43–46.
42 Ibid, 47–49.
43 Ibid, 51–52.
44 Ibid, 53–54.
45 William Epley, interview with Dr. Richard K. Wright, Jr., 13 and 18 September 2002, CMH.
46 Ibid.
47 Ibid and "Military Records, Records of U.S. Forces in Southeast Asia, 1950–1975 RG 472, NARA.
48 Interview, Epley with Wright.
49 Ibid and "Renegade Woods," Historical Resources Branch CMH, https://history.army.mil/documents/vietnam/reneg/reni.htm.
50 Interview, Epley with Wright.
51 Ibid.
52 Ibid.
53 Vietnam War Campaigns, Vietnam War Campaigns | U.S. Army Center of Military History and"III Corps tactical zone," III Corps tactical zone – Citizendium.
54 Interview, Epley with Wright.
55 Ibid and Vietnam War Campaigns, CMH, Vietnam War Campaigns | U.S. Army Center of Military History and "III Corps tactical zone," III Corps tactical zone – Citizendium.
56 Interview, Epley with Wright.
57 Renegade Woods, https://history.army.mil/documents/vietnam/reneg/reni.htm.
58 Interview, Epley with Wright.
59 Ibid.
60 After Action Interview Report, Ambush at the Dak Po, 21–22 January 1969, CMH
61 After Action Interview Report, Ambush at the Dak Po, 21–22 January 1969, CMH.
62 Oral History Interview VNIT 259, Serial Interview, 1st Battalion, 27th Infantry, 25th Infantry Division, CMH, 1st Battalion, 27th Infantry, 25th Infantry Division (army.mil).
63 The Separate Brigade S-2 in Vietnam, VNIT-398, CMH.
64 Oral History Interview, VNIT 101, End of-Tour Interview, CPT Joseph W. Kinzer, Advisory Team 163, Liaison Officer, 3d Airborne Brigade, Airborne Division, CMH, https://history.army.mil/documents/vietnam/vnit/vnit0101.htm.
65 Exit Interview with LTC Douglas S. Smith, Commander, 2d Battalion, 47th Infantry, 9th Infantry Division VNIT 457, CMH, 1st Battalion, 27th Infantry, 25th Infantry Division (army.mil).
66 Gough, Terrence J. "The U.S. Army Center of Military History: A Brief History," Army History, PB-20-96-2 (No.37).
67 Memorandum, Lieutenant Colonel Leonard Wegner to Secretary of the General Staff, U.S. Army Vietnam Headquarters, Subject: Status of the Historical Program, 13 April 1970. RG 472, Records of the U.S Forces in Southeast Asia, NARA.
68 Major Godwin P. McLaughlin, subject: USARV Command Historian—Newsletter No. 19, 22 December 1971. RG 472, General Records, USARV Command Historian Newsletters, Box 298, Records of the U.S Forces in Southeast Asia, NARA.
69 Major Godwin P. McLaughlin, subject: USARV Command Historian—Newsletter No. 19, 11 February 1972. General Records, USARV Command Historian Newsletters, RG 472, Box 298, Records of the U.S Forces in Southeast Asia, NARA.

Afterword

1   Hackworth and Sherman, *About Face,* 548-549.
2   Ibid, 549.
3   Ibid, 582.
4   "Military History Detachments," Office of Army Reserve History, U.S. Army Reserve Command, Military History Detachments (army.mil).
5   Major David Hanselman, "The Tip of the History Spear: Capturing the Combat History of the Army in Current Operations," The Campaign for the National Museum of the United States Army (armyhistory.org).
6   Ibid.
7   Ibid.
8   Ibid.
9   Ibid.
10 Ibid.
11 Ibid.
12 Ibid.
13 Ibid.
14 Letter, S.L.A. Marshall to Dr. Ken Hechler.
15 Hanselman, "The Tip of the History Spear."

Bibliography

Primary Sources

National Archives and Records Administration (NARA)

Enlisted Record and Report Of Separation. Record Group (RG) 407, Records of The Adjutant General's Office, Honorable Discharge, Eva C. Spencer, November 1944, National Personnel Records Center.

Operations Reports, RG 407, Records of The Adjutant General's Office, World War II, 1941–1948, Information and Historical Service.

Report of Casualty. RG 407, Records of The Adjutant General's Office, Ganoe, William A., 17 Oct 66, National Personnel Records Center.

General Records, RG 472, Records of the U.S Forces in Southeast Asia, 1950–1975.

Military Records, RG 472, Records of U.S. Forces in Southeast Asia, 1950–1975.

Military Records RG 338, Records of U.S. Army Operational, Tactical, and Support Organizations (World War II and Thereafter).

Military Records, RG 498, Records of Headquarters, European Theater of Operations, United States Army (World War II).

U.S. Army Center of Military History (CMH)

10th Information and Historical Service, Headquarters Eighth Army. "Special Study of The Yokohama War Crimes Trials, December 1945–September 1947." Historical Manuscripts Collection (HMC) 8-5.1A.

_____. "Staff Study of Japanese Operations In Zamboanga (1944–1945)," HMC 8-5.1A.

_____. "Staff Study of Japanese Operation on Panay Island.

8086 Army Unit (AFFE) Military History Section, Headquarters, U.S. Army Forces, Far East. "Evacuation of Refugees and Civilians from Seoul, June 1950 and December 1950 to January 1951," HMC 8-5.1A.

After Action Interview Report, Ambush at the Dak Po, 21-22 January 1969, CMH.

Alexander, 2d Lieutenant Bevin. "Engineer Construction of General L.K. Ladue Bridge," HMC, 8-5.1A.

_____."Operations of 8th Army Quartermaster Service Center Number 3," HMC, 8-5.1A.

AG 322, Adjutant General, War Department to Commanding General USAF, Central Pacific Area, subject: Organization of Information and Historical Service in Central Pacific Area, 11 July 1944, Force Structure and Unit History Branch.

Bauer, Theodore; Oliver Frederiksen; and Ellinor Anspacher, "The Army Historical Program In The European Theater, 8 May 1943–31 December 1950," Occupations Forces in Europe Series, Historical Division, European Command, Karlsruhe, Germany, 1951.

Blumenson, Captain Martin. "Action at Chinju on 31 July 1950," HMC 8-5.1A.

_____. "Withdrawal from Taejon on 20 July 1950," HMC 8-5.1A.

EUSAK. Military History Newsletter, Number 1, 25 June 1952, HMC 8-5.1A.

_____. Military History Newsletter, Number 2, 30 September 1952, HMC 8-5.1A.

Fetchman, Robert. "The Value of Historical Detachments," Student Monograph, Advanced Infantry Officers Course, Fort Benning, Georgia, 1952.

Field Manual 0-0 Military History, no date, 228.01, Historical Research Collection (HRC) 314.7.

Gough, Terrence. "Military Historians and Lessons-Learned Activities In World War II, Korea, and Vietnam," 2 June 1980, Histories Division.

Grant, 1st Lieutenant Donald P. and Captain Richard A. Hill. "A Chronology of the Historical Detachments in Korea, October 1950 to January 1954," HMC-1 8-5.1A DO.

Letter, Harry S. Truman to Dr. Morrison, 22 December 1950, copy in 228.01, HRC 314.72.

Mossman, Bill. "The Military History Detachments in Korea," 28 April 1980, Terence Gough Collection.

Office Center of Military History, The Military Historian in the Field, 1953.

Podesta, Major Edward. Command Report No. 13 "Covering the Period of 1 October to 31 October 1952 for IX Corps Attached to the Eighth U.S. Army Throughout the Period," HMC 8-5.1A.

Starr, Lieutenant Colonel Chester to Chief, Historical Division, War Department, subject: Report on the Activities of the Historian Section, Fifth Army during the Italian Campaign, 1943–1945, 25 November 1945, 228.01, HRC 314.7.

The Adjutant General Office, War Department, AG 322 (20 June 1946), AO-IWDGOT-M, subject: Redesignation, Constitution, Activation and Reorganization of Certain Units in the Pacific Theater, 1 July 1946, Force Structure and Unit History Branch.

Thompson, Royce L. Establishment of the War Department Historical Formation for World War II, Documentation, no date, HRC 314.72.

_____. Establishment of the War Department's Historical Program for World War II, August 1947, HRC, 314.72.

_____. "History of the Historical Section, European Theater of Operations," Historical Section, European Theater of Operations, no date, HRC 314.72.

_____."History of the Historical Section, ETO," Documentation Vol. I (Parts 1 and 2), Historical Section, ETO, no date, HRC 314.72.

War Department. T/O&E20-12S, October 3, 1944, Force Structure and Unit History Branch.

Williamson, Major Edward, Major Pierce Briscoe, Captain Martin and 1st Lieutenant John Mewha. "Action on Heartbreak Ridge," HRC 8-5.1A.

Wiley, Bell. Historical Program Of the U.S. Army 1939 To Present [1945]. no date, HMC, 2-3.7 AB.A.

Department of the Army

Army Regulation 345-105. Military Records: Historical Records and Histories of Organizations, 18 November 1929, and 22 November 1930.

Special Regulation 525-45-2 Combat Operations: Command Report, 24 March 1953.

T/O&E 20-17A, 8 March 1952.

T/O&E 20-17R, 12 April 1955.

T/O&E 20-17D, 20 February 1959.

T/O&E 20-17D, Military History Detachment, 20 February 1959.

T/O&E, 20-17E, Military History Detachment, 19 July 1963.

George C. Marshall Foundation

Dr. Forrest Pogue, Normandy, 1944.

University of Texas at El Paso (UTEP)

Eva Spencer Ostenberg Papers. UTEP Library, Special Collections Department.
SLA Marshal Papers. UTEP Library, Special Collections Department.

Books

Alexander, Bevin. *Korea: The First War We Lost*. New York: Hippocrene Books, 1986.

Anderson, Franklin D. Preface to Forrest C. Pogue, *Pogue's War: Diaries of a WWII Combat Historian*. Lexington, Kentucky: The University Press of Kentucky, 2001.

Barber, Noel Barber. *A Sinister Twilight: The Fall of Singapore 1942*. Boston, Massachusetts Houghton Mifflin Company, 1968.

Birtle, Andrew James. *The Korean War: Years of Stalemate, July 1951- July 1953*, Washington, D.C., CMH, 2012.

Blair, Clay. *The Forgotten War: America in Korea, 1950-53*. New York: Doubleday, 1987.

Conn, Stetson. *Historical Work in the United States Army, 1862–1954*. Washington, D.C.: CMH, 1980.

Fehrenbach, T. R. *This Kind of War: A Study in Unpreparedness*. New York: Macmillan, 1963.

Ganoe, William A. *The History Of The United States Army*, New York City: D. Appleton-Century Company, Incorporated, 1924.

Gugeler, Russell A. *Combat Actions in Korea*. Washington, D.C.: CMH, 1970.

Greenfield, Kent. *The Historian and the Army*. Rutgers University Press; Rutgers College, New Jersey, 1954.

Hackworth, Colonel David, H. and Julie Sherman. *About Face: the Odyssey of an American Warrior*. New York: Simon and Schuster, 1989.

Hastings, Max. *The Korean War*. New York: Simon and Schuster, 1987.

Hechler, Kenneth. *The Bridge At Remagen*. Ballantine, New York, 1957.

_____. *The Enemy Side of the Hill, The 1945 Background on Interrogation of German Commanders*, 30 July 1949, CMH.

Hornfischer, James D. *Neptune's Inferno—The U.S. Navy at Guadalcanal*. Random House, NY, Bantam Books, 011.

Marshall, S. L. A. Bringing *Up the Rear, A Memoir*. Presidio Press, San Rafael, California, 1979.

_____. Pork Chop Hill. Permabooks, New York, 1959.

_____.*Victory Island: The Battle of Kwajalein* with an Introduction by Joseph Dawson III, to the Bison Books printing. Lincoln: University of Nebraska Press, 2001.

Pogue. Forrest C. *Pogue's War: Diaries of a WWII Combat Historian*. Lexington, Kentucky: The University of Kentucky Press, 2001.

Spector, Ronald H. *United States Army in Vietnam, Advice and Support: The Early Years 1941–1960*, CMH, Washington, D.C., 1985

Stewart, Richard W. Deepening Involvement, *1945–1965*, Washington, D.C., CMH, 2012.

Sun Tzu. *The Art of War*, translated by Thomas Cleary. Boston and London: Shambhala Publications, 1988.

Westover, John G. *Combat Support in Korea*. Washington, D.C.: CMH, 1987.

Williams, Major F.D.G. *SLAM: The Influence of S.L.A. Marshall on the United States Army*. Office of the Command Historian, U.S. Army Training and Doctrine Command, Fort Monroe and CMH, 1994.

Articles

Anonymous. "Chester G. Starr," *The Friday Review*, October 15, 1999.

_____. "Chester G. Starr, noted historian, dies," University of Michigan News Service, September 29, 1999.

Cole, Hugh, M. "Writing Contemporary Military History," *Military Affairs*, Volume 12, No 3, Autumn 1948, 164-166.

Ferguson, James. "The U.S. Army Historical Program In Vietnam, 1954–1968."

Gough, Terrence. "The U.S. Army Center of Military History: A Brief History," *Army History*, Spring 1996, 1-5.

Greenfield, Kent. "For the Future: A Memory of the Present," *Johns Hopkins Magazine*, November 1959, 28-ff.

Greer, Richard. "Fort Shafter: Scholars in Khaki," *Hawaiian Journal of History*, Vol. 3, 1969, 146-155.

Hunt, Richard. "The Military History Detachment in the Field," in Robert Coakley, *A Guide to the Study and Use of Military History*, CMH, Washington, D.C.: Government Printing Office, 1982 reprint.

Schudel, Matt. "World War II Historian, Patton Expert Blumenson Dies," *Washington Post*, April 17, 2005, C 11.

Siemon, Bruce. "Focus on the Field," *Army History*, Winter 1991/92, 28-31.

Wright, Robert. "Clio in Combat: The Evolution of the Military History Detachment," *The Army Historian*, No. 6, Winter 1985, 3-ff.

Oral History Interviews

Alexander, Bevin with Kathryn Roe Coker, April 6, 2009. U.S. Army Reserve Historical Research Collection (USARHRC), U.S. Army Reserve Command (USARC).

Alexander, Bevin with Kathryn Roe Coker, May 6, 2009. USARHRC, USARC.

Cochley, Edward D. with Frank R. Shirer. MISC-CMH-2000-001, CMH.

Gugeler, Richard with Kathryn Roe Coker. May 15, 2009, USARHRC, USARC.

Hechler, Kenneth with Kathryn Roe Coker, June 19, 2009. USARHRC, USARC.

Middleton, Harry with Kathryn Roe Coker, October 30, 2009. USARHRC, USARC.

Wright, Jr., Richard K with William Epley, September 13 and 18, 2002, CMH.

Online sources

"III Corps tactical zone," CMH, III Corps tactical zone—Citizendium.

"Arthur L. Conger," Arthur L. Conger - Wikipedia.

Associated Press, "Ken Hechler, congressman who fought for miners and marched with Martin Luther King, dies at 102," December 12, 2016, https://www.chicagotribune.com/news/obituaries/la-na-ken-hechler-20161212-story.html.

Burdett, Thomas. "Marshall, Samuel Lyman Atwood," Texas State Historical Association, https://www.tshaonline.org/handbook/entries/marshall-samuel-lyman-atwood.

"Forrest C. Pogue," National Museum of the United States Army (thenmusa.org).

"Forrest Pogue," Wikipedia, https://en.wikipedia.org/wiki/Forrest_Pogue.

Gough, Terrence J. "The U.S. Army Center of Military History: A Brief History," *Army History*, Spring 1996.

Hanselman, Major David. "The Tip of the History Spear: Capturing the Combat History of the Army in Current Operations," The Campaign for the National Museum of the United States Army (armyhistory.org).

"Ken Hechler," https://en. wikipedia.org/wiki/Ken_Hechler#cite _note-5.

"Ken Hechler," Wikipedia, Ken Hechler—Wikipedia.

Hechler, Kenneth with Niel M. Johnson, November 29, 1985, http://www.trumanlibrary.org/oralhist/hechler.htm.

"Military History Detachments," Office of Army Reserve History, U.S. Army Reserve Command, Military History Detachments (army.mil).

"Oliver Lyman Spalding, Jr., Brigadier General, United States Army," http://www.arlingtoncemetery.net/ospauldingjr.htm.

Oral History Interview VNIT 259, Serial Interview, 1st Battalion, 27th Infantry, 25th Infantry Division, 1st Battalion, 27th Infantry, 25th Infantry Division, CMH, (army.mil).

Oral History Interview. Kenneth Hechler with Niel M. Johnson, 29 November 1985, http://www.trumanlibrary.org/oralhist/hechler.htm.

Oral History Interview, VNIT 101. End of-Tour Interview, CPT Joseph W. Kinzer, Advisory Team 163, Liaison Officer, 3d Airborne Brigade, Airborne Division, CMH, https://history.army.mil/documents/vietnam/vnit/vnit0101.htm.

Oral History Exit Interview VNIT 457 with LTC Douglas S. Smith, Commander, 2d Battalion, 47th Infantry, 9th Infantry Division, CMH. 1st Battalion, 27th Infantry, 25th Infantry Division (army.mil).

Oral History Interview VNIT-398. The Separate Brigade S-2 in Vietnam, CMH, Selections from the Vietnam Interview Tape (VNIT) Collection (army.mil).

"Renegade Woods," CMH, https://history.army.mil/documents/vietnam/reneg/reni.htm.

"Vietnam War Campaigns," CMH, Vietnam War Campaigns | U.S. Army Center of Military History.

Index